"This book equips all current and potential [...] approach to unleashing resources to help indi [...] move toward optimal functioning. Lucey's and Burke's app [...] leadership is comprehensive, rooted in the latest research, and practically useful. It is a must have resource for anyone aspiring to become more impactful and effective as a leader by bringing out the best in teams and individuals."

Prof. Emerita Jane Dutton, Business Administration and Psychology, University of Michigan

"Original and intellectually stimulating, *Positive Leadership in Practice* presents to us a new, innovative leadership model, termed Alight. This model enables a leader to make sense of six essential resources, further breaking down into 18 components. Grounded in research and benefiting from great coaching questions, this book is a pleasure to read."

Pr. Ilona Boniwell – CEO Positran; Professor of positive psychology and coaching psychology, University of East London

"Sometimes books come along which are 'right up your street', and this is one of those books. Lucey and Burke have produced an insightful model for taking positive psychology research to inform daily leadership practice. Fusing research evidence with what managers, leaders, trainers and coaches need to bring this alive through practical actions that can be applied in the dynamic, hybrid-working, diverse world most leaders now find themselves in. A recommended read for 2022."

Prof Jonathan Passmore, Senior Vice President CoachHub

"Written by leading thinkers in the field of positive psychology, this timely and incisive text brings a welcome focus on the practical aspects of positive leadership. This book makes a valuable contribution to the field of positive organisational scholarship."

Prof. Christian van Nieuwerburgh, Centre for Positive Psychology and Health, Royal College of Surgeons in Ireland

"Congratulations Lucey & Burke on a much needed book on Positive Leadership. Building on the groundbreaking work of Professor Kim Cameron, Jane Dutton & Gretchen Spreitzer, this book is a go-to text for leaders, coaches and consultants. Whilst the field of Positive Organisational

Scholarship and Positive Leadership are not yet fully embraced in business schools, this book, along with those before it, will provide a guide and inspiration to further develop and apply the many concepts that form part of Lucey & Burke's own Positive Leadership model ALIGHT. I know it will be a key text in my own professional library."

Dr Suzy Green, D Psych (Clin) MAPS, Founder and CEO The Positivity Institute, Australia

"This book is a timely, insightful, and practical addition to our understanding of leadership. Diving into some of the less well understood or defined aspects of what great leaders do, the authors bring the credibility of powerful research insights, giving us tangible ways to consider our own, and others', approaches. At a time when evidence-informed practice can lead to overly-simplistic analyses, Lucey and Burke have given us a rich resource to navigate some of the more complex dimensions of leadership. With tools to support personal reflection as well as practical action, this book deserves to become a staple of any leader committed to their own, and their organisation's, learning and development."

Liz Robinson, Co-CEO Big Education Trust

"Never has the need for positive leadership been greater in ourselves, our teams, our organisations and our communities. This engaging book demystifies the concept of 'Positive Leadership' and fills the existing gap with a comprehensive framework underpinned by a robust evidence base. The six element ALIGHT framework is a clear and practical guide for leaders and aspiring leaders to develop their 'positive leadership' approach. This book is a 'must read' for anyone serious about developing best practice leadership skills."

Dr Mary E Collins CPsychol EdD, Senior Executive Development Specialist, Graduate School of Healthcare Management, Royal College of Surgeons in Ireland

"Positive leaders contribute to the world around them. Their impact is deeply felt by their teams, communities, organisations and beyond. Yet, positive leadership is not sufficiently encouraged or appreciated. This is a timely book for leaders, leadership development practitioners and academics. It proposes a new positive leadership model (ALIGHT), which brings a balanced and well-researched overview of the ingredients of positive leadership. The book is also practical and reflective, and it offers the perspectives and experiences of leaders across different industries."

Dr Ana Paula Nacif, Leadership and Wellbeing Coach, Course Leader and Lecturer, MSc Applied Positive Psychology and Coaching Psychology, University of East London

"Every leader or potential leader should read this book! Best practice in leadership is captured beautifully by the authors and the pages are packed full of great content. There is a wonderful mix of evidence based knowledge, and guidance on how to apply this in practice. The logical and consistent structure of Chapters 2–7, guided by the ALIGHT model, made it easy and enjoyable to read, and will make it easy to refer back to as the reader reflects on their practice and growth as a leader in the future. Chapter 8 helps the reader to see how it all fits together, and Chapter 9 provides a plethora of resources that can help leaders to embody positive leadership."

Dr Marie Stopforth, Chartered Psychologist and Coach, Associate Fellow of the British Psychological Society, founder of The School of Coaching Psychology

"*Positive Leadership in Practice* is landing on bookshelves at exactly the right time. Lucey and Burke's book will be one I recommend in my graduate leadership classes and use as a handbook with clients!

Lucey and Burke don't shy away from the pressure that intersecting social movements and pandemic-related crises are placing on leaders globally. Instead, drawing on their extensive personal, professional and academic experience, they proffer an innovative, evidence-based, and ambitious ALIGHT model of positive leadership. Thankfully, Lucey and Burke do not provide a sugar-coated model of positive leadership. Perfection is not required and the authors approach all topics with positive and negative examples. In short, readers will be hard pressed to walk away from *Positive Leadership in Practice* without an expanded or deepened repertoire of leadership knowledge and ambitions.

Lucey and Burke profile each component of the ALIGHT model in its own chapter. Helpful graphic organisers shape each unfolding narrative with infusions of research evidence and thought-provoking snippets from interviews with a cross-section of leaders. Within each chapter, readers are guided to pause and reflect on powerful questions that strike at the heart of individual and collective practices underpinning positive leadership. Throughout, the authors skilfully signpost resources and tools for readers to extend their own learning and reflection. The culmination of their work is the new ALIGHT framework *Positive Leadership Resources Scale.*"

**Dr Karen Edge, UCL Centre for Educational Leadership,
UCL Institute of Education**

"An inspiring, thoughtful and provocative book for leaders, coaches, consultants and change agents interested in helping employees and communities flourish and reach their highest potential."

**Dr Andrea Giraldez-Hayes, Director Wellbeing and Psychological
Services Clinic, University of East London**

Positive Leadership
in Practice

This book aims to help leaders become the best versions of themselves, achieve extraordinary results, and help their team accomplish the same. Packed with research and practical advice from real-life positive leaders, it offers an extensive look into both what high-performance leadership is and how it can be achieved.

Positive Leadership in Practice is a resource that all leaders can tap into to be more effective. The book introduces an ALIGHT model that guides leaders through six fundamental resources that can alight their own and their team's motivation and transform their performance to an extraordinary level. Further breaking down the six resources into 18 core components, the book expands on what constitutes the six resources to make them tangible and accessible. The book also offers leaders the opportunity to self-assess their own levels of resources and levels of positive leadership through a questionnaire, as well as opportunities to reflect on how to further develop these levels of resources and positive leadership. Finally, the book signposts practical strategies to tap into on the back of their reflections to take action to become their best possible positive leader.

This book is for those starting out in their professional leadership journey to those with well-established leadership responsibilities and careers. It is for existing and aspiring managers, leaders, team leaders, senior leaders, CEOs, and all those with people development related roles such as in learning and development, leadership development, organisational development, coaching and wider human resources roles. This book is also for anyone in a more informal leadership position who may not recognise themselves as a leader; as really we are all leaders in some capacity whether we know that yet or not.

Cornelia Lucey, FRSA, is an award-winning leadership psychologist, chartered coaching psychologist, and consultant delivering transformational and bespoke positive psychology leadership development programmes for large-scale multinationals, charities, small and medium-sized enterprises (SMEs), and start-ups. Her research specialisms are in wellbeing, resilience, and positive leadership, and she has published in all of these fields. For more information on her work and company Cornelia Lucey Positive Leadership (CLPL), go to www.cornelialucey. com or connect on LinkedIn.

Jolanta Burke, PhD, is a Chartered Psychologist specialising in positive psychology and an Associate Professor at the Centre for Positive Psychology and Health, RCSI University of Medicine, and Health Sciences, Ireland. She has authored eight books and was acknowledged by *The Irish Times* as one of 30 people who make Ireland a better place. For more information, go to www.jolantaburke.com.

Positive Leadership in Practice

A Model for Our Future

Cornelia Lucey and Jolanta Burke

Routledge
Taylor & Francis Group

LONDON AND NEW YORK

Cover image: © Cornelia Lucey

First published 2022
by Routledge
4 Park Square, Milton Park, Abingdon, Oxon OX14 4RN

and by Routledge
605 Third Avenue, New York, NY 10158

Routledge is an imprint of the Taylor & Francis Group, an informa business

British Library Cataloguing-in-Publication Data
A catalogue record for this book is available from the British Library

Library of Congress Cataloging-in-Publication Data
Names: Lucey, Cornelia, 1984–author. | Burke, Jolanta, author.
Title: Positive leadership in practice : a model for our future / Cornelia Lucey
    & Jolanta Burke.
Description: First Edition. | New York, NY : Routledge, 2022. | Includes
    bibliographical references and index.
Identifiers: LCCN 2021057901 (print) | LCCN 2021057902 (ebook) |
    ISBN 9780367772499 (hardback) | ISBN 9780367772468 (paperback) |
    ISBN 9781003170433 (ebook)
Subjects: LCSH: Leadership—Psychological aspects. | Teams in the
    workplace—Management. | Organizational effectiveness.
Classification: LCC BF637.L4 L83 2022 (print) | LCC BF637.L4 (ebook) |
    DDC 158/.4—dc23/eng/20220302
LC record available at https://lccn.loc.gov/2021057901
LC ebook record available at https://lccn.loc.gov/2021057902

ISBN: 9780367772499 (hbk)
ISBN: 9780367772468 (pbk)
ISBN: 9781003170433 (ebk)

DOI: 10.4324/9781003170433

Typeset in Optima
by Apex CoVantage, LLC

To my enormous and inspiring family; to my wonderful husband, James, for always championing me; to our firstborn, Ophelia, who came along whilst I was writing this; and to all the positive leaders I have worked with who have taught me everything I know and everything I have yet to know.

Cornelia

To all the leaders I have worked with, past, present, and future.

Jolanta

Contents

Foreword

Early in my career I found myself a new and inexperienced leader in charge of an organisation under threat from rapidly changing market conditions. How I wish I'd had this book then. The inability of the organisation to adapt and change fast enough was in large part due to the unarticulated, but deeply embedded, beliefs I held about the role and responsibility of leadership. In a nutshell, I thought it was up to me, and me alone, to come up with the answers. That, I thought, was what I was paid to do. And I failed.

Some years later I was running a thriving business offering change consultancy to all manner of organisations. I quickly realised that many of the leaders I met were constrained by the same imprisoning and limiting beliefs that I had been. Not only that, but the prevalent belief was that to promote change, they needed to create a 'burning platform'. In other words, that the way to get people to do something different was to scare them into it. Conversations with leaders about change were full of references to 'resistance to change' and 'the need to get buy-in' as if the staff were a mindless lump of reluctant toilers and the leader's job was to relentlessly pump motivation into them. I frequently walked into organisations of exhausted senior management and confused, demoralised staff.

What these leaders lacked was a model of leadership that allowed them to cultivate growth and change from within their organisation, that helped them recognise and make productive use of the strengths and unique assets of each and every employee, and that allowed them to engage everyone in identifying and tackling organisational challenges. They needed help to understand their organisation as a mosaic of uniquely talented people who, with positive leadership, would flourish. In other words, they needed help to see leadership as a relational activity, expressed through an integrated pattern of beliefs, behaviour, and affect that could act to release and shape the motivation of others to achieve wholesale organisational change.

Cornelia Lucey and Jolanta Burke, drawing on their backgrounds in leadership and psychology, have created just such a model for understanding and living positive leadership. Acting as guides, they draw the reader through the many findings from positive psychology that can be fruitfully applied in an organisational context to create flourishing workplaces where people can be at, and give of, their best.

The book contains a beautifully balanced mix of a wealth of carefully selected research, illuminating case studies from their own practice, a self-assessment tool for leaders, and practical guidance with supporting resources on how to move towards ever more effective positive leadership. Taking the descriptive knowledge of how we are when we are at our best, it creates practical pathways of prescriptive activity. One of the aspects I particularly like about this book is that it tackles the myth that positive ways of being are only good for positive times, showing instead how these approaches can be applied in dire situations to create improvements and turnarounds in feelings and fortunes at team and organisational levels. All these elements are held together by their innovative and memorable model: ALIGHT.

In our current benighted times, the need for a leadership that can maintain hope and optimism in the face of adversity may never have been greater; this is the promise of positive leadership and the value of this book.

Sarah Lewis, C.Psychol,
Author of *Positive Psychology at Work*
London, 2021

About the authors

Cornelia Lucey is a highly experienced Senior European Mentoring and Coaching Council (EMCC) practitioner and British Psychological Society (CPsychol) leadership psychologist with over 15 years of experience coaching and developing senior executives and their teams across a range of commercial, corporate, charity, and public-sector organisations. She is an award-winning leadership development consultant, delivering transformational and bespoke positive psychology leadership development programmes for large-scale multinationals, charities, small and medium-sized enterprises (SMEs), and start-ups. Her research specialisms are in wellbeing, resilience, and positive leadership, and she has published in all of these fields. As a former senior executive and current business owner herself, Cornelia has first-hand experience of the challenges leaders at the senior level face. She supports organisations cross-sector such as Rothschild & Co.; BNP Paribas; Google; Siemens Gamesa (Renewable Energy); British Film Institute; Schneider Electric; Insead; and Teach First, as well as local government, education, and not-for-profit charitable organisations. She is an ambassador for the education charity Teach First and an invited fellow of the Royal Society for the encouragement of Arts, Manufactures and Commerce (RSA), a London-based organisation committed to finding practical solutions to social challenges. She is a regularly invited speaker to conferences worldwide and committed to supporting the improvement of educational outcomes for young people and the lifetime development of adults. Please see www.cornelialucey.com for more.

Dr Jolanta Burke is a Chartered Psychologist with the British Psychological Society specialising in positive psychology and an Associate Professor at the Centre for Positive Psychology and Health in RCSI University of

Medicine and Health Sciences. She has authored eight books, her latest is "Positive Psychology and Health: 100+ research-based Tools for Enhancing Wellbeing" published by Routledge; and has contributed over 200 academic, professional, and popular publications, for such publications as *The Guardian*, *New Zealand Herald*, and *Irish Independent*; and she writes a regular blog for *Psychology Today*. She is an editor-in-chief of *Journal of Happiness and Health* and writes an regular blog "The Good Life Ritual: A Healthy Mind, One Step at a Time" for Psychology Today. Over the years, Dr Burke has led state-funded research projects, and consulted in the private sector for organisations in healthcare, technology, financial, pharmaceutical, insurance, not-for-profit, retail, and hospitality. Dr Burke has won a range of educational rewards, such as the prestigious Trinity Teaching Excellence Award many years in a row. For her work in Ireland, she has been acknowledged by *The Irish Times* as one of 30 people who make it better place. For more information, please go to www.jolan taburke.com.

Acknowledgement

With thanks to our talented graphics designer, Anna Tsunematsu, for the figures you find in these pages. Also, sincere thanks to all our interviewees for taking the time to speak with us and willingness to share their stories with you.

Interviewees

Sarah Blomfield, General Counsel, Evercore LLP

Sarah is general counsel, EMEA, at the leading global independent investment banking advisory firm Evercore LLP, London, and has over 20 years' experience spanning legal, compliance, and risk. Prior to joining Evercore in 2020, Sarah was managing director and regional head of compliance at Rothschild & Co in London. She started her legal career at Slaughter and May and Allen & Overy in London, where she focussed primarily on mergers and acquisitions, financial regulation, and private equity. Sarah holds an MA in history from the University of Cambridge, is a school governor of Shiplake CE Primary and Shiplake College, and is on the development board of the English National Ballet. Sarah is also a mum to three teenage girls and enjoys travelling, yoga, and tennis.

Sean Corrigan, Engineer, Founder of the "Let It Bee" Project

Sean is an engineer with over 20 years' experience working with communities and stakeholders on environmental projects. He has developed educational programmes and community initiatives which have led to sustainable change, such as water conservation, water source protection, enhanced biodiversity, and climate change mitigation. His latest initiative is the group water scheme "Let It Bee" project, which resulted in farmers and thousands of school children planting trees and hedgerows to protect water, bees, and other pollinators in their community. The project received support from the government in the Republic of Ireland and won the European Bee Award for the protection of pollinators. Other projects that Sean has managed have won awards from the construction industry for the best managed water project, the National Geographic, and the Local Authority Management Awards.

In his spare time Sean likes to spend time with his wonderful daughters. He is also a beekeeper; an EU Climate Pact Ambassador; a champion of inclusion; and a voluntary director with Variety Ireland, a children's charity that helps children with mobility, learning, and environmental needs.

Russell Hobby CBE, Charity CEO, Teach First UK

Russell joined Teach First as CEO in September 2017 building on more than 15 years developing and promoting leadership in schools. Prior to joining Teach First Russell was general secretary of the National Association of Head Teachers (NAHT), which represents over 29,000 school leaders in the UK, and before that worked as a management consultant, founding Hay Group's education practice. In recent years Russell has run marathons and triathlons in a bid to deny the onward march of time. Before this sounds too energetic, he appears to have achieved the record for the slowest ever triathlon time at his most recent outing.

Orla Deering, Co-founder, Reba Reborn Hair and Beauty Chain

Orla is a co-founder of Reba Reborn Hair and Beauty. Over a decade ago, she ventured to open her first salon with husband John Deering, and within a few years she moved to a larger venue and opened an additional salon to meet the demands of her customers. Over the years, her team won a range of awards, such as the Phorest Award for receiving the highest amount of five-star reviews online, RCVP Magazine Award for best customer service in Leinster region, The Irish Hair and Beauty Salon of the Year award, and more. She has turned her salons into educational hubs for future hairdressers and beauticians. In her spare time, Orla loves to meditate.

Professor Luke O'Neill, Chair of Biochemistry, Education

Professor Luke O'Neill is an immunologist who holds the Chair of Biochemistry in Trinity College Dublin. He is a founding director of Trinity Biomedical Sciences and a winner of a range of international awards, such as the European Federation of Immunology Societies Medal and the Milstein Award of the International Cytokine and Interferon Society. He was listed in Thompson/Reuters as one of the top 1% of scientists in the world. He has a passion to engage with the general public on scientific topics and has a science slot with Pat Kenny on the Irish national radio station Newstalk. Professor O'Neill published several books, including a book for children: The Great Irish Science Book. In his spare time, he plays in a rock band.

Eartha Pond, Entrepreneur and Athlete

Eartha is a highly successful elected local government councillor, athlete, and educator. Her continuous work and dedication both in schools and local communities across London has gone on to be recognised at a national as well as international level. Eartha counts being named a School Sports Matters Teacher of the Year and a Global Teacher Prize Finalist among her many accolades. A bona fide people's person who disrupts the status quo, Eartha cherishes opportunities to support others in making a difference whilst also priding herself on leaving a legacy fuelled with integrity.

Martine Rose, Founder, Fashion Designer

Martine Rose is a British menswear fashion designer and founder of the label by her same name, established in 2007 and now distributed worldwide, partnering with many of the leading retailers such as Barneys, Dover Street Market, SSENSE, Matches Fashion, KM20, Isetan, Nordstrom Space, and Joyce. Martine has always been drawn to people on the periphery of society, subcultures, marginalised groups, and people who for whatever reason choose to do it their way. Family and community are at the heart of the company, and Martine is inspired by her Jamaican-British heritage and her deep interest and personal involvement in the music and high/low melting-pot cultures of London.

Charley Stoney, CEO, Advertising

Charley Stoney is a CEO of the Institute of Advertising Practitioners in Ireland (IAPI). She has held managing director roles in marketing and advertising over the last 20 years. IAPI is the body for the commercial creativity and communications industry in Ireland, whose purpose is to firmly position the industry as a fundamental engine of Ireland's future growth. This is even more important at present as the economy and industry emerge from the coronavirus pandemic. Charley is also a board member of the Advertising Standards Authority for Ireland (ASAI), as well as a board member and joint CEO of the Central Copy Clearance in Ireland (CCCI).

1 Introduction

Introduction

The world faced a catastrophic pandemic in COVID-19, and society will live with the challenges this presented in years to come. Yet even before this happened, we were facing dire straits, living on the brink of an ongoing climate crisis (Worland, 2020), and desperately seeking ways for more effective and sustainable living. More people than ever in the so-called developed parts of the world are disengaged at work and experiencing levels of anxiety and depression. More students leave school feeling ill-equipped for their fast-moving futures (Slee, Nazareth, Freemantle, & Horsfall, 2021). As consistently indicated by leadership research, leadership has a fundamental influence on all corners of society and organisations, from schools to businesses. Leaders offer a golden opportunity to influence a more positive future at school and in workplaces. Today, more than ever, we need positive leaders.

The social upheaval of the #BlackLivesMatter movement, which commenced in 2013, gained increasing popularity following the 25 May 2020 murder of George Floyd by a police officer. The aggressions exposed by the #MeToo movement from 2017 onwards left millions of people feeling alienated and denigrated as reflections of daily injustices and micro-aggressions that billions face daily came hurtling to the foreground. At the core of these political and social movements is the sentiment that people want their lives and opinions to matter (Prilleltensky & Prilleltensky, 2021). Their angry reactions indicate that society seeks holistic and pro-social leadership (Syed, 2020) to address these ongoing inequalities of race, gender, and wider persistent societal disparities. But what can leaders do when faced with or are even

DOI: 10.4324/9781003170433-1

part of endemic and often overwhelming social challenges? This is where our behaviour as leaders becomes so essential and where a positive leadership – a more conscious way of bringing the best out of ourselves and others – offers a pathway forward in paving better ways forward for managers, leaders, their reports, and for us all.

The pursuit of wellbeing has become the most endorsed goal in western society (Ford et al., 2015). It extends beyond our domain, seeping into our career lives and raising our expectations about the meaning of work (Steger, 2017). Now for employees, it is not enough that a job provides one with an income. It is not enough that it offers career progression. It is also not enough that a job gives one security. Given that we spend more time at work than sleeping, resting, or enjoying our families, we expect our work to contribute significantly to our wellbeing (Bailey & Madden, 2016; A Wrzesniewski, 2014). Yet these expectations are not being met; therefore, we urgently need to focus on how organisations, managers, and leaders help redress this situation through how we manage and lead ourselves and others.

At the same time, leaders in organisations are flailing in the dark, blindly trying to navigate the VUCA environment (volatile, uncertain, complex, and ambiguous), and they seek practical, evidence-based ways to increase their wellbeing and performance and the wellbeing and engagement of their teams, organisations, and communities. Outdated models of leadership no longer serve the challenges we face as an evolving human race. How do we bring the best out of ourselves and others? What does the most up-to-date psychology tell us about the behaviours that lead us to function in life optimally? Approaches to leadership which will fundamentally transform the way we learn, educate, and work are critical for a more sustainable and positive future.

Over the past 30 years, positive psychology has brought more to the fore in academic circles on what creates optimum functioning at individual, teams, and system levels (Green & Palmer, 2019), and there is now a pertinent opportunity to integrate and embed this knowledge into our personal and professional lives moving forward. Our pursuit of wellbeing has also resulted in an explosion of positive psychology in work research in the past decade (Burke, 2021; Johnson, Robertson, & Cooper, 2018), a part of which is evidence-based positive leadership. However, while some researchers have already begun to mark the contours of the rapidly growing field of positive leadership (Boniwell & Smith, 2018; Burke, 2020; Cameron, 2008), what is missing is a comprehensive and cohesive framework of positive leadership that will inform leaders of what it means to be a positive leader in the contemporary world, as well as the 'how' in which we can do so; this is what this book aims to provide.

Furthermore, whilst academic publications about positive leadership have increased eightfold over the last two decades (2001–21), and today the search engine spews over 2 million online entries about positive leadership, relatively little is known about its practical applications. Case studies of organisations that do the right thing guiding their staff towards extraordinary performance do exist; there are some evidence-informed examples of how they practice this, which we can replicate ad hoc in our organisations; there are also have leadership questionnaires loosely related to positive leadership, such as Authentic Leadership. However, what we miss is a comprehensive framework we can follow to help us make sense of the positive leadership research and practice; a framework that leaders and organisations could follow to start slowly implementing positive changes; a framework that provides us with a validated scale we can use to learn more about how positive leadership relates to other organisational outcomes. This is the gap that our book addresses.

Creating a new positive leadership model

The most prevalent model of positive leadership to date is Cameron's (2008), according to which positive leadership comprises (1) facilitating the extraordinary positive performance, (2) affirmative bias, and (3) facilitating the best human condition. Facilitating extraordinary performance relates to leaders becoming focused not only on being 'good enough' and displaying mediocre performance but helping their team achieve their potential and become the best versions of themselves. Affirmative bias is about leaders focusing on strengths instead of 'fixing' their team's deficits. Finally, facilitating the best human condition refers to creating (1) a positive climate, (2) positive relationships, (3) positive communication, and (4) positive meaning. The model is used extensively in research worldwide.

The ALIGHT model we have developed complements Cameron's model concerning our focus on facilitating extraordinary performance and the best human condition. However, it builds further on it by delving deeper into the 'how' of this facilitation. Many organisations we have worked with wanted to apply positive leadership, but despite reading many books about it, didn't know what steps they could take. Drawing from the literature relating to the potential application of Cameron's positive leadership model (Cameron, 2008), Murphy and Louis's less prevalent model of positive school leadership (2018), and Burke's (2020) comprehensive outline of positive leadership research, as well as the latest positive psychology research, some of which was applied in leadership, we designed a theoretical model that helps readers apply the newest research in their organisations. Furthermore, in developing this model we drew on our collective experience of 40 years of practice and 25 years of research in supporting managers and leaders nationally and internationally to bring the best out of themselves and others. While our model is not yet exhaustive, it incorporates the main developments in the theory and practice of positive leadership to date.

We took a deductive approach to our research. In step 1, we reviewed the last 20 years of positive psychology research; its prevalence of topics; and their impact on individuals, organisations, and society. We drew on our research and professional experiences in the hundreds of workplaces we have worked within or consulted for. In step 2, we reviewed the literature for each one of the topics and explored its application in leadership. We included research that related to either leaders, organisations, or their team members. In step 3, we narrowed down the themes and created the six-element ALIGHT model presented in this book (Figure 1.1). ALIGHT is an acronym that stands for abundance, limberness, inspiration, grand design, health, and tribe. We will delve deeper into the framework we created in the next section.

To best illustrate the diverse and cross-sector application of the model, we then interviewed eight extraordinary ordinary leaders across a range of sectors and explored their perspectives and reflections on leadership practice. We deliberately chose leaders that other senior leaders in their fields nominated; they were selected as being positive leaders who demonstrated behaviours that brought the best out of themselves and others and that were representative of different sectors, genders, and cultures to illustrate the application of positive leadership in various aspects of our worlds and lives. We analysed these interviews using a deductive thematic analysis approach that provided evidence of practice for the ALIGHT elements of our positive leadership model. Moving on from this, we have covered in this book the what, the why, the how, and the application of positive leadership. This practical dimension has been missing from books referencing positive leadership to date, and therefore we hope it will have much broader application in creating positive

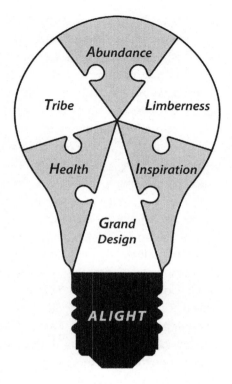

Figure 1.1 The ALIGHT model

organisational cultures. The current book tells a story of our journey and the journey of thousands of other leaders to date, a journey that will undoubtedly continue as we learn more about what it is like to be a positive leader.

Positive leadership: a definition

Positive leadership does not refer to a person, a style, or a trait. If we were to consider positive leadership as a trait, it would imply that leadership is an innate quality, a stable part of who we are, a trait that we were born with. However, positive leaders are not born positive. Research indicates that characteristics such as optimism or gratitude need to be developed over time (Greif & Gleason, 1980; McGrath & Noble, 2017). Children are not born grateful. They need to be taught in what situations society expects them to say 'thank you' or how they can react optimistically to their circumstances.

We are all genetically predisposed to specific behaviour and responses, but our outcomes are an exciting cocktail of our genes, circumstances, culture, learnt behaviours, and intentional efforts (Pluess & Boniwell, 2015; Sheldon & Lyubomirsky, 2021; Shin, Wong, Yancura, & Hsu, 2020). Some of us learn positive leadership early in life; others acquire it later. Epigenetic research shows us that regardless of age, we can change our ways, unlearn, and relearn new attitudes and behaviours, with some of us being more susceptible to that change than others (Belsky et al., 2009; Jay Belsky & Pluess, 2009). Therefore, positive leadership is not about 'being'; instead, it is about 'becoming'.

Similarly, it is not about practising a style of leadership. Positive leaders don't put on a suit of clothes and behave in a specific, positive manner. It is quite the opposite. A positive leader is a person who dares to be themselves. They realise the danger of becoming alienated from themselves and pursue the 'authentic becoming' that allows them to be true to their desires (Eriksen, 2012; Kasser, 2004). Authentic becoming is a complex matter. First, it requires leaders' awareness of who they are and what they want to do to put a dent in this world (Ryan & Deci, 2004). Second, it requires the courage to pursue it regardless of other people's approval (Kasser, 2004), perhaps resulting in temporary negativity and frustrations at times. Finally, it requires an ability to manage negative thoughts and emotions that can derail us and prevent authentic becoming (Ivtzan, Lomas, Hefferon, & Worth, 2016); sometimes staying with these negative thoughts and emotions for a while until we figure out the solution to our problems (David, 2017). This is why each one of the elements of the ALIGHT model of positive leadership is expressed by leaders differently. While they all go in a similar direction, how they pursue and reach them may vary, as we shall illustrate later in this book.

Positive leaders are not toxically positive people who do not recognise the reality of pain, disappointment, and suffering. They do not practice "the tyranny of positive thinking" (Held, 2002) that makes others uncomfortable and may be deemed unrealistic. They do not seek out only positive feedback nor do they seek or offer few opportunities for development and growth for themselves or others. Instead, the 'positive' aspect of the label stands for a more nuanced approach to leadership. It specifically draws from the field of positive psychology – the study of what makes humans optimally function (Seligman & Csikszentmihalyi, 2000). 'Positive' means that leaders create a 'safe' environment for their team to be themselves and share their worries, speak up, and voice their opinion, otherwise known as psychological safety (O'Donovan & McAuliffe, 2020). It means that they go against the common grain by not only fixing the 'weaknesses' but also thoroughly engaging with 'strengths' and 'resources' – and using these strengths and resources to address challenges and shortcomings (Ryan M. Niemiec & Pearce, 2021). They do not focus on the mediocre, but aim at helping people and organisations become the best versions of themselves (Cameron, 2008) – however hard it may sometimes feel, their intention guides them. Their actions create lasting outcomes that allow them, people around them, organisations, and societies to flourish. Therefore, positive leadership is a balanced way of leading that negotiates challenges, conflict, and suffering, with optimal performance, flourishing, and compassionate being.

Positive leaders are aware of their positive resources and can use them effectively to maximise their own, their team's, and their community's potential to instigate positive change and outcomes. Positive leadership is a blended and integrated set of intellectual, psychological, emotional, and social resources that leaders can tap into to transform their outcomes and the outcomes of their team, organisation, and society. Intellectual resources refer to the knowledge and information leaders have that help them get the best out of themselves, their people, their organisation, and the community they live in. Psychological resources refer to the beliefs and associated behaviours that help leaders transform their practice. Emotional resources refer to the tools leaders employ to attend to their emotions and maximise their usefulness at any given time. Finally, social resources are the wherewithal that assists leaders in connecting with others and creating a tightly knitted and energising environment in which individuals and teams are more likely to thrive. All these resources in tandem allow leaders to create an environment where they can thrive and help their communities thrive.

The ALIGHT model identifies six such resources which leaders can use to start a journey of positive transformation. Each ALIGHT component requires and is an amalgamation of: intellectual resources (we require knowledge to practise it); psychological resources (we need to activate our beliefs and behaviour); emotional resources (we need to maximise the usefulness of our emotions); and social resources (we need to do it with people). We need to fully utilise the range of these resources to flourish.

To practise positive leadership, leaders need to become fully aware of the resources at their disposal and make wise choices to activate them when required. The awareness of help comes from self-awareness, as well as ongoing reflection and feedback from within themselves and from others. Without this awareness, leaders are not able to make the transformational changes they need to fully develop to their potential as positive leaders. Furthermore, leaders need to feel comfortable with the resources and integrate them authentically into their lives. Authentic integration refers to leaders perceiving the resources as suitable for them, saying that 'this is me', 'it feels OK to use this resource', and in receiving feedback from others that this is the case. Sometimes, leaders may be so alienated from themselves that they may not feel comfortable with using their positive leadership resources despite it feeling right to use them. We hope that this book will take you on a journey that will help you assimilate these new or developing (for we are always developing ourselves) resources into your lives.

Positive leaders are individuals who can see the bigger picture by both noting weaknesses and identifying strengths and resources. Conversely, leading with purely identifying faults resembles reaching out for low-hanging fruit. Admittedly, bad is more potent than good (Baumeister, Bratslavsky, Finkenauer, & Vohs, 2001), which is why it is easy to notice and pay attention to. This 'negative' bias offers us plenty of benefits. It helps us attend to danger, it prepares us for tackling obstacles, it allows us to make our environment safer, and ultimately, it helps us survive. However, it also comes at a price. When we focus dominantly on weaknesses, we do not attend to strengths and resources, which offers us an incomplete picture of a person and a situation. That negative bias is prevalent in our research and practice. By 2011, only one out of ten studies focused on the 'positive' aspects of management and leadership (Rusk & Waters, 2013), meaning that we have developed a skewed view of what it means to be a good leader. Similarly, if we perceive leadership as managing weaknesses, we will not see a complete picture of the powerful resources at our disposal. This is why positive leaders' ability to also and most importantly perceive strengths and enact them has the potential of making a huge and fundamental difference to their people, their organisation and society.

When positive leaders can tap into positive leadership resources, they become open to and adapt to change. They do not stubbornly stick with their goals and persist for the sake of it, but practise flexibility when required. They constantly assess the environment and decide when a change of direction and tweaking of goals are needed. They are aware of their emotions and the emotions of others and are able to adjust their reactions to ensure positive outcomes for all involved (David, 2017). Finally, they have a resilience that allows them to constantly adjust their sails and progress on their journey without falling apart (albeit there may be moments or times where it feels things are falling apart).

Positive leaders who use their positive resources are self-inspiring through their self-efficacy. In addition, they tap into their psychological resources to practise optimism which helps them and others around them become unstuck in adversity. They also evoke hope, which allows them to find motivation and a pathway for making a change. This positive and abundant forward-thinking motivates other people and reassures them that a change is possible. Add to it their energising practices, and positive leaders become persistently inspiring in the eyes of others.

Positive leaders who use their positive resources are in touch with the grand design. They can transform their thinking from the monotony of daily tasks towards a transcendental level of their own and other people's performance. They can link their daily duties to a higher meaning and purpose. For example, creating surgical sponges in a factory is not only about producing a product but saving other people's lives. At the same time, they can reverse this process by moving from 'transcendental' towards the 'practical' levels of turning the meaning and purpose into action.

Positive leaders who use their positive resources promote health; they encourage consideration of health at every level in their actions and decision-making processes related to physical, emotional, or environmental contexts. They are deliberate in ensuring healthy environments for themselves, their teams, and other stakeholders. A positive leader ensures that they authentically have a work-life balance that they role model, and encourage and actively support all team members to do the same. Their interactions are in all broadest senses of the word – be it verbal, written, or behavioural – healthy between themselves and their widest tribes; they walk the health talk.

Positive leaders who use their positive resources create connections through their daily processes and habits. They are conscious of checking in on others and making moments to connect, be it through kind inquiry, gratitude, humour, or a sense of compassion. They don't think the conversation in passing is a waste of their valuable time; they know it is valuable time. They make time to deepen connections over time. They are unafraid to engage in conflict and see the value in it for themselves, others, and the development of ideas because for them, conflict is positive, in that it is always a positive conflict.

Positive leadership resources

Positive leadership is a set of resources, associated attitudes, and behaviours that allow individuals to achieve optimal performance. The ALIGHT model is an acronym and mnemonic consisting of the following components and resources: A – Abundance, L – Limberness, I – Inspiring, G – Grand design,

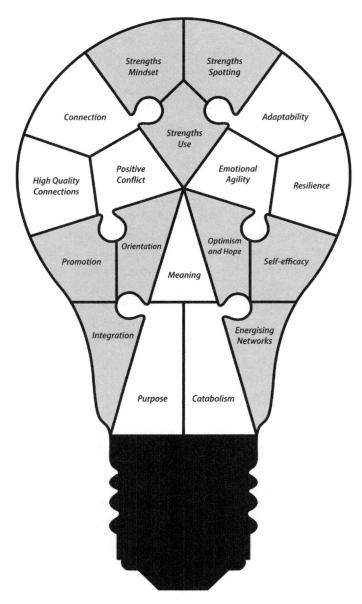

Figure 1.2 The ALIGHT positive leadership model: 18 components

H – Health, T- Tribe. The model is a map and a gauge of how positive leaders behave; it is a set of skills individuals develop to maximise their outcomes. The six resources can be broken down into 18 components (3 components within each resource) (Figure 1.2). And we shall detail these in Chapters 2–7.

In the early noughties, a model was created that helped researchers and practitioners make sense of the benefits of positive emotions (Fredrickson, 2001). According to the model, positive emotions served an essential purpose to broaden our perspective and provide us with an ability to generate a solution; build our resources, including intellectual, physical, social, and psychological; and undo the impact of negative emotions. This theoretical model was then tested, advancing the research and practice in this area. In the same vein, we hope that the ALIGHT resource model will help researchers and practitioners conceptualise the field of positive leadership, narrow down their focus concerning further developments in this area, and provide practitioners with a set of resources they can use to improve their leadership practice and outcomes.

In combination with the resources and components, positive leaders can set their team ALIGHT. The words and actions arouse passion in people around them and get them fired up and ready to go beyond what they believed they were capable of. However, it is not necessarily charisma that drives their influence, but the meaningful connection with others. Being a positive leader is like witnessing Mary Wollstonecraft's publication of one of the earliest examples of feminist philosophy, *A Vindication of the Rights of Woman*, in 1792. Wollstonecraft's suggestion that men and women should be considered equal as rational beings was radical and revolutionary, and challenged traditional assumptions. It didn't take long for a backlash to occur, and it wasn't reprinted until the mid-19th century. It is also like watching Reinhold Messner climb mountains without oxygen. He was the first man to climb all the peaks over 8,000 m without bottled oxygen: up until then, nobody believe it was humanly possible. Yet his achievement left a legacy helping hundreds of mountaineers to climb further without oxygen and break more records. It is not the personality of these trailblazers, but their actions that made it happen. The same applies to positive leaders who inspire courage and outstanding performance in their team. And the way they do it is by leaning on the resources we have identified and summarised in the six-step ALIGHT acronym. Positive leaders focus on abundance and pay attention to their emotional and cognitive limberness; they offer inspiration, grand design, and foreground health and tribe.

Developing positive leadership

We are aware that you will want to know what one needs to do to develop positive leadership. Positive leadership is not technical skill development; it is not about domain-specific leadership development – acquiring knowledge and skills within leadership (e.g. telling us what makes a good strategy). Nor is positive leadership developed horizontally, where we might expand our toolkit by adding to the tools we have, by gaining more skills, knowledge, and competence (e.g. this is how we lead change). Positive leadership instead is developed through a vertical approach to leadership development (Jones, Chesley, & Egan, 2020); that is, we build its six resources through experiences where we have the opportunity to exercise our ability to be adaptable and flex these resource muscles. Developing positive leadership is about transforming our mindsets, shifting our frames of reference from these two types of leadership, which focus on *what* knowledge leaders make sense of (e.g. if this person is angry, what does that tell me), to the *how* leaders make sense of the knowledge acquired (e.g. what is it about this situation that might be triggering this anger and what are the options for this reaction, what resource do I need to practise or exercise here?). It's about development that opens our eyes to adopting more complex and inclusive viewpoints, developing self-awareness, expanding mindset, learning more about the how in which we understand one another; going beyond forming the 'basis' of conversations, relationships (what can I see), and rather get to the heart, root, and mind of helping us to explore what is going on for deepest understanding (how could this situation be playing out for different people?). In being developed vertically, it operates beneath the surface. Positive leaders choose to ask 'how' rather than 'what' knowledge can help me here; they look below the surface and into the matrix for more possibilities to complex problems – and positive leadership development prepares them for this.

Who is this book written for?

We wrote this book for all leaders and aspiring leaders who want to lead in a way that best serves themselves, their team, their organisation, and their community. We recognise that the book will be particularly attractive to existing and aspiring managers, leaders, team leaders, senior leaders, CEOs, and all those with people development related roles such as in learning and development, leadership development, organisational development, coaching and wider human resources roles, and academics in the field interested in this growing research. However, we must also highlight that, in our eyes, every human being has the potential to be a positive leader, no matter their age, background, or context and that we will all at any one point in our lives take a leadership role – and more often than we realise – be it as a mother, sister, brother, friend, we are all leaders. Therefore, even though our examples refer to individuals in formal leadership positions, the framework for positive leadership applies to everyone who leads ideas and people in a specific direction.

Let's consider some fantastic leaders who have not held a formal leadership position yet made a significant difference in people's lives. Nicolaus Copernicus (1473–1543), a Polish mathematician and astronomer, suggested that the earth circles around the sun, not the other way round. His courage of conviction led scientists beliefs and methods long until we had evidence for his theory's existence. Second, the Beatles, whose music has influenced the industry and led a social revolution in the 1960s, by creating awareness and spreading wisdom believed by millions. Finally, Roger Bannister, who in 1954, ran a mile in four minutes. Before he accomplished it, people thought it was impossible. Not only has he proven that human beings are capable of doing it, but he led the way, resulting in Hicham El Guerrouj from Morocco achieving the current world record of running one mile in 3 minutes and 43 seconds. Leaders are individuals whom others follow, regardless of their formal position. This book is for and about all these types of leaders, the influencers and energisers who make a positive difference to individuals, families, teams, organisations, communities, or the world.

Nonetheless, this book goes beyond leadership. Even though it was written with a leader in mind, leaders' attitudes towards the resources they choose to use and their actions permeate their organisation, team, and communities. This is why, in addition to leadership development, the ALIGHT resources presented in this book can also be applied by teams, organisations, and communities to make a positive change. Communities may engage in abundance (A) thinking to get the best out of their members. Organisations may choose to take steps towards developing organisational limberness (L) and, as such, prepare themselves for the challenges of the future. Teams may practise inspiring (I) dialogues to keep each other motivated, whilst individuals on the team may choose to tap into the resource of grand design (G) to support them in creating meaningfulness at work. Organisations may choose to implement a series of health interventions (H) that support their employees in boosting physical and mental capacities. Finally, departments may implement tribe (T) practices to help people tap into their social capital. We hope that the ALIGHT model we created will help individuals, teams, and organisations make positive changes. This model can become a map for anyone wanting to tap into the positive leadership resources to achieve their full potential and help others do the same.

The structure of the book

This book's objective is to provide readers with a clear evidence-based framework for positive leadership practice (the what and the why), share the how, and offer examples from a range of well-known leaders who depict various aspects of positive leadership (the application).

Chapter 1, this chapter, is the introduction – where you will read our case and an overview of the research on positive leadership. Next, you will be offered a brief introduction to the field of positive leadership, which details the reasons for its growth, the scope and the outcomes of this rapidly evolving field, and the people we will be speaking to that imbue positive leadership behaviours. Finally, we will introduce you to the framework and the evidence upon which it was built, along with the rationale for selecting each framework aspect.

The following six chapters will take each component of the six-part framework and support you to review it: detailing the research behind it; the characteristics required of leaders to practise it; the leadership behaviours demonstrated by it; and finally, the outcomes achieved through it. The descriptions you read will be intertwined with quotes from the leaders interviewed to give the framework life and meaning. In Chapters 2–7, we will guide you through the key behaviours and resources that have been identified in the research and will explain to you their research roots and presentations so that they are clear to understand; you will then read an outline of how these behaviours play out, including reading real-life case studies of positive leaders in action. In each of these chapters, you will also have the opportunity for three different moments of self-reflection on each of the 18 components of the ALIGHT framework; this will be presented to you through 18 further 'reflection on practice' boxes to add reflexivity to your reading experience.

In Chapter 8, you will understand the integration of the components of this framework and how each resource and its components can flow into and from the next, showing the fluidity and self-fulfilling possibilities of the framework when applied, as well as understanding the need for intentional and careful application of the six resources, considering the cautious volume and balance positive leaders apply to the six resources and what can hinder or get in the way of their careful application.

In Chapter 9, you will move from understanding the theoretical framework and practical applications of positive leadership to looking at ways you can assimilate positive leadership into your workplace practice. You will undertake an evidence-based self-assessment of positive leadership to decide which aspect of the framework you want to self-improve. We will provide you with further reflection opportunities with self-coaching guidance on developing this for yourself or working with leaders and colleagues. Chapter 10 addresses the 'so what' of what we have shared and where the research into this interdisciplinary field is yet to go.

In terms of where you start and how much you read, you are the reader; thus, you can choose. You may want to start by understanding the research, or understanding the model, or reading about the model in practice through our case studies, or jump straight to Chapter 9 to self-assess yourself before beginning. You can take the path that suits you, based on your levels of positive leadership right now and come back to the different elements as you go through. We recommend starting from the beginning of the book and working your way through it to give yourself the best chance to understand the nuances of what we will present.

References

Bailey, C., & Madden, A. (2016). What makes work meaningful – or meaningless. *MIT Sloan Management Review, 57*(4), 53.

Baumeister, R. F., Bratslavsky, E., Finkenauer, C., & Vohs, K. D. (2001). Bad is stronger than good. *Review of General Psychology, 5*(4), 323–370. doi:10.1037/1089-2680.5.4.323

Belsky, J., Jonassaint, C., Pluess, M., Stanton, M., Brummett, B., & Williams, R. (2009). Vulnerability genes or plasticity genes? *Molecular Psychiatry, 14*(8), 746–754. doi:10.1038/mp.2009.44

Belsky, J., & Pluess, M. (2009). Beyond diathesis stress: Differential susceptibility to environmental influences. *Psychological Bulletin, 135*(6), 885–908.

Boniwell, I., & Smith, W.-A. (2018). Positive psychology coaching for positive leadership. In S. Green & S. Palmer (Eds.), *Positive psychology coaching in practice* (1st ed., pp. 159–178). London: Routledge.

Burke, J. (2020). *Positive psychology and school leadership: The new science of positive educational leadership*. New York City: Nova Science.

Burke, J. (2021). *The ultimate guide to implementing wellbeing programmes for school*. London: Routledge.

Cameron, K. (2008). *Positive Leadership: Strategies for extraordinary performance*. San Francisco: Berrett-Koehler Publishers, Inc.

David, S. (2017). *Emotional agility: Get unstuck, embrace change and thrive in work and life*. London: Penguin Books Ltd.

Eriksen, M. (2012). Facilitating authentic becoming. *Journal of Management Education, 36*(5), 698–736. doi:10.1177/1052562911423883

Ford, B. Q., Dmitrieva, J. O., Heller, D., Chentsova-Dutton, Y., Grossmann, I., Tamir, M., . . . Mauss, I. B. (2015). Culture shapes whether the pursuit of happiness predicts higher or lower well-being. *Journal of Experimental Psychology. General, 144*(6), 1053–1062. doi:10.1037/xge0000108

Fredrickson, B. L. (2001). The role of positive emotions in positive psychology: The broaden-and-build theory of positive emotions. *American Psychologist, 56*(3), 218–226. doi:10.1037/0003-066X.56.3.218

Green, S., & Palmer, S. (2019). *Positive psychology coaching in practice*. London: Routledge.

Greif, E. B., & Gleason, J. B. (1980). Hi, thanks, and goodbye: More routine information. *Language in Society, 9*(2), 159–166. doi:10.1017/S0047404500008034

Held, B. S. (2002). The tyranny of the positive attitude in America: Observation and speculation. *Journal of Clinical Psychology, 58*(9), 965. doi:10.1002/jclp.10093

Ivtzan, I., Lomas, T., Hefferon, K., & Worth, P. (2016). *Second wave positive psychology: Embracing the dark side of life*. London: Routledge.

Johnson, S., Robertson, I., & Cooper, C. L. (2018). *Well-being: Productivity and happiness at work*. Manchester: The Palgrave Macmillan.

Jones, H. E., Chesley, J. A., & Egan, T. (2020). Helping leaders grow up: Vertical leadership development in practice. *The Journal of Values-Based Leadership, 13*(1), 8.

Kasser, T., & Sheldon, K. M. (2004). Nonbecoming, alienated becoming, and authentic becoming: A goal based approach. In J. Greenberg, S. L. Koole, & T. Pyszczynski (Eds.), *Handbook of experimental existential psychology* (pp. 486–499). New York: Guildford Press.

McGrath, H., & Noble, T. (2017). *Bounce Back! Years F-2* (3rd ed.). Australia: Pearson Education Australia.

Murphy, J. F., & Louis, K. S. (2018). *Positive school leadership: Building capacity and strengthening relationships*. Canada: Teachers College Press.

Niemiec, R. M., & Pearce, R. (2021). The practice of character strengths: Unifying definitions, principles, and exploration of what's soaring, emerging, and ripe with potential in science and in practice. *Frontiers in Psychology, 11*, 3863.

O'Donovan, R., & McAuliffe, E. (2020). A systematic review exploring the content and outcomes of interventions to improve psychological safety, speaking up and voice behaviour. *BMC Health Services Research, 20*(1), 1–11. doi:10.1186/s12913-020-4931-2

Pluess, M., & Boniwell, I. (2015). Sensory-processing sensitivity predicts treatment response to a school-based depression prevention program: Evidence of vantage sensitivity. *Personality and Individual Differences, 82*, 40–45. doi:10.1016/j.paid.2015.03.011

Prilleltensky, I., & Prilleltensky, O. (2021). *How people matter: Why it affects health, happiness, love, work, and society.* Cambridge, UK: Cambridge University Press.

Rusk, R. D., & Waters, L. E. (2013). Tracing the size, reach, impact, and breadth of positive psychology. *The Journal of Positive Psychology, 8*(3), 207–221. doi:10.1080/17439760.2013.777766

Ryan, R. M., & Deci, E. L. (2004). Autonomy is no illusion: Self-determination theory and the empirical study of authenticity, awareness, and will. In J. Greenberg, S. L. Koole, & T. Pyszczynski (Eds.), *Handbook of experimental existential psychology* (pp. 449–479). Guilford: Guilford Press.

Seligman, M. E. P., & Csikszentmihalyi, M. (2000). Positive psychology: An introduction. *American Psychologist, 55*(1), 5–14. doi:10.1037/0003-066X.55.1.5

Sheldon, K. M., & Lyubomirsky, S. (2021). Revisiting the sustainable happiness model and pie chart: Can happiness be successfully pursued? *Journal of Positive Psychology, 16*(2), 145–154. doi:10.1080/17439760.2019.1689421

Shin, M., Wong, Y. J., Yancura, L., & Hsu, K. (2020). Thanks, mom and dad! An experimental study of gratitude letter writing for Asian and White American emerging adults. *Counselling Psychology Quarterly, 33*(3), 267–286. doi:10.1080/09515070.2018.1542519

Slee, A., Nazareth, I., Freemantle, N., & Horsfall, L. (2021). Trends in generalised anxiety disorders and symptoms in primary care: UK population-based cohort study. *Br J Psychiatry, 218*(3), 158–164. doi:10.1192/bjp.2020.159

Steger, M. F. (2017). Meaning in life and wellbeing. In M. Slade, L. Oades, & A. Jarden (Eds.), *Wellbeing, recovery and mental health* (pp. 75–85). New York: Cambridge University Press.

Syed, J. (2020). *Diversity management and missing voices handbook of research on employee voice.* Cheltenham, UK: Edward Elgar Publishing.

Worland, J. (2020). 2020 Is our last, best chance to save the planet. *Time.*

Wrzesniewski, A. (2014). Engage in job crafting. In G. M. Spreitzer & J. Dutton (Eds.), *How to be a positive leader: Small actions, big impact* (pp. 65–75). San Francisco: Berrett Koehler.

2 | **Abundance**

Charley Stoney, CEO of the Institute of Advertising Practitioners in Ireland, is naturally inclined towards people's strengths. She knows it is easy to see impairment, weakness, and shortcomings, yet feels it is considerably more rewarding to see strengths, assets, and virtues. She takes it up a level when she talks about her commitment to seeing abundance and celebrating it. She refers to her team's strengths as "beautiful weirdness". This way, she acknowledges the value of their diversity and uniqueness. It allows her to focus on the exceptional assets that her team has (abundance) instead of their shortcomings (deficits), thus tweaking the environment to feel authentic and appreciated. Only in an abundant climate can her team truly be themselves and achieve their potential.

What is abundance?

Abundance is a leader's inclination towards seeing, developing, and using their own, other people's, and organisational strengths. It comprises three components (Figure 2.1): (1) strengths mindset, which refers to a leader's belief that strengths are malleable; (2) strengths spotting, meaning an ability for leaders to notice and name their strengths and the strengths of others; and (3) strengths use, which refers to a leader's ability to apply strengths in their daily life and encourage others to do the same (Figure 2.2). These resources allow leaders to achieve extraordinary performance and tap into their employees' potential. Furthermore, they are enacted at personal, collective, and organisational levels, meaning that positive leaders can act the components of abundance concerning themselves, use it in their daily communication with

DOI: 10.4324/9781003170433-2

Figure 2.1 The Abundance resource piece of the ALIGHT jigsaw

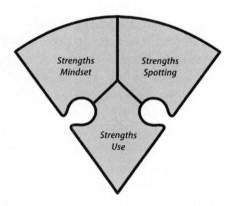

Figure 2.2 The Abundance components

their team, and promote it when making decisions at an organisational level. Let us now delve deeper into each one of the components.

Mindset

The placebo effect has puzzled academics and practitioners for years. It refers to our ability to achieve positive outcomes that do not derive from medical treatment (Crane, 2016). The theories as to why they are effective are plentiful, with one of them drawing from the power of our expectations that inform our outcomes, as they allow us to summon our emotional, cognitive, and behavioural resources to make it happen (Crane, 2016).

Imagine if medical doctors told you that the work you do benefits your health. This is precisely what accommodation attendants across seven US hotels were told (Crum & Langer, 2007). In a short conversation, a group of researchers told them that their work had been carefully analysed by a medical doctor, who confirmed that carrying out their daily duties, such as cleaning hotel rooms, cleaning bathrooms, changing sheets, and hoovering the carpets was comparable to doing a daily requirement of exercise. Subsequently, two months later, they reported physiological changes, such as improving cardiovascular health and weight loss. At the same time, another group of accommodation assistants who did the same amount of physical activity, but were not told of the benefits of their work on their health, reported no such change. The first group's changed mindset worked just like the placebo effect; it provided them with enough belief to make a change happen. Mindset is therefore a powerful resource for initiating change.

A growth mindset is one such example of a placebo effect. According to Dweck (2006), we are all on a continuum in relation to the perspectives on our abilities, intelligence, and talent at one end. We perceive them as stable, unchangeable qualities that define us; at the other end, we see them as malleable. Depending on our views, our intellectual, emotional, and social resources are activated and result in different behaviour and outcomes. In a classic study, Mueller and Dweck (1998) put participants into growth or fixed mindsets by giving specific feedback on their tasks. For example, researchers told group 1 (fixed mindset) that they did well on their mathematical test because they were smart; therefore, their results were due to their stable characteristics. Researchers told group 2 (growth mindset) that they were successful because they worked hard.

As soon as all the participants' performance declined, the fixed mindset people blamed their intelligence for not doing well. After all, if they did well because they were smart, they must have done poorly because they are not smart enough. Subsequently, they did not enjoy the activity and saw it as a measure of their intelligence. When given a choice of doing an easier or more difficult task, they opted for an easy one to maintain their positive self-image. When asked at the end of the experiment about their final scores, over 50% of them lied and claimed their results were better than they were. At the same time, the growth mindset participants enjoyed the challenge of the activity and wanted to keep going with a more challenging task. The task reflected their hard work, not their capacity, which is why only 1% of them lied about their results. A growth mindset is therefore an openness to the idea that our qualities are malleable.

If we translate these results into workplace outcomes, their impact can be potentially staggering. Simple feedback from a leader, colleague, or self-evaluation deemed to be fixed may lead to dire consequences concerning individual and group performance. When everything is going well, there is not much of a difference between the groups. However, when individuals experience a setback, those with a fixed mindset avoid activities that may imply their deficits and prevent them from looking 'dumb' in front of their colleagues (Yeager & Dweck, 2012; Yeager et al., 2014). On the other hand, those with a growth mindset are more likely to challenge themselves and persevere through challenges, thus focusing on their competence, not an ability that may have a negative effect on their outcomes (Dweck, 2006).

Unfortunately, some organisations continue to promote a fixed mindset. Many years ago, one of our employers used a number of personality and talent assessment tools to recruit new staff. We would talk about the new starters in terms of who they were in a type casting way, e.g. "She is persistent and perfect for this job", we would say when analysing the results of her talent assessment, or "He is INTJ, so here are his strengths and weaknesses", referring to the Myers Briggs type indicator, which did often seem to describe the team member's personality accurately. While these assessment tools were validated and valuable tools to learn about the type of people our new colleagues were, we tended to assume that the team employees would *always* behave in a specific way, which – in the long term – was not a helpful assumption. What we often forget is that various factors influence our behaviour.

Think of yourself with your work colleagues, family, and friends. You behave differently with people you trust than you do with strangers. Consider a physical environment where you work. The office design, colour, light, symmetry, or shapes may be conducive to creative thinking, or not; they may encourage collaboration or prevent it; they may help us to become effective or get in the way of our productivity (Lee, 2018), not to mention our differences associated with our capacity to learn and change. The latest developments in epigenetics, which studies the environmental influence of genetic changes, suggest that some are particularly sensitive to our environment and have a greater aptitude to alter our behaviour (Pluess, 2015). Therefore, some of the people you employed three years ago may behave very differently today than they initially did. This is because their behaviour may have adjusted to the environment.

When we view employees' strengths as stable characteristics, personalities, and talents that cannot alter much, our mindset becomes more fixed on who the people are instead of their potential. In other words, we may have a fixed or growth mindset towards our strengths or the strengths of people around us, which will influence how we engage with strengths (Biswas-Diener, Kashdan, & Minhas, 2011; Jach, Sun, Loton, Chin, & Waters, 2018). When leaders consider their strengths as fixed, they are focused on demonstrating to others what they are good at, proving themselves to them, and doing their jobs the same way they have done before to be praised for what they are good at. When leaders see their strengths as malleable, they know that if they can't do something well today, it is because they can't do it yet. The more effort they put into developing their strengths, applying them to their daily lives, the better they will become at using them in the future. Furthermore, their strengths are just a resource they have which they continue to tap into and become better at applying as they practise it every day. To do it effectively, they need to start with a strengths mindset.

Similarly, when leaders perceive their team's strengths as malleable, they are not fixated on judging their people, labelling individuals, or making decisions based on the assumption that people do not change. Instead, they are focused on the process of their development and see them on a journey to becoming their best possible selves. This, in turn, allows them to tap into their potential and help their team reach a higher level of performance via the Pygmalion effect, which posits that leaders' expectations of followers' high performance result in the improvement of their performance (Whiteley, Sy, & Johnson, 2012). This effect is even more potent for less experienced leaders. Among students, awareness of strengths is associated with higher levels of perceived leadership development. It makes them more involved in community service, leadership training, and voluntary organisations to practice their leadership skills (Soria, Roberts, & Reinhard, 2015). Therefore, the benefits to young people who actively develop their leadership capacity are even more powerful (Kouzes & Posner, 2019). Let us see how positive leaders embrace this strength mindset.

Sean Corrigan is a wastewater and environmental engineer in Ireland and an unofficial leader of the award-winning "Let It Bee" project. He is passionate about keeping watercourses clean. Over the last decade, the landscape in rural Ireland has changed significantly. Farmers have been incentivised through their government-managed essential farm payments to maximise their land utilisation. Non-productive land, such as land with hedgerows, trees, and marginal land, is deemed ineligible for payment. This has led to the removal and destruction of many biodiverse habitats. Breaching these guidelines results in the government ceasing European Union payments to their farm, and thus a significant reduction in their annual income. They farm their land to the edge of a watercourse without leaving any idle patches. This, in turn, results in the slurry from their farm, filled with chemicals, spilling into the Irish lakes and rivers, killing off their natural habitat. Given that farming was their livelihood, Sean has faced a big dilemma in motivating farmers to cease water pollution.

In his approach, he has decided to work with farmers' strengths. Farmers are very hard-working people and part of a tight-knit community. Even though their farming was being associated with water pollution, they genuinely did not want to be part of the problem, but become part of a solution. Sean introduced one farmer to an additional revenue stream for him, which was keeping beehives. Since bees needed clean air to survive, the farmer and Sean planted a 1200 sq m area of wild meadow and trees between the farm and the water. This meadow prevented the slurry from entering the water system, creating an excellent environment for the farmers' children to play, provided an additional income to the farmer from the honey that the bees produced, and made the farmer proud about his contribution to enhancing their environment.

Drawing from the strengths of the farming community, Sean watched as the first farmer convinced the second farmer to do the same. The second farmer convinced the third farmer, and soon, 21 farmers in the area began to protect the local river from pollution. The success of this project resulted in Sean receiving several Irish and European awards. To tap into the strengths of the farming community, he had first to believe that a change can happen, which is what a strength mindset is all about. We will talk more about this bee project and its healthy, fully integrative approach in Chapter 6. Before we move to look at strengths spotting, take some time now to reflect on your strength mindset – how well does this integrate into your work?

> **Reflection on practice**
> *Begin by identifying what your strengths mindset is like – do you lean towards a "fixed" or "growth" perception of your strengths? How likely do you believe that people's strengths can change? Think of colleagues or your practice; how have you or others developed their strengths in the past? On a scale from 1 to 10, how likely are you (or others you have in mind) to develop their strengths? The closer you are to 10, the more you or others display a growth strength mindset.*

If you scored around 5, over the next few weeks search for examples of people who have developed their skills significantly over time. Reflect on how they have done it. How much effort have they put into their personal and professional growth? Some claim it takes 10,000 hours to become experts. What does it look like in practical terms?

Strength spotting

Positive leaders have an awareness of their strengths and can spot other people's strengths well. Some people find it particularly easy to do. Charley Stoney, a CEO of the Institute of Advertising Practitioners in Ireland (IAPI), is proud of the programme she developed along with the IAPI Board: 'Ireland: Where Creative Is Native'. After taking over the leadership position in IAPI, she reflected on how Ireland, a small country of just over 4 million people, has already contributed significantly to the world. Many Irish writers have become household names: Oscar Wilde, Samuel Beckett, W. B. Yates, and James Joyce, to more recently Seamus Heaney, Roddy Doyle, Iris Murdoch, Maeve Binchy, and others. Ireland has produced some of the top names in the music industry, such as U2, Van Morrison, Enya, The Cranberries, The Script, Snow Patrol, The Pogues, The Corrs, Damien Rice, and many more. St Patrick's Day celebrations also have a huge international influence where places such as the Eiffel Tower, Niagara Falls, or the Sydney Opera House light up in green and millions of people go out on the streets of New York, London, Montserrat (Caribbean), Buenos Aires, Montreal, Auckland, Sydney, Munich, and Singapore join the Irish in the annual parade to celebrate the Irishness. 'Ireland: Where Creative Is Native' is a perfect example of the abundance approach where a starting point is what is great about Ireland to capitalise on magnifying that, rather than focusing on its comparative size or population.

For advertisers, searching for strengths in their product or people they promote is natural. They find that special something and put a spotlight on it, thus bringing it to the consumer's attention. When they get it right, they have the general public buy into their ad campaign. When they get it wrong, their campaign often falls flat. The same applies to salespeople. When selling a product, they need to find out what the product's strengths are and how these strengths can be helpful to the potential buyers. Nevertheless, when it comes to people they work with, sometimes leaders forget to follow the same logic and focus on what works well. For positive leaders, the process of strength spotting is similar, whereby they search for what is working, and their role is to amplify it and replicate it as much as possible.

Focusing on strengths at work garnered significance in the 1970s when a social worker, Saleeby, suggested they should be used in practice. As a result, many practitioners began to focus on what is good about people rather than what does not work. This strength-based approach continues in the appreciative inquiry approach to growing individuals, teams, and organisations. We will discuss it later in this chapter. However, the biggest obstacle to the generic strength-based approach is that we often are either unaware of our strengths or unable to articulate them. Therefore, an assessment of strengths comes in useful in such situations.

There are five main strength assessments that leaders can apply in their practice. The most prevalent theory of strengths derives from positive psychology, and it perceives strengths as values in action (VIA). There are 24 such strengths, divided into six virtues that can be analysed using a free assessment of strengths (www.viacharacter.org). An example of a strength includes perseverance, kindness, or leadership. Using this model, the definition of strengths is complex and includes ten defining criteria, such as that a strength needs to contribute to the good life, be morally valued, and that the display of strength by one person would not diminish another person. Usually, leaders identify employees' top strengths and help them apply their strengths more frequently at work.

The second model of strengths comes from the Strengths Profile (Linley & Bateman, 2018). It is based on strengths that describe behaviours associated with daily personal or work life. It offers 60 strengths to choose from, and they include organisation, writing, and resilience. They are organised into four categories: realised strengths, unrealised strengths, learnt behaviours, and weaknesses. Realised strengths are those that your employee is aware of and uses frequently. Unrealised strengths are potential strengths that your employee can use if they put their mind to it. Learnt behaviours are developed over the years, which are not strengths, but behaviours that the person is good at. Weakness are exactly that, weaknesses.

For leaders, the guidance is to utilise their team's strengths to help them achieve high performance, tap into their unrealised strengths to set up stretch goals, and challenge their teams. They use the learnt behaviours as a great resource when needed, and use their weaknesses only to compensate for the lack of strengths on the team. According to this model, the definition of strengths is that strength is something that energises employees. Therefore, weaknesses and learnt behaviours are draining when used too frequently.

The third model of strengths comes from StrengthFinder, which was the first strength assessment ever created. It consists of 34 strengths and provides a comprehensive profile of strengths that employers can tap into (Hodges & Clifton, 2004). It has been used by organisations worldwide and defines strengths as talents refined with knowledge and skills.

The fourth model is the StrengthsScope, the only strengths profile accepted by the British Psychological Society as a psychometric test. It was also the first strengths instrument that acknowledged the challenge of over-using strengths. The strengths in this model are divided into relational, emotional, execution, and thinking strengths (Brook & Brewerton, 2016). They are highly oriented towards the workplace and business and some of the strengths can also read like competencies.

While these four models provide data and help us assess our own and our team's performance, sometimes we do not need to complete any assessments, but base our judgement of ourselves and other people's strengths on our perception. For example, strength assessments are suitable for creating a vocabulary of strengths and creating consistency of use and language across a team or organisation, but they are not always necessary. Employees can decide what they believe they are good at, and leaders can do the same. The most important thing is to use what helps, what we excel at, and keep improving our use of this whilst enjoying the increased performance.

Performance reviews are the bread and butter of leadership. We often secretly or openly moan when they come up and then dutifully tick all the boxes and fill in all the blank spaces to provide employees with clarity as to what we expect them to do and what we want them to avoid doing. However, in a study with almost 20,000 managers across five continents, researchers found that feedback we offer employees is counterproductive (Council, 2002). We taught leaders to provide constructive feedback (Kunich & Lester, 1996; Ovando, 2005), i.e. they were asked to specify what was not working, focus on behaviours that employees needed to change, and discuss how it should be accomplished. However, when we focus When we focus on the negatives during a performance review, employees begin to make less effort and they question their suitability for the job, all of which has a negative impact on their performance, which drops to as much as 26.8%. On the other hand, when a leader emphasises employees' performance strengths, their performance soars to 36.4%. Therefore, positive feedback matters, and strengths can help leaders guide their team's performance, and boost the effectiveness and power of performance reviews to make them more meaningful.

Becoming aware of one's strengths boosts self-confidence (Clifton, Anderson, & Schreiner, 2006), a fundamental leadership quality. This is why positive leaders have full awareness of what is good about them and how they can use it. When we asked him about his strengths, a professor of biochemistry and immunology and a chair of biochemistry in Trinity College Dublin did not even flinch. He listed them one by one, explaining briefly what each of his strengths meant and how it added value to his daily work and team. Orla Deering, co-founder of Reba Reborn Hair and Beauty chain in Ireland, could also clearly identify what she was good at and what she needed help with. There was no reflection required, as she had it all thought through thought it all through. She divides the tasks she is involved in at work between herself and her husband, the co-owner of the business, based on what each of them is good at. This 'owning' of strengths allows positive leaders to fully accept themselves, regardless of their strengths. Knowing what resources they can tap into allows them to transform their performance and lead their team towards success.

Awareness of leaders' strengths provides them with a solid foundation to help others identify, develop, and apply strengths, enhancing the team's effectiveness (Rath & Conchie, 2009). Strength focus is a crucial resource for positive leaders. Experts in road safety say that when we lose control of a car, we search for trees or lampposts to avoid them. However, by focusing on them, we are more likely to crash into them. Instead, we should pay attention to the space between the trees or lampposts. This is because whatever we focus our attention on, we are more likely to be drawn towards. Our brain does not understand the language of negation: "Do not go there". Instead, we see the image of the tree, and that is where we are heading. The same applies to strengths.

When we focus on strengths, we are more likely to see them in ourselves and others – for example, priming teachers to notice their students' strengths before a class enhances students' engagement, autonomy, and wellbeing (Quinlan, Vella-Brodrick, Gray, & Swain, 2019). Likewise, priming therapists to consider their clients' strengths ten minutes before their therapy session resulted in more profound outcomes for both clients and therapists and a sense of greater mastery (Flückiger, Caspar, Holtforth, & Willutzki, 2009). Imagine what would happen if, in addition to recognising their own strengths, leaders considered the strengths of others in the same way.

When we become aware of our strengths and the strengths of others, it is crucial not to perceive them in silos. It is not a single strength that guides our behaviour, even though it may seem predominant, but the entirety of the strength constellation (Biswas-Diener et al., 2011). For example, say that one of your top strengths is tenacity. It is a beautiful quality to have, as it allows us to persevere and keep going when others have already given up. However, if our flexibility is underdeveloped at the same time, tenacity without flexibility may result in rigidity that will not serve us well when trying to accomplish goals. Equally, we may display the strength of courage. We are brave in the face of adversity or perhaps can stand up for other people (especially if we have developed the strength of fairness). However, courage without prudence will result in reckless behaviour and will harm the people around us if we are not careful. This is why it is crucial to view strengths in the context of other strengths and various situations in which we use them. This will ultimately help us understand ourselves and other people's behaviours better.

Reflection on practice

Complete one of the strengths questionnaires outlined earlier (VIA, Strengths Profile, Strengthsfinder, or StrengthScope).

Reflect on the results or contact a coach to reflect on the results together. What are your top strengths? How do you know they are your strengths? Think of examples of situations when you have recently displayed your strengths. What did it feel like? What other situations would your strengths be useful in? How do your strengths interact with each other?

Now, reflect on others, you could reflect on: your colleagues, a team, a whole organisation, family members, a film or book characters, etc. Think of what top strengths that they display. How do you know it? What situations led you to believe what their strengths were? Do they overuse or underuse any strengths? How do their strengths interact with each other?

Strength use

Strength use relates to how we tap into the potential of our strengths daily. In other words, how effectively we use strengths in our lives. Being aware of our strengths does not guarantee their use. We apply strengths differently in our personal and work lives and often need help to do it (Huber et al., 2020). For example, we once worked with a coaching client who used many of her strengths when engaging with her knitting hobby. However, she used hardly any of her strengths at work, which resulted in her not enjoying it. We slowly tried to figure out a way to transfer her excellent strength use from her personal life to another domain of her life during our sessions. This resulted in her enjoying her work much more and getting much more satisfaction from her life overall. Sometimes, these tiny changes in our practice can make a huge difference.

Using strengths at work and helping others use strengths at work can significantly impact their wellbeing. For centuries we have debated the meaning of wellbeing. Philosophers perceived it from various perspectives. For example, some viewed it as the prudential value of human beings, whereby experiencing pleasure is more valuable than experiencing pain (hedonism); others considered wellbeing as desire fulfilment, and yet some spoke about wellbeing as an objective list of what they believed made people happier (Fletcher, 2016). On the other hand, anthropologists viewed wellbeing from the cultural perspective, whereby they appreciated the individual within a specific cultural context (Fujimura & Nommensen, 2019). Nevertheless, another widespread point of reference comes from psychologists, for whom wellbeing is a construct comprising various elements of what is considered wellbeing (Burke, 2021).

These elements are derived from various approaches to assessing wellbeing. Some theories stem from a review of past literature, such as the psychological wellbeing theory, which draws from the readings of Freud, Jung, and similar classic psychologists; other theories arise from the assessment of the general public, who postulated wellbeing to be their sense of life satisfaction and frequent experiences of positive emotional states (Diener, Suh, Lucas, & Smith, 1999; Ryff & Keyes, 1995). Regardless of the origin, they were constructed to help people conceptualise how they felt and identify what could be done to help them feel better every day.

In recent decades, new models have emerged, created by positive psychologists and combining several perspectives on wellbeing. They are referred to as flourishing models. Flourishing is understood as the highest level of emotional, psychological, and social functioning (Keyes, 2002). Whilst the vast majority of people experience moderate levels of wellbeing, whereby they may reach two out of three elements of wellness, flourishing individuals are at their best across all the main aspects of wellbeing.

Experiencing flourishing protects us from mental health problems, such as depression (Keyes, Yao, Hybels, Milstein, & Proeschold-Bell, 2020). It also helps us live a more fulfilling life and is associated with a higher level of performance (Keyes et al., 2012). However, it is essential to note that this does not mean that flourishing individuals would have the highest performance at work, and the performance of those who are moderately well or unwell would be inferior. On the contrary, there are many circumstances whereby employees with lower levels of wellbeing may become highly effective in their job. However, the consistency of performance may be more visible with individuals who are flourishing.

Furthermore, employees who are doing well, especially concerning their emotional wellbeing, are also more engaged and more efficient in applying themselves at work. Thus, they are more likely to contribute to the organisational results (Harter, Schmidt, & Keyes, 2003). These are just some of the reasons why wellbeing and flourishing matter.

One way in which positive leaders can help employees flourish at work is by helping them use their strengths at work. In a study with 10,000 employees in New Zealand, team members who identified their strengths were nine times more likely to flourish psychologically than those who did not (Hone, Jarden, Duncan, & Schofield, 2015). Furthermore, the employees who regularly used their strengths at work were 18 times more likely to experience flourishing than those who were not. Whilst most participants were aware of their strengths, using them effectively was challenging for many. However, it yields particularly positive results.

In addition to wellbeing and flourishing, using strengths at work is associated with perceiving work as more meaningful (Harzer & Ruch, 2012, 2016). When it is meaningful, we can experience more intrinsic motivation, which boosts our wellbeing further; a job is no longer just a job, but has a deeper purpose. Furthermore, when we use strengths at work, they have the power to buffer us against stress and help us find more satisfaction in what we do every day (Harzer & Ruch, 2015). We use these strengths to help us enjoy our work and become better at it due to the relational aspect of the role we play on the team and how our strengths can help us belong (Ruch, Gander, Platt, & Hofmann, 2018).

Strengths can be viewed in the context of individuals, as well as groups. Let us consider them concerning productivity and performance, which are the foundations of sustainable organisations, which is why they have become a focal point for so many leaders. Over the years, leaders have heard of many approaches to enhancing employees' performance, one of which was the famous Tuckman's model for team creation (Bonebright, 2010). According to the model, for a team to achieve a high level of performance, they need to go through four stages of development: (1) forming, (2) storming, (3) norming, and (4) performing. Forming relates to individuals being pulled together into a group that may become a team at some point in the future. Storming is the part of a process associated with disagreement, discord, and subgroups being created with an opposite purpose. After the storming stage, teams move into norming, whereby consensus is created along with role clarification, and finally, they reach the stage of performing. The model suggests that teams must go through the stage of conflict and resolve their problems in order to perform to their full potential. This approach is echoed by other leadership models, such as situational leadership, transformational leadership, and bounded leadership (Korzynski, Kozminski, Baczynska, & Haenlein, 2021; Lehmann-Willenbrock, Meinecke, Rowold, & Kauffeld, 2015; Malik & Singh, 2017), which presuppose that leaders need to focus on the problem at hand and find solutions to help teams perform. All these models are so well established in business that their efficacy is rarely questioned. However, what if they were not correct? This is a question that one researcher asked himself as he designed an experiment with ten new project teams.

The average size of the project teams he worked with was between 5 and 14 employees (Pavez, 2017). He divided them into two groups, one that followed the problem-solving approach and another group that engaged in an appreciative inquiry process. The second group's starting point was focusing on the resources they had, figuring out what had worked for them in the past, and finding ways in which they could replicate it and amplify their past success in their future project. This approach to managing a project promptly illuminated each team member's potential, whereby in a short space of time, everyone knew what each other's strengths were. It also increased connectivity between each member, which allowed the team to develop purpose and build trust quickly. Furthermore, it inspired the team's transformation and enhanced their potency by increasing their collective efficacy, which was related to everyone on the team believing that they could achieve more together. All these positive changes resulted in the team performing at much higher levels compared to a traditional team. Their performance occurred sooner than the teams focusing on solving problems, as they did not waste too much time and energy on what was not working but rather understood more what could and what was working well for them. This is how the power of an abundance strengths mindset can make a significant difference to your team's life.

Abundance mindset is therefore associated with believing that people around us can change their ways, resulting in extraordinary outcomes. In addition, it is believed that our qualities and characteristics are malleable, and we are all capable of growth and development. Most importantly, however, it is about tapping into our strengths and using them effectively to influence our performance.

Creativity and innovation are of particular interest to many employers. We live in a competitive environment where we have seen more innovation in the last 100 years than in the last 20 centuries. Creativity has thus become a highly sought-after commodity, which is why many organisations engage in a war for talent. Allowing employees to use their strengths at work evokes innovative thinking and behaviour (Ding, Lin, & Su, 2021; Ge & Sun, 2020). Furthermore, developing specific strengths, such as hope or wisdom, is associated with an improvement in innovative thinking and reduced stress and enhanced performance (Avey, Luthans, Hannah, Sweetman, & Peterson, 2012).

In this section, we considered the importance of individuals using strengths and teams applying strengths in their work practice. Positive leaders' abundance approach is crucial; however, strengths focus comes with a note of caution. There is a 'golden mean' of using strengths (Niemiec, 2019) meaning that like the goldilock's principle, we would do well to use our strenghts "just right". Strengths underuse or overuse is associated with adverse outcomes, such as social anxiety and social withdrawal (Freidlin, Littman-Ovadia, & Niemiec, 2017; Matsuguma & Niemiec, 2021). They may also lead to a range of counterproductive behaviours (Niemiec, 2018). For example, when we practise too much kindness, it may lead to us experiencing compassion fatigue or being perceived as intrusive; if we show too much perseverance, we may be viewed as stubborn; if we are too honest, we may be seen as inconsiderate, rude, or self-righteous. Therefore, strengths can become our weaknesses when we overuse them.

This can also become a good way of discussing employees' weaknesses by focusing on how they have overused some of their strengths. After all, most, if not all, of the behaviours that got us into trouble are usually associated with overusing strengths. Employees were late for work; it is not because they were lazy but because they overused their appreciation of beauty. When walking past the park to work, they slowed down to be with nature, hence losing track of time. When they argued with a colleague in the canteen, it was not because they were argumentative, but because they had overused their strength of fairness. Booking a room for a client without a credit card confirmation was not because they were naïve, but because they overused their trust towards the strangers. Therefore, each negative thing we have ever done can be explained by strength overuse to ensure a more inclusive and developmental language.

Reflection on practice
How did you or could you recently have used your strengths? Consider some of your most challenging situations in the last week. Which strengths have you under or overused? How have your strengths got you in trouble?

Abundance in action

Positive leaders practice abundance in various ways. Your greatest challenge will be to 'believe' that strengths can be developed for some of you. Years of conditioning has made you think that we are set in our ways for life. Alternatively, you may even believe that the older we get, the less likely we will change. This type of thinking leaves very little room for change. If you see your strengths as traits or characteristics rather than attributes, it may take you much thinking, reflection, more evidence, and extra effort to process it. The good news is that even if you practise a fixed-strengths mindset, you will still be able to strength spot and use your own and other people's strengths. These three elements are not exclusive of each other.

Some of the leaders we have worked with as coaches have also taught us a valuable lesson about their abundance of resources. They may have used it well with their team, but not so well concerning themselves. This may have been due to their lack of confidence, awareness, or the value of modesty they practised. As such, they had to overcome the psychological obstacles standing in the way of 'owning' their own strengths before they fully engaged with this resource. And we have worked with other leaders who fully flourished with their teams. On the spot, these leaders were able to identify their own strengths and the strengths of other people, teams, community, an organisation, and in some cases, the strengths of projects they have worked on. We see what we fully pay attention to. Therefore, strengths spotting is not a universal or complete skill. However, once we become aware of the extent of our strengths spotting capacity both within ourselves or in others, we can develop this further and, it is helpful to transfer this skill into other contexts of our lives.

Knowledge is not a skill; therefore, just because we believe we can boost our strengths and recognise them easily does not mean that we can apply them in our daily lives. Furthermore, our application of the abundance resource is domain-specific, whereby we may be good at applying them in one project or one aspect of our lives but not so good at applying them elsewhere. This is why it is important to continually consider ways in which our abundance skills can be developed. Initially, it may take us more reflection and effort to do it. However, as we begin to use the resource of abundance more actively, it will become easier.

For some of us, our strengths are associated with our profession. However, researchers do not know if we are attracted to specific jobs depending on our strengths or because we develop our strengths by actively engaging with them. As such, differences were found between nurses, physicians, supervisors, clinical psychologists, office workers, social workers, economists, teachers, leaders, service and sales workers, skilled agricultural, forestry and fishery workers, craft and related trades workers, managers, supervisors, and others (Gander, Hofmann, & Ruch, 2021; Heintz & Ruch, 2020). If the jobs we do impact our strengths, leaders helping employees tap into their strengths can escalate this process. On the other hand, if we are attracted to the jobs that suit our strengths, developing them will come easy. Either way, leaders recognising the team's strengths and helping the team to develop them further will be further assisted and enabled by the work environment. This is one specific condition that allows for the strengths to develop.

When introducing the abundance resource into an organisation, what matters is whether or not an organisation where you work fully supports your employees' strength use. When it does, employees' self-evaluations of strength use are effective in helping them apply more strengths at work; when the organisation does not support strength use, then the change associated with an abundance perspective is not fully embedded in the tapestry of organisational life (Ding & Lin, 2019). This is why it is essential to incorporate the strength culture in an organisation to ensure robust outcomes.

Another condition that helps employees engage more effectively with strength use is their supervisor or manager supporting them (Ding & Yu, 2020; Lavy, Littman-Ovadia, & Boiman-Meshita, 2017). However, that support needs to be active and authentic. It is not enough for you as a leader to 'talk the talk'; you need to 'walk the walk'. When employees feel that their leaders actively support them in using their strengths at work, they begin to apply discretionary strengths beyond their work requirements. Only active support from a leader can make this positive difference.

Last word

In conclusion, positive leaders tap into the resource of abundance regularly. They are aware of the influence of negative self-evaluation, negative feedback and weakness, or deficit focus in daily interactions. Subsequently, they make a considered effort to see their own, their team's, and other people's and organisations' strengths. They also firmly believe that strengths are not a stable characteristic, but a malleable quality that can alter with time. Therefore, they make extra effort to apply their strengths and help their team do the same. They develop habits that enable them to do it. However, they are also wary about keeping a strength balance and not overusing strengths, so they practise regular communication with their team about the strengths they have overused and their impact on others. Thus, their abundance approach allows them to view their people and situations from various perspectives instead of being blinded to the just the negative or positive aspects of life.

References

Avey, J. B., Luthans, F., Hannah, S. T., Sweetman, D., & Peterson, C. (2012). Impact of employees' character strengths of wisdom on stress and creative performance. *Human Resource Management Journal*, *22*(2), 165–181. doi:10.1111/j.1748-8583.2010.00157.x

Biswas-Diener, R., Kashdan, T. B., & Minhas, G. (2011). A dynamic approach to psychological strength development and intervention. *The Journal of Positive Psychology, 6*(2), 106–118. doi:10.1080/17439760.2010.545429

Bonebright, D. (2010). 40 years of storming: A historical review of Tuckman's model of small group development. *Human Resource Development International, 13*(1), 111–120. doi:10.1080/13678861003589099

Brook, J., & Brewerton, P. (2016). *Optimize your strengths: Use your leadership strengths to get the best out of you and your team.* New York: Wiley.

Burke, J. (2021). *The ultimate guide to implementing wellbeing programmes for school.* London: Routledge.

Clifton, D. O., Anderson, E. C., & Schreiner, L. A. (2006). *StrengthsQuest: Discover and develop your strengths in academics, career, and beyond* (2nd ed.). Princeton, NJ: Gallup Press.

Council (2002). *Performance management survey.* Washington DC: CAPP.

Crane, G. S. (2016). Harnessing the placebo effect: A new model for mind-body healing mechanisms. *The International Journal of Transpersonal Studies, 35*(1), 39–51.

Crum, A. J., & Langer, E. J. (2007). Mind-set matters: Exercise and the placebo effect. *Psychological Science (0956–7976), 18*(2), 165–171. doi:10.1111/j.1467-9280.2007.01867.x

Diener, E., Suh, E. M., Lucas, R. E., & Smith, H. L. (1999). Subjective well-being: Three decades of progress. *Psychological Bulletin, 125*(2), 276–302. doi:10.1037/0033-2909.125.2.276

Ding, H., & Lin, X. (2019). Can core self-evaluations promote employee strengths use? *Journal of Psychology in Africa, 29*(6), 576–581. doi:10.1080/14330237.2019.1691792

Ding, H., Lin, X., & Su, W. (2021). Employee strengths use and innovative behavior: A moderated mediation model. *Chinese Management Studies, 15*(2), 350–362. doi:10.1108/CMS-05-2019-0191

Ding, H., & Yu, E. (2020). How and when does perceived supervisor support for strengths use influence employee strengths use? The roles of positive affect and self-efficacy. *Journal of Psychology in Africa, 30*(5), 384–389. doi:10.1080/14330237.2020.1821307

Dweck, C. S. (2006). *Mindset: The new psychology of success.* New York: Random House.

Fletcher, G. (2016). *The philosophy of wellbeing.* London: Routledge.

Flückiger, C., Caspar, F., Holtforth, M. G., & Willutzki, U. (2009). Working with patients' strengths: A microprocess approach. *Psychotherapy Research, 19*(2), 213–223. doi:10.1080/10503300902755300

Freidlin, P., Littman-Ovadia, H., & Niemiec, R. M. (2017). Positive psychopathology: Social anxiety via character strengths underuse and overuse. *Personality and Individual Differences, 108*, 50–54. doi:10.1016/j.paid.2016.12.003

Fujimura, C. K. & Nommensen, S. (2019). *Cultural dimensions of wellbeing: Therapy animals as healers.* London: Lexington Books.

Gander, F., Hofmann, J., & Ruch, W. (2021). Character strengths: Person – Environment fit and relationships with job and life satisfaction. *Frontiers in Psychology, 11*, 1582. doi:10.3389/fpsyg.2020.01582

Ge, Y., & Sun, X. (2020). The relationship of employees' strengths use and innovation: Work engagement as a mediator. *Social Behavior & Personality: An International Journal, 48*(5), 1–6. doi:10.2224/sbp.9083

Harter, J. K., Schmidt, F. L., & Keyes, C. L. M. (2003). Well-being in the workplace and its relationship to business outcomes: A review of the Gallup studies. In C. L. M. Keyes & J. Haidt (Eds.), *Flourishing: Positive psychology and the life well-lived* (pp. 205–224). American Psychological Association. doi:10.1037/10594-009

Harzer, C., & Ruch, W. (2012). When the job is a calling: The role of applying one's signature strengths at work. *Journal of Positive Psychology, 7*(5), 362–371. doi:10.1080/17439760.2012.702784

Harzer, C., & Ruch, W. (2015). The relationships of character strengths with coping, work-related stress, and job satisfaction. *Frontiers in Psychology, 6*.

Harzer, C., & Ruch, W. (2016). Your strengths are calling: Preliminary results of a web-based strengths intervention to increase calling. *Journal of Happiness Studies, 17*(6), 2237–2256.

Heintz, S., & Ruch, W. (2020). Character strengths and job satisfaction: Differential relationships across occupational groups and adulthood. *Applied Research in Quality of Life, 15*(2), 503–527. doi:10.1007/s11482-018-9691-3

Hodges, T. D., & Clifton, D. O. (2004). Strengths-based development in practice. In P. A. Linley & S. Joseph (Eds.), *Positive psychology in practice* (pp. 256–268). John Wiley & Sons, Inc.

Hone, L. C., Jarden, A., Duncan, S., & Schofield, G. M. (2015). Flourishing in New Zealand workers: Associations with lifestyle behaviors, physical health, psychosocial, and work-related indicators. *Journal of Occupational and Environmental Medicine, 57*(9), 973–983. doi:10.1097/JOM.0000000000000508

Huber, A., Strecker, C., Hausler, M., Kachel, T., Höge, T., & Höfer, S. (2020). Possession and applicability of signature character strengths: What is essential for well-being, work engagement, and burnout? *Applied Research in Quality of Life, 15*(2), 415–436. doi:10.1007/s11482-018-9699-8

Jach, H. K., Sun, J., Loton, D., Chin, T.-C., & Waters, L. E. (2018). Strengths and subjective wellbeing in adolescence: Strength-based parenting and the moderating effect of mindset. *Journal of Happiness Studies, 19*(2), 567–586.

Keyes, C. L. M. (2002). The mental health continuum: From languishing to flourishing in life. *Journal of Health and Social Behavior, 43*(2), 207–222. doi:10.2307/3090197

Keyes, C. L. M., Eisenberg, D., Perry, G. S., Dube, S. R., Kroenke, K., & Dhingra, S. S. (2012). The relationship of level of positive mental health with current mental disorders in predicting suicidal behavior and academic impairment in college students. *Journal of American College Health, 60*(2), 126–133. doi:10.1080/07448481.2011.608393

Keyes, C. L. M., Yao, J., Hybels, C. F., Milstein, G., & Proeschold-Bell, R. J. (2020). Are changes in positive mental health associated with increased likelihood of depression over a two year period? A test of the mental health promotion and protection hypotheses. *Journal of Affective Disorders, 270*, 136–142. doi:10.1016/j.jad.2020.03.056

Korzynski, P., Kozminski, A. K., Baczynska, A., & Haenlein, M. (2021). Bounded leadership: An empirical study of leadership competencies, constraints, and effectiveness. *European Management Journal, 39*(2), 226–235. doi:10.1016/j.emj.2020.07.009

Kouzes, T. K., & Posner, B. Z. (2019). Influence of managers' mindset on leadership behavior. *Leadership & Organization Development Journal, 40*(8), 829–844. doi:10.1108/LODJ-03-2019-0142

Kunich, J. C., & Lester, R. I. (1996). Leadership and the art of feedback: Feeding the hands that back us. *Journal of Leadership Studies, 3*(4), 3–22. doi:10.1177/107179199600300402

Lavy, S., Littman-Ovadia, H., & Boiman-Meshita, M. (2017). The wind beneath my wings: Effects of social support on daily use of character strengths at work. *Journal of Career Assessment, 25*(4), 703–714. doi:10.1177/1069072716665861

Lee, I. F. (2018). *Joyful: The surprising power of ordinary things to create extraordinary happiness*. London, UK: Penguin Random House.

Lehmann-Willenbrock, N., Meinecke, A. L., Rowold, J., & Kauffeld, S. (2015). How transformational leadership works during team interactions: A behavioral process analysis. *Leadership Quarterly, 26*(6), 1017–1033. doi:10.1016/j.leaqua.2015.07.003

Linley, A., & Bateman, T. (2018). *The strengths profile book: Finding what you can do + love to do and why it matters*. Birmingham: CAPP Press.

Malik, A. R., & Singh, P. (2017). Transformational leadership and cultural minorities: A conceptual model. *European Business Review, 29*(5), 500–514. doi:10.1108/EBR-12-2015-0181

Matsuguma, S., & Niemiec, R. M. (2021). Hikikomori from the perspective of overuse, underuse, and optimal use of character strengths: Case reports. *International Journal of Applied Positive Psychology, 6*, 219–231. doi:10.1007/s41042-020-00047-3

Mueller, C. M., & Dweck, C. S. (1998). Praise for intelligence can undermine children's motivation and performance. *Journal of Personality and Social Psychology, 75*(1), 33–52. doi:10.1037/0022-3514.75.1.33

Niemiec, R. M. (2018). *Character strengths interventions: A field guide for practitioners*. Boston, MA: Hogrefe Publishing.

Niemiec, R. M. (2019). Finding the golden mean: The overuse, underuse, and optimal use of character strengths. *Counselling Psychology Quarterly, 32*(3/4), 453–471. doi:10.1080/09515070.2019.1617674

Ovando, M. N. (2005). Building instructional leaders' capacity to deliver constructive feedback to teachers. *Journal of Personnel Evaluation in Education, 18*(3), 171–183. doi:10.1007/s11092-006-9018-z

Pavez, I. (2017). *An empirical understanding of appreciative organizing as a way to reframe group development*. Paper presented at the 5th World Congress on Positive Psychology, Montreal, Canada.

Pluess, M. (2015). *Genetics of psychological well-being the role of heritability and genes in positive psychology* (M. Pluess, Ed.). Oxford: Oxford University Press.

Quinlan, D., Vella-Brodrick, D. A., Gray, A., & Swain, N. (2019). Teachers matter: Student outcomes following a strengths intervention are mediated by teacher strengths spotting. *Journal of Happiness Studies, 20*(8), 2507–2523. doi:10.1007/s10902-018-0051-7

Rath, T., & Conchie, B. (2009). *Strengths based leadership: Great leaders, teams, and why people follow*. Omaha, NE: Gallup Press.

Ruch, W., Gander, F., Platt, T., & Hofmann, J. (2018). Team roles: Their relationships to character strengths and job satisfaction. *The Journal of Positive Psychology, 13*(2), 190–199. doi:10.1080/17439760.2016.1257051

Ryff, C. D., & Keyes, C. L. M. (1995). The structure of psychological well-being revisited. *Journal of Personality and Social Psychology, 69*(4), 719–727. doi:10.1037/0022-3514.69.4.719

Soria, K. M., Roberts, J. E., & Reinhard, A. P. (2015). First-year college students' strengths awareness and perceived leadership development. *Journal of Student Affairs Research and Practice, 52*(1), 89–103.

Whiteley, P., Sy, T., & Johnson, S. K. (2012). Leaders' conceptions of followers: Implications for naturally occurring pygmalion effects. *Leadership Quarterly, 23*(5), 822–834. doi:10.1016/j.leaqua.2012.03.006

Yeager, D. S., & Dweck, C. (2012). Mindsets that promote resilience: When students believe that personal characteristics can be developed. *Educational Psychologist, 47*(4), 302–314. doi:10.1080/00461520.2012.722805

Yeager, D. S., Johnson, R., Spitzer, B. J., Trzesniewski, K. H., Powers, J., & Dweck, C. S. (2014). The far-reaching effects of believing people can change: Implicit theories of personality shape stress, health, and achievement during adolescence. *Journal of Personality and Social Psychology, 106*(6), 867–884. doi:10.1037/a0036335.supp (Supplemental)

3 | **Limberness**

Taking time to observe, note, reflect, and learn from our own words and actions and those of others in a curious and non-reactive way is a harder feat than it sounds. Russell, the chief executive officer (CEO) of the UK-based education charity Teach First has worked on building this limberness muscle. Russell says we need to get to know the people we work with and be as open as possible; we also need to be reflective about our own reactions and behaviours and that of others in an open-minded and curious way – not jumping to conclusions and assumptions. Russell says this limberness enables a flow in relationships and means that colleagues will come and talk to you about matters you will not have anticipated because they trust they will be listened to in good faith. He suggests that to get a true picture of what is going on in any organisation, rather than reacting to somebody's outburst or concern by reflecting on their emotion, we can separate this out and realise there will be something happening below the surface that's triggering a person's email, outburst, or concern rather than taking it at face value: "Increasingly, if you approach that [situation instead] with a viewpoint that these are smart people, acting in good faith just doing something that you find hard to explain or understand . . . what that means is that there's something in that context which is making that [irrational behaviour] seem like rational behaviour to them." Russell is aware that behaviour can signify information, and by being adaptable and emotionally agile as leaders, we can learn more – be resilient and grow – in any given situation – all of which results in limberness.

DOI: 10.4324/9781003170433-3

What is limberness?

Limberness is a leader's ability to adapt, be emotionally agile, and become resilient in changing contexts (Figure 3.1). Limberness is three-fold and multidimensional in how it empowers leaders to be agile and flexible. It comprises (1) adaptability, which involves an intentional shift in behaviour or mindset; (2) emotional agility, which is the ability to choose a reaction – a selection of an emotional or, indeed, a cognitive response – that best or better fits the scenario we find ourselves in; and (3) resilience – learning and growing from an experience, be it adverse or positive (Figure 3.2). These combined resources allow leaders to achieve extraordinary performance and tap into their employees' optimum potential through limberness. They are enacted at subjective, collective, and organisational levels, meaning that positive leaders are able to enact the components of limberness in relation to themselves, use them in their daily communication with their team, and promote them when making decisions at an organisational level. These three components lead to growth – a growth that leads to better performance for ourselves and others than a rigid mindset. We will now delve more deeply into these components, describing what they are, why they are important,

Figure 3.1 The Limberness resource piece of the ALIGHT jigsaw

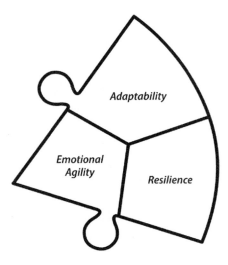

Figure 3.2 The Limberness components

and how they show up for positive leaders before giving you the opportunity to reflect on your own practice.

Adaptability

Adaptability is defined as "the capacity to adjust oneself readily without great difficulty to fit circumstances" (Rettew, 2009). This implies merely the capacity for change rather than heralding a *positive* change. A positive change may indeed occur when individuals are adaptable, but adaptability may as well result in a negative or neutral change. For example, we may adapt to practising a gratitude activity (counting blessings) to an extent when, after doing it every day for two weeks, this activity will cause boredom and thus result in a negative outcome (Lyubomirsky, Sheldon, & Schkade, 2005). Alternatively, a leader overusing "thank you" or "well done" may see these motivating statements devalued to such an extent that they make no difference or, worse, make a negative impact on employees. The nature of adaptability is well depicted in the Serenity Prayer, which is about providing "the serenity to accept the things one cannot change, the courage to change the things one can, and the wisdom to know the difference" (Shapiro, 2014). This is what adaptability is about: accepting or adapting to changed circumstances.

Adaptability is about individuals and teams being able to maintain their wellbeing, especially emotional wellbeing, in response to adversity, setback, and even when facing traumatic events (Thompson, 2021). It is about them feeling in control, despite having diminished control. Thus, this resource supports leaders by prompting them to take action, change direction, and solve problems instead of dwelling on the outcome which they did not expect or feared. Adaptability is the opposite of saying: "never, ever give up". It is about realising when the time for giving up has arrived and when leaders feel comfortable to change the course.

At the same time, adaptability is not a predictor of the actual change or a degree of change that occurs in an individual's or team's lives (Rettew, 2009). Just because people are capable of adapting, does not mean that they will initiate change. Adaptability is the realisation that they need to take action to change their circumstances.

There are various types of adaptability. Career adaptability, for example, implies individuals' readiness to adapt to changes at work such as expansion of their role or additional duties (Johnston, 2018). Interpersonal adaptability is the individuals' capacity to modify their emotional, behavioural, and cognitive regulation in response to changed circumstances, novel situations, or people (Martin, Nejad, Colmar, & Liem, 2013; VandenBos, 2016). These two types of adaptability are a great example of the limberness resource as they imply the need for leaders to become ready to change direction.

The links between adaptability and greater job satisfaction and performance are increasingly evidenced (Sony & Mekoth, 2016), along with improved relationships through building trust and increased understanding (Erikson, Pender, & Bradbury, 2020) and better leaders, as they are more likely to respond effectively in crisis situations (Yukl & Mahsud, 2010). Limber leaders are open to change and adapt and recognise the increase in performance that this openness to experience and adaptability brings. This is sometimes described as a 'driven benevolence' (Bercial, 2017), an ability to move between compassion and accountability at appropriate moments flexibly. And the good news for us is that adaptability is not a fixed trait: we can learn to develop this capacity to be adaptable (Goleman, Boyatzis, Davidson, Druskat, & Kohlrieser, 2017). In a study examining the moderating role of social support in the relationship between adaptability and life satisfaction, a positive relationship between adaptability and life satisfaction was stronger for individuals with higher levels of social support than for individuals with lower levels of social support (Zhou & Lin, 2016).

Russell regularly talks about the need for leaders to first and foremost be adaptable in how they respond to situations, to be reflective, and to act on real-life reflections with a flexibility of mind. He says:

> You lead, and you see what effect it has and being able to be open and seeing what impact you have on others, being aware of that and then being prepared to adjust to it, you learn as much from that as from anything else.

This centres on adaptability. The opposite of adaptability is 'fixedness' or 'rigidity', where leaders refuse to shift their thinking and feel 'my way is the only way'. Adaptable behaviour, by contrast, can flex and shift into being *both* disciplined *and* creative, thoughtful *and* expressive, spontaneous *and* logical. The positive impact of this adaptability includes better relationships, performance, mental health, transitions, and – as most relevant to our positive leaders – better leadership (Burnell, 2020). In addition, adaptability allows us to remain calm under pressure and display curiosity amid change, being more thoughtful and less reactive (Brassey et al., 2021).

Concerning relationships, people view others who can change the way they communicate based on who their audience is more favourably; this adaptability helps to build an understanding between people (Erikson et al., 2020). In relation to performance, studies have shown that adaptability can support the way individuals approach tasks that are new to them (Grover, 2005), developing creativity (McArdle, Waters, Briscoe, & Hall, 2007) and problem-solving (Mumford, Connelly, Baughman, & Marks, 1994), all aiding performance under pressure (Holland, Woodcock, Cumming, & Duda, 2010). All of these outcomes lead us to the unsurprising identification of the relation between adaptability and better mental health: some studies in the adult population show the link between adaptability and increased job satisfaction (Zhou & Lin, 2016); another highlights adaptability as a potential protective factor against mental health difficulties (Kashdan & Rottenberg, 2010). Finally, in relation to transitions, adaptability can also help with leaders' transitions to retirement, with redundancy, from education to the workplace, and when relocating (Burnell, 2020).

Martine Rose is a British menswear fashion designer and founder of the international label by her same name. She grew up in South London often surrounded by an eclectic mix of family characters and friends that she says all had a critical influencing factor on her creativity and inclusion of all of life's diversity. She would often find herself at her West Indian grand-mother's home with a wide array of the local community spilling in for food, rest, and conversation. Martine's grandmother rented rooms out in the 1970s and 1980s to the West Indian diaspora, who found themselves in London struggling to find rooms to rent due to the abhorrent racism that confronted them in the rental market. Martine says, because of being in that house and seeing her grandmother's generosity in action, she is a person who is adaptable, living with a full acceptance of the array of humanity that anyone can fall on hard times. She says being part of that community taught her that everyone deserves kindness and that there's a space for everyone at the table. As a result, she is perpetually adaptable in the way she manages herself and works with her team. "I'm not a really rigid person. I don't have fixed ideas on people. I have realistic expecta-tions of people, and I don't mind failing [. . .] and I don't hold people up against unachievable goals. I'm okay for people to stumble." For Martine, adaptability is essential to creating trust and enabling creativity, innova-tion, and connection.

Crucially, there is much research to support the relationship between adaptability and better leadership for the combined effect of adaptable individuals being more effective in crisis situations (as already men-tioned) (Yukl & Mahsud, 2010), able to create better relationships with colleagues, and able to foster better employee engagement (Goleman et al., 2017). Adaptable leaders are able to move outside of their comfort zone to employ non-habitual methods of responding to others and tap into other types of leadership behaviours (Sugerman, Scullard, & Wilhelm, 2011), all whilst maintaining their authenticity (Burnell, 2020). Further-more, this adaptability muscle is well flexed by positive leaders. Russell explains that because of the nature of power dynamics and relationships in organisations, leaders inescapably do have power over people's careers and prospects and make choices about people. Consequently, he says that people naturally alternate and adjust their behaviour around him and other leaders. This means leaders can end up being very insulated from the reality of both their own impact and what is really going on – lacking in the desire to develop their own adaptability muscles. "And I think that is much more prevalent than a lot of leaders realise [. . .] the steps that you take to remove the barriers between you and your colleagues are critical." Russell tries to go above and beyond to reduce the impact his power has on the honesty and authenticity of how people present themselves. He

45

says: "I think if you want to learn well, you have to have an environment and culture of transparency and honesty inside the organisation, which is harder than we might think". Here Russell unpicks what he describes as the 'CEO prism' – where people conceal their true thoughts and feelings in a self-protective mechanism. He says leaders can protect themselves from this by being more adaptable and recognise what is getting in the way of their adaptability too.

Overplayed strengths can get in the way of our ability to be adaptable (Kaiser & Overfield, 2011). When leaders overplay their strengths, they become their biggest weakness, as they stop adapting to the context or situation before them (Kaplan & Kaiser, 2013). A strengths approach over-played can be a colleague's worst nightmare. Take an enthusiastic leader; if they become overenthusiastic, their overenthusiasm in getting their point across can drown out the voice of others through volume, intensity, or making others feel overpowered and disempowered – they stop adapt-ability in its tracks. Take another leader who has a strength of developing others; if they overuse this strength, their focus can become tilted towards development at the detriment of delivery, perhaps detracting colleagues or employees from executing their task-related activity when deadlines are looming, preventing adaptability of mindset from shifting towards the most important priority. Maximising our strengths requires a careful balance, as leaders can turn their strengths into weaknesses through overuse and neglecting shortcomings that can degrade the performance of employees, teams, and organisations. Some research has shown that there can be a tendency for managers and leaders to overdo their strengths while under-doing opposing but complementary behaviours. Kaiser and Overfield (2011) signalled a tendency of leaders to do too much of the behaviours related to their strengths with less of a tendency to do too little of opposing but complementary behaviours. Therefore, the leaders may miss out on an opportunity to adapt the degree to which they use strengths or apply dif-ferent strengths to changed circumstances. This research shows that over-abundance and the adaptability of limberness need to be considered to promote balance. We will discuss balance in positive leaders' resources further in Chapter 8.

And how do we develop the adaptability muscle? Some initial research has shown that self-reflection can aid adaptability in the context of careers (Kim & Shin, 2020), management approaches (Karaevli & Hall, 2006), and how the similar but otherwise termed 'insight' can support our positive adaptation of thought patterns (Grossmann & Kross, 2010; Kross & Ayduk, 2017; Nakajima, Takano, & Tanno, 2017). It appears that leaders being actively self-aware of their own thoughts, feelings, and personality preferences may be the first step in flexing away from natural preferences when a different perspective is required. The self-reflection and insight of the positive leaders we spoke to were actively reflective, where leaders spoke of choosing to know themselves better and learn from experience. All our interviewees were able to evidence this intentional self-reflection or insight. Self-reflection represents a genuine curiosity about the self, where the person is intrigued and interested in learning more about his or her emotions, values, thought processes and attitudes (Dahl, Wilson-Mendenhall, & Davidson, 2020). This type of introspection mostly leads to positive consequences associated with good mental health, such as self-knowledge and self-regulation (Morin, 2011).

On the other hand, leaders that overthink this or go beyond the balance of self-reflection can lead to imbalanced self-rumination. Self-rumination is anxious attention paid to the self, where the person is afraid to fail and keeps wondering about his or her self-worth. Through introspection (at moderate levels) and self-reflection, we can increase our self-awareness, knowledge, and understanding of how we may react in certain situations – both our awareness and our insight (Dahl et al., 2020). This may help us better manage our reactions – to be adaptable – and understand why others may react in that way.

Adaptability and self-awareness then are inherently linked (Karaevli & Hall, 2006). More specifically, one major adaptive function of self-awareness is self-regulation, which includes altering one's behaviour, resisting temptation, changing one's mood, selecting a response from various options, and filtering irrelevant information (Baumeister & Vohs, 2004). This moves us to think about emotional agility, the second key component in developing limberness. So while adaptability signposts our openness to seeing things differently, emotional agility enables us to choose and select the most appropriate emotional or cognitive response. It is the self-regulation piece of emotional agility that gives adaptability its positive power. Whilst adaptability is about accepting or adapting to changed circumstances, emotional agility enables the adaptability to become a positive lever for change. Let's now take a moment to reflect on your own adaptability before we turn to look at how emotional agility gives wings to adaptability, transforming its power.

Reflection on practice
Think back to the last time you were feeling uncertain or had to change a course of action.
- *What was the silver lining when you chose to embrace the change?*

- *What information, resources, or support allowed you adapt to this new situation?*

- *What did you do to minimise your disappointment, frustration, fear, or anger in this situation?*

- *On reflection, what can you do more of/less of in the future to help you adapt to a changed situation more effectively?*

Emotional agility

Emotional agility is the capacity to choose a reaction – a selection of an emotional or indeed a cognitive response – that best or better fits the scenario we find ourselves in (David, 2017). It's a process that puts you here and now and enables you to change or keep behaving in a way that best aligns with your intentions and values. Moreover, this is not about pushing away or ignoring difficult thoughts and emotions, but holding them more lightly so you can bend and flex to do the things that matter to you. Emotional agility has been interchangeably referred to across different sectors as psychological flexibility, emotional intelligence (van Hugten et al., 2021), and more recently, emotional agility (David, 2017). These terms are similar but imply a different aspect of emotional engagement. Psychological flexibility implies acceptance of thoughts and feelings, be they negative or positive. Emotional intelligence extends the emotional experiences and their impact on self and others. In contrast, emotional agility incorporates both concepts and builds on them by ensuring that our actions are authentic and reflective of our values. We chose to use the term because it provides the most comprehensive perspective on how to cope effectively with emotions.

We ask the reader to recognise and remember through our discussion that there is both an emotional and cognitive layer to this term of emotional agility. Therefore, there is also both an emotional and cognitive process through which the positive leader goes to be limber. Different parts of our brain are responsible for supporting us to be emotionally agile: the 'emotional' parts (the parts responsible for different aspects of perceiving and learning and regulating emotions; our habits; and those involved in pleasure, reward, and motivation); and the 'cognitive' parts (responsible for high-level cognition, including attention and processing, and those responsible for consolidating short-term memory to long-term memory (Brann, 2017)). So, while adaptability signposts our openness to seeing things differently, emotional agility enables us to choose (or move ourselves into the right space) to actively be limber and select the best emotional OR cognitive response for us in any given moment and with reduced reactivity.

Developing emotional flexibility skills in the working context has shown very encouraging results in public-sector settings; effectiveness in a private-sector setting; and more recently effectiveness of developing these skills as well as self-efficacy amongst high-paced, high-demanding, and highly-educated knowledge workers (Jacqueline Brassey, Witteloostuijn, Huszka, Silberzahn, & Dam, 2020). Entrepreneurs with greater psychological flexibility (or to use our term, emotional agility) are, on average, more satisfied with their work and lives (van Hugten et al., 2021). In a study of 244 entrepreneurs Hugten et al. demonstrated that emotional agility substantially helped explain entrepreneurs' satisfaction over and above existing explanatory variables. Emotional agility has been shown to help people with negative self-image, procrastination, and tough transitions (David, 2017). Emotionally agile colleagues demonstrate flexibility in dealing with the constant changes we face in the world and workplace, managing stress and setbacks better, and remaining open to what is next instead of being derailed by any anger and sadness, remaining curious, accepting, and self-compassionate (David, 2017). Therefore, it can be useful in the work context.

Emotional agility works at both the emotional and cognitive levels to create limberness. Being aware of the natural triggers and responses that we all have can help us consider how we can resource ourselves as positive leaders to be more emotionally agile and conscious about how we interpret our own or others' triggers in a more positive perspective for the benefit of ourselves and others. Positive leaders are conscious that they and others have an unconscious that influences all of our thoughts, feelings, and behaviours. They are adept at acknowledging and working with their emotions and feelings. They recognise that we have a more conscious cognitive brain and a less conscious emotional brain. Van Hugten et al. discuss the connections between psychological capital and emotional agility (2021), explaining that while psychological capital is composed of (work-related) self-efficacy, optimism, hope, and resilience (Luthans, Youssef, & Avolio, 2007; Chadwick & Raver, 2020), emotional agility can be seen as a more in-depth approach to the resilience aspect of psychological capital – that emotional agility refers to concrete behaviours and mental processes that underlie individual resilience.

Positive leaders are limber as they practise the intentionality of thinking slow, which relates to systematic integration of the information available to them, instead of practicing an autopilot response (Kahneman, 2011). Their ability to not respond to their own reactions, but to recognise the need to breathe, step back from initial reactions, and take in a broader perspective helps them adapt. The limber leader is also emotionally agile, mindfully aware of their thoughts and feelings, of their impact on others, and notices others struggling or managing to regulate their emotions and thoughts in daily and complex situations. They develop flexibility and agility in their emotions and thoughts for the given context to get the best from themselves and in helping others get the best from themselves. This does not mean that limber leaders do not have challenging thoughts or feelings or lean away from the difficult challenges and conversations we all face that can inevitably lead to anxious feelings. In fact, they lean into them, with balanced consideration for their own and others' thoughts and feelings too. Tough feedback and tough decisions such as delivering role or even redundancies news are part and parcel of managers' and leaders' work today.

Russell says

Sometimes you have to go to someone with tough feedback or explain there's a role that's no longer needed inside the organisation. And actually, by avoiding those situations, you can create an undercurrent of dishonesty and meaninglessness [. . .] there's a level of hard honesty that underpins this (limberness), it's about treating people like adults that they can take the news, they deserve the honesty.

Whilst no positive leader will 'like' to deliver these tough messages, they ensure they manage the people involved in the conversation (both themselves and others) with the intention of limberness and emotional agility to aim for the most positive outcome possible.

A recent study of multimedal-winning coaches in Olympic sport found that behind their success was the ability to move along the continuum between 'drivenness' (e.g. unwavering high standards) and benevolence (e.g. a people-first culture) (Bercial, 2017). To do this, coaches relied on being highly attuned to their athletes' needs and the desire to then choose to move along this continuum to meet their needs. This 'chameleon-like' ability to move between contrasting personality styles is what leaders require to get the most out of their teams, grow organisations, or, in these cases, win Olympic gold. Finding that emotional resonance with colleagues and choosing to adapt behaviours is yet another evidence of agility.

Maximising their potential, positive leaders are able to balance their thought processes as well as their emotions when the time is needed. Russell regularly talks in his role as CEO as needing to be conscious about balancing his thoughts processes when holding onto thoughts that need to be let go of for the sake of healthy energy management for all. He explains that "actually knowing when to let go about things and to know that what's outside of your control [. . .] is incredibly important". He says that whilst all leaders go through moments of crisis, make mistakes, and experience suffering and criticism, very few are invulnerable to how much time they spend worrying and thinking about what others may think, with the press and social media sometimes compounding this exposure and worry over time. He says that scandal and controversy and fury can be forgotten in a short period of time, helping to restore perspective, yet "the danger is you get paralyzed in that running through the thoughts of what will people think?" Instead, he says having a limber attitude in these moments – adapting and being emotionally agile – and reassuring yourself and others that this moment and feeling too shall pass, can help a leader navigate the inevitable challenges of leading.

Likewise, leaders can also develop schemata akin to ongoing internal narrators that can hinder or help their leadership: inner critics (Figure 3.3) or inner champions (Figure 3.4). Figures 3.3 and 3.4 represent some of the thought patterns, narratives, and schemata the human brain can develop. These can be thought of as memories, experiences, and others' advice held in our mind, often things that others have said to us (either intending to be consciously helpful or unhelpful) at different stages of our life. Whilst positive leaders may have both, they are aware of both and work with them to give cognitive limberness and perspective towards themselves and others (Dahl et al., 2020). As we have seen in Chapter 2, they learn to lean dominantly into their internal champions. Using these emotional and cognitively agile adjustments, they can move to a greater phase of adaptability, emotional agility, and resilience to grow. Next, we will explain how resilience is aided through the support and relationships of others that surround positive leaders, that resilience helps positive leaders to build and grow, and that resilience that leads to growth can come from adverse as well as positive events. Let us first reflect on our emotional agility.

Figure 3.3 The inner critic

Figure 3.4 The inner champion

Reflection on practice

Think of the last time you have experienced a challenging event.

- *How much were you able to notice your emotions and thoughts as an observer in the moment and to make choices about them?*

- *How much were you able to reflect instead of reacting in the moment?*

- *What thought patterns have you noticed that best served you or hijacked you at the time?*

Resilience

Resilience is a complex and much-debated construct, with hundreds of definitions offered (Southwick, Bonanno, Masten, Panter-Brick, & Yehuda, 2014). Our research identifies resilience in positive leaders as broader than adapting well in the face of adversity or bouncing back and much more nuanced than many existing definitions. It can be different for a particular individual, family, team, organisation, or culture; varies across domains and phases of life; and is context dependent (Southwick et al., 2014). Resilience in positive leadership contains precursors of adaptability and emotional agility and is followed by growth – the learning and growing from the experience, be it adverse or positive. It is more than an individual trait and is affected by the interactions within and between organisations (Day, 2012), aided through the support and relationship with others (Quinlan & Hone, 2020); it can develop through both adverse and positive events and is developable through key tested techniques. In summary, resilience for positive leaders is a process of adaptability and emotional agility leading to a way back – or indeed a way forward – from a trigger event.

Resilience increases through social support, teams, and organisations that foster this rather than via individuals alone, as some limited definitions would suggest and create debate (Southwick et al., 2014). Quinlan and Hone (2020) argue that helping others is key to growth in times where resilience is required: 'help yourself by helping others'; they state that "by helping others we take the attention off ourselves and at the same time feel useful and needed" (p. 50).

Resilience can also be seen as being a multiplier of resources and has a building effect. Waters et al. describe how resilience multiplies us as a 'building effect' (Waters et al., 2021) for individuals, their teams, and organisations. Limber leaders are not only resilient, but they are also so to their advantage – building on and through their experiences to better things. In terms of the building effect, much research has shown that traumatic events can be a trigger for positive growth in personal development areas such as self-perception, interpersonal relationships, knowledge of one's strengths, life philosophy, appreciation of life, and spirituality. This multifaceted understanding of how resilience leads to greater things and a range of positive outcomes has been described in research studies as adversarial growth (Joseph & Linley, 2008), stress-related growth (Park, Cohen, & Murch, 1996), and/or post-traumatic growth (PTG) (Helgeson, Reynolds, & Tomich, 2006).

One such empirical study conducted on PTG during COVID-19 (Vazquez et al., 2021) found that PTG was higher when people believed they were living in a good world and had a positive outlook for the future. This shows a link between limberness and inspiration, which we will discuss in Chapter 8.

Some people will get stuck by an adverse event, but resilience is the active choice to move forward from this. Resilience is where the growth happens, and we know that this resilience and growth can happen from both adverse and positive events. The positive leaders we spoke to did not just grow from 'negative' adverse or traumatic events either – they grew from positive events too, a phenomenon described as 'post-ecstatic growth' (PEG) (Roepke, Jayawickreme, & Riffle, 2014). PEG was shown in one study of 605 participants to lead to deeper spirituality, increased meaning and purpose in life, improved relationships, and greater self-esteem. Any important event – whether it is experienced as positive or negative – might lead to growth. This study showed substantial overlap between the positive changes people reported after both the worst and best experiences of their lives, with positive experiences particularly impacting eudemonic wellbeing (wellbeing most associated with the deeper happiness found in meaning and purpose) and worldviews. Participants reported that their positive experiences had opened their eyes to new opportunities, goals, roles, and values and that they felt they had grown more.

Importantly, some distinctions between the type of positive emotion experienced from a positive event trigger can lead to different outcomes. Roepke's study found that feeling a sense of inspiration, awe, and elevation is an especially important positive emotion for growth: the more a person experiences these during an important event, the more growth they see in themselves (2013). No wonder then we also see that inspiration is a key resource of a positive leader (see Chapter 4).

The good news is that resilience for positive leaders is developable, and consistently across the research we see it is developable through buffering, bolstering, and building positive processes and capacities (Dahl et al., 2020; Waters et al., 2021). This can happen through processes and capacities such as meaning, coping, self-compassion, courage, gratitude, character strengths, positive emotions, positive interpersonal processes, and high-quality connections (Waters et al., 2021). Many of these processes and capacities are discussed elsewhere in this book, and coping, self-compassion, and courage most closely align with strategies that can build adaptability, emotional agility, and resilience, developing our overall limberness. So how do we develop our coping, self-compassion, and courage to be more limber?

Coping strategies are cognitive and behavioural efforts that foster adaptation in times of challenge. Coping is developed through increasing the experience of positive cognitions (e.g. positive reappraisal) and through increasing positive emotions (e.g. gratitude) (Waters et al., 2021). Self-compassion involves treating yourself with the same kindness, care, and concern you would show to a good friend when they are struggling in some way (Neff, 2003). Self-compassion helps us over the long run by reducing the negative effects of perceived stress over time (Stutts, Leary, Zeveney, & Hufnagle, 2018). Self-compassion can be developed in three different ways through being mindful of our pain (Neff & Dahm, 2015) (acknowledging it, e.g. this is a moment of suffering); recognising the shared nature of suffering and that everyone is imperfect and encounters challenges in life (Neff & Germer, 2018) – thus seeing our situation with perspective and balance rather than exaggerating how bad things are (e.g. suffering is a part of life); and, finally through giving love to ourselves, offering soothing and kindness (e.g. may I be kind to myself).

Courage is about taking a worthwhile risk (Pury & Saylors, 2017), acting towards valued goals despite the possibility of personal negative consequences and resulting negative emotional states. Courage can be developed by reminding oneself of the value of the goal they are pursuing (Pury et al., Forthcoming). Other research has shown that being reminded of a time where one successfully faced their fears (Kramer & Zinbarg, 2019) and being rewarded for getting closer to a phobic object (Chockalingam & Norton, 2019) help to increase courage. Additionally, drawing on other strengths can likely make that path easier. Ensuring the worth and value of one's own goals, reminding oneself of them, and taking steps to mitigate risk – including the risk to others – can likely foster courage in these difficult times.

Reflection on practice
Think back to the last challenging situation:
- *How did you react?*

- *What were the benefits of experiencing this challenging situation? What have you learnt?*

- *What coping, self-compassion, or courage strategies helped you develop your resilience, or could help you do so if you experienced the same or a similar situation in the future? For example, cognitive reappraisal, practising self-compassionate words towards yourself, or drawing on your strengths to take a worthwhile risk?*

Limberness in action

Several critical organisational and social conditions can support the development of limberness in leaders: diversity, wellbeing, psychological safety, and emotional support systems. Firstly, in order for leaders to tap into their adaptability, emotional agility, and resilience to be limber, organisations need to offer an environment where diversity is embraced (Yang et al., 2016). A diverse workforce in gender, race, sexual orientation, and ways of thinking will support organisations and leaders to remain adaptable and open to different perspectives. By only having the same types of people or ways of thinking, an organisation is limiting itself and its leaders in the opportunity and advancements it can make in being adaptable. Meeting culture can also signal this diversity. Leaders can create opportunities for not just listening to 'yes' people but asking for different opinions, listening to people who challenge your way of thinking (Brassey et al., 2021).

Another condition that needs to be in place is for wellbeing to be valued as a foundational practice for leaders, where leaders have daily practices to foster their wellbeing and support their performance in an era of constant change, including body, mind, and spiritual practices (Brassey et al., 2021). Again, we will discuss this more in Chapter 6.

One might argue that in culmination, the most essential condition for the development of limberness is the presence of psychological safety – a culture where openness to experience and a learning mindset is encouraged, where there is a willingness to be wrong (Edmondson & Lei, 2014). Psychological safety is about organisations having the conditions that enable teams to admit when things haven't gone right, to give and receive feedback regularly, to learn from failure, and to feel safe taking risks (Edmondson, 2019). This creates a willingness to challenge the status quo and each other. To create environments that are psychologically safe, learning cultures are essential (Edmondson & Lei, 2014). This leads to an openness to the fact that we are all learners and that risk and things not going as planned are inevitable in moving forwards. According to Edmondson and Lei (2014), this has a positive impact on our creativity, as we feel less restricted, receive regular feedback, and are therefore more likely to be open to things going wrong.

Finally, as with the component of resilience being fostered and promoted by social support, emotional support systems need to be available to support leaders through the tough times (Mathieu, Eschleman, & Cheng, 2019). Leaders need to be encouraged to develop deep connections through being vulnerable, empathetic, and meeting others with compassion where appropriate and authentic (Brassey et al., 2021). Again, we will discuss more on this Chapter 7.

Building on the previous breakdown of the three components of limberness (adaptability, emotional agility, and resilience) and drawing them together, limberness is the positive leader's ability to:

a. Stretch and flex their emotions to the given situation and context to adapt into a more optimal psychological space (adaptability);
b. Mindfully and through awareness to choose to make space between any distorted perspectives and truth by being open to multiple and different perspectives (emotional agility);
c. Move through change and grow to be better for it (resilience).

Adaptability is a readiness to respond to the feeling of being stuck – emotional agility provides an awareness to see and act on choices. Resilience is growing from the choice chosen in response to the feeling of being stuck and the adverse event. Whilst adaptability is openness to change and a capacity to grow, resilience is where the growth happens. To only be able to flex one of the limberness resource's components cannot lead us to limberness. Imagine somebody is adaptable but not emotionally agile or resilient; this would result in a leader being willing to present as flexible but not make emotional or cognitive choices to act on this flexibility and then not learn from this action. Imagine somebody is adaptable and resilient but not emotionally agile; this would offer a leader who has the desire to alter their mindset or behaviour and learn from this but lacks the skills of being able to emotionally or cognitively flex their reaction – a very frustrated leader perhaps. Imagine somebody is adaptable and emotionally agile but not resilient; they will flex their approach and choose better emotional and cognitive responses, but will not learn and grow from their adaptation and agility, perhaps repeating mistakes or having to learn over and over again to change their approach in similar situations. All three of these resources – adaptability, emotional agility, and resilience – are therefore essential to integrate into full limberness.

Last word

In conclusion, positive leaders tap into the resource of limberness on a daily, if not hourly, basis. The limber leader adapts their mindset when the context is called for and then vacillates purposefully along a continuum of emotional and psychological flexibility for a given situation and context. They support their co-workers and teams to gain emotional or cognitive control or recovery for the best outcomes. That is not to say that positive leaders do not have the wild emotional and cognitive reactions and filters we all do, but they take time to get to know their own brains and others and learn to adapt and then respond appropriately and compassionately as much as possible and are armed with this inner self and inner other knowledge to learn and grow through resilience. The limber leader harnesses "whatever emotions she believes are necessary to achieve her goal" (Doorley, Goodman, Kelso, & Kashdan, 2020, p. 4). Furthermore, the limber leader does not push away or avoid emotions or thoughts, but works with them for her advantage; "if we cannot control the presence of negative emotions and other potential barriers to goal pursuit, perhaps the best we can do is creatively use them to our advantage" (Doorley et al., 2020, p. 5). Moderate emotional and physiological arousal (compared to none) facilitates task performance in a range of contexts, and likewise, the limber leader works with their arousal as if it were a traffic light signpost to recalibrate and respond with flexibility and astound with their limber performance.

References

Baumeister, R. F., & Vohs, K. D. (2004). *Handbook of self-regulation: Research, theory, and applications*. New York: The Guilford Press.

Bercial, S. L. (2017). *Leadership lessons from serial winning coaches*. Retrieved from https://leadersinsport.com/performance/leadership-lessons-serial-winning-coaches/

Brann, A. (2017). *Neuroscience for coaches: How to use the latest insights for the benefit of your clients* (2nd ed.). London: Kogan Page.

Brassey, J., De Smet, A., Kothari, A., Lavoie, J., Mugayar-Baldocchi, M., & Zolley, S. (2021). Future proof: Solving the 'adaptability paradox' for the long term. *Organization Practice*, Retrieved from https://www.mckinsey.com/business-functions/people-and-organizational-performance/our-insights/future-proof-solving-the-adaptability-paradox-for-the-long-term

Brassey, J., Witteloostuijn, A. V., Huszka, C., Silberzahn, T., & Dam, N. V. (2020). Emotional flexibility and general self-efficacy: A pilot training intervention study with knowledge workers. *PLoS One, 15*(10), e0237821. doi:10.1371/journal.pone.0237821

Burnell, L. (2020). *The science of adaptability: A white paper*. London: Mindflick.

Chadwick, I. C., & Raver, J. L. (2020). Psychological resilience and its downstream effects for business survival in nascent entrepreneurship. *Entrepreneurship Theory and Practice, 44*(2), 233–255. doi:10.1177/1042258718801597

Chockalingam, M., & Norton, P. J. (2019). Facing fear-provoking stimuli: The role of courage and influence of task-importance. *The Journal of Positive Psychology, 14*(5), 603–613. doi:10.1080/17439760.2018.1497685

Dahl, C. J., Wilson-Mendenhall, C. D., & Davidson, R. J. (2020). The plasticity of well-being: A training-based framework for the cultivation of human flourishing. *Proceedings of the National Academy of Sciences, 117*(51), 32197. doi:10.1073/pnas.2014859117

David, S. (2017). *Emotional agility: Get unstuck, embrace change and thrive in work and life*. London: Penguin Books Ltd.

Day, C. (2012). The importance of teacher resilience to outstanding teaching and learning in schools. *SecEd, 11*.

Doorley, J. D., Goodman, F. R., Kelso, K. C., & Kashdan, T. B. (2020). Psychological flexibility: What we know, what we do not know, and what we think we know. *Social and Personality Psychology Compass, 14*(12), 1–11. doi:10.1111/spc3.12566

Edmondson, A. (2019). The role of psychological safety. *Leader to Leader, 2019*(92), 13–19. doi:10.1002/ltl.20419

Edmondson, A., & Lei, Z. (2014). Psychological safety: The history, renaissance, and future of an interpersonal construct. *Annual Review of Organizational Psychology and Organizational Behavior, 1*, 23–43. doi:10.1146/annurev-orgpsych-031413-091305

Erikson, T., Pender, M., & Bradbury, R. (2020). *Surrounded by idiots: The four types of human behavior and how to effectively communicate with each in business (and in life)*. London: Penguin.

Goleman, D., Boyatzis, R. E., Davidson, R. J., Druskat, V., & Kohlrieser, G. (2017). *Adaptability: A primer*. Florence, MA: Key Step Media/More Than Sound.

Grossmann, I., & Kross, E. (2010). The impact of culture on adaptive versus maladaptive self-reflection. *Psychological Science, 21*(8), 1150–1157. doi:10.1177/0956797610376655

Grover, S. M. (2005). Shaping effective communication skills and therapeutic relationships at work: The foundation of collaboration. *AAOHN Journal, 53*(4), 177–182. doi:10.1177/216507990505300410

Helgeson, V. S., Reynolds, K. A., & Tomich, P. L. (2006). A meta-analytic review of benefit finding and growth. *Journal of Consulting and Clinical Psychology, 74*(5), 797–816. doi:10.1037/0022-006X.74.5.797

Holland, M. J. G., Woodcock, C., Cumming, J., & Duda, J. L. (2010). Mental qualities and employed mental techniques of young elite team sport athletes. *Journal of Clinical Sport Psychology, 4*(1), 19–38. doi:10.1123/jcsp.4.1.19

Johnston, C. S. (2018). A systematic review of the career adaptability literature and future outlook. *Journal of Career Assessment, 26*(1), 3–30. doi:10.1177/1069072716679921

Joseph, S., & Linley, P. A. (2008). Psychological assessment of growth following adversity: A review. In S. Joseph & P. A. Linley (Eds.), *Trauma, recovery, and growth: Positive psychological perspectives on posttraumatic stress*. (pp. 21–36). Hoboken, NJ: John Wiley & Sons Inc.

Kahneman, D. (2011). *Thinking, fast and slow*. London: Allen Lane.

Kaiser, R. B., & Overfield, D. V. (2011). Strengths, strengths overused, and lopsided leadership. *Consulting Psychology Journal: Practice and Research, 63*(2), 89–109. doi:10.1037/a0024470

Kaplan, R. E., & Kaiser, R. B. (2013). *Fear your strengths: What you are best at could be your biggest problem*. San Francisco: Berrett-Koehler Publishers.

Karaevli, A., & Hall, D. T. T. (2006). How career variety promotes the adaptability of managers: A theoretical model. *Journal of Vocational Behavior, 69*(3), 359–373.

Kashdan, T. B., & Rottenberg, J. (2010). Psychological flexibility as a fundamental aspect of health. *Clinical Psychology Review, 30*(7), 865–878. doi:10.1016/j.cpr.2010.03.001

Kim, J. H., & Shin, H. S. (2020). Effects of self-reflection-focused career course on career search efficacy, career maturity, and career adaptability in nursing students: A mixed methods study. *Journal of Professional Nursing, 36*(5), 395–403. doi:10.1016/j.profnurs.2020.03.003

Kramer, A., & Zinbarg, R. (2019). Recalling courage: An initial test of a brief writing intervention to activate a 'courageous mindset' and courageous behavior. *The Journal of Positive Psychology, 14*(4), 528–537. doi:10.1080/17439760.2018.1484943

Kross, E., & Ayduk, O. (2017). Self-distancing: Theory, research, and current directions. In J. M. Olson (Ed.), *Advances in experimental social psychology* (Vol. 55, pp. 81–136). Boston: Academic Press.

Luthans, F., Youssef, C. M., & Avolio, B. J. (2007). *Psychological capital: Developing the human competitive edge*. New York: Oxford University Press.

Lyubomirsky, S., Sheldon, K. M., & Schkade, D. (2005). Pursuing happiness: The architecture of sustainable change. *Review of General Psychology, 9*(2), 111–131. doi:10.1037/1089-2680.9.2.111

Martin, A. J., Nejad, H. G., Colmar, S., & Liem, G. A. D. (2013). Adaptability: How students' responses to uncertainty and novelty predict their academic and non-academic outcomes. *Journal of Educational Psychology, 105*(3), 728–746.

Mathieu, M., Eschleman, K. J., & Cheng, D. (2019). Meta-analytic and multiwave comparison of emotional support and instrumental support in the workplace. *Journal of Occupational Health Psychology, 24*(3), 387–409. doi:10.1037/ocp0000135

McArdle, S., Waters, L., Briscoe, J. P., & Hall, D. T. (2007). Employability during unemployment: Adaptability, career identity and human and social capital. *Journal of Vocational Behavior, 71*(2), 247–264. doi:10.1016/j.jvb.2007.06.003

Morin, A. (2011). Self-awareness part 1: Definition, measures, effects, functions, and antecedents: Self-awareness. *Social and Personality Psychology Compass, 5*(10), 807–823. doi:10.1111/j.1751-9004.2011.00387.x

Mumford, M. D., Connelly, M. S., Baughman, W. A., & Marks, M. A. (1994). Creativity and problem solving: Cognition, adaptability, and wisdom. *Roeper Review, 16*(4), 241–246. doi:10.1080/02783199409553589

Nakajima, M., Takano, K., & Tanno, Y. (2017). Adaptive functions of self-focused attention: Insight and depressive and anxiety symptoms. *Psychiatry Research, 249*, 275–280. doi:10.1016/j.psychres.2017.01.026

Neff, K. D. (2003). Self-compassion: An alternative conceptualization of a healthy attitude toward oneself. *Self & Identity, 2*(2), 85. doi:10.1080/15298860309032

Neff, K. D., & Germer, C. K. (2018). *The mindful self-compassion workbook: A proven way to accept yourself, build inner strength, and thrive*: New York: The Guilford Press.

Neff, K. D., & Dahm, K. A. (2015). Self-compassion: What it is, what it does, and how it relates to mindfulness. In *Handbook of mindfulness and self-regulation* (pp. 121–137). New York: Springer.

Park, C. L., Cohen, L. H., & Murch, R. L. (1996). Assessment and prediction of stress-related growth. *Journal of Personality, 64*(1), 71–105. doi:10.1111/j.1467-6494.1996.tb00815.x

Pury, C. L. S., Bryant, R., Chapman, A. J., Haliburton, K. L., Reimer, G. P., Swartzwelter, C. J., . . . Thompson, M. I. (Forthcoming). Narrative reports of actions taken to increase one's courage.

Pury, C. L. S., & Saylors, S. (2017). Courage, courageous acts, and positive psychology. *Positive Psychology*, 153–168.

Quinlan, D. M., & Hone, L. C. (2020). *The educators' guide to whole-school wellbeing: A practical guide to getting started, best-practice process and effective implementation* (1st ed.). London: Routledge. doi:10.4324/9780429280696

Rettew, J. G. (2009). Adaptability. In S. Lopez (Ed.), *The encyclopedia of positive psychology*. Chichester, UK: Blackwell Publishing Ltd.

Roepke, A. M. (2013). Gains without pains? Growth after positive events. *The Journal of Positive Psychology, 8*(4), 280–291. doi:10.1080/17439760.2013.791715

Roepke, A. M., Jayawickreme, E., & Riffle, O. M. (2014). Meaning and health: A systematic review. *Applied Research in Quality of Life*, *9*(4), 1055–1079. doi:10.1007/s11482-013-9288-9

Shapiro, F. R. (2014). *Who wrote the serenity prayer?* Retrieved from www.chronicle.com/article/who-wrote-the-serenity-prayer/

Sony, M., & Mekoth, N. (2016). The relationship between emotional intelligence, frontline employee adaptability, job satisfaction and job performance. *Journal of Retailing and Consumer Services*, *30*, 20–32. doi:10.1016/j.jretconser.2015.12.003

Southwick, S. M., Bonanno, G. A., Masten, A. S., Panter-Brick, C., & Yehuda, R. (2014). Resilience definitions, theory, and challenges: Interdisciplinary perspectives. *European Journal of Psychotraumatology*, *5*. doi:10.3402/ejpt.v5.25338

Stutts, L. A., Leary, M. R., Zeveney, A. S., & Hufnagle, A. S. (2018). A longitudinal analysis of the relationship between self-compassion and the psychological effects of perceived stress. *Self and Identity*, *17*(6), 609–626. doi:10.1080/15298868.2017.1422537

Sugerman, J., Scullard, M., & Wilhelm, E. (2011). *The 8 dimensions of leadership: DiSC strategies for becoming a better leader*. San Francisco: Inscape Publishing.

Thompson, S. C. (2021). The role of personal control in adaptive functioning. In C. R. Snyder, S. J. Lopez, L. M. Edwards, & S. C. Marques (Eds.), *The Oxford handbook of positive psychology* (3rd ed.). New York: Oxford University Press.

van Hugten, J., el Hejazi, Z.-N., Brassey, J., Vanderstraeten, J., Cannaerts, N., Loots, E., . . . van Witteloostuijn, A. (2021). What makes entrepreneurs happy? Psychological flexibility and entrepreneurs' satisfaction. *Journal of Business Venturing Insights*, *16*, e00263. doi:10.1016/j.jbvi.2021.e00263

VandenBos, G. R. (2016). *APA college dictionary of psychology* (2nd ed.). Washington, DC: American Psychological Association.

Vazquez, C., Valiente, C., García, F. E., Contreras, A., Peinado, V., Trucharte, A., & Bentall, R. P. (2021). Post-traumatic growth and stress-related responses during the COVID-19 pandemic in a national representative sample: The role of positive core beliefs about the world and others. *Journal of Happiness Studies*, 1–21. doi:10.1007/s10902-020-00352-3

Waters, L., Algoe, S. B., Dutton, J., Emmons, R., Fredrickson, B. L., Heaphy, E., . . . Steger, M. (2021). Positive psychology in a pandemic: Buffering, bolstering, and building mental health. *Journal of Positive Psychology*, 1–21. doi:10.1080/17439760.2021.1871945

Yang, Y. C., Boen, C., Gerken, K., Li, T., Schorpp, K., & Harris, K. M. (2016). Social relationships and physiological determinants of longevity across the human life span. *Proceedings of the National Academy of Sciences*, *113*(3), 578. doi:10.1073/pnas.1511085112

Yukl, G., & Mahsud, R. (2010). Why flexible and adaptive leadership is essential. *Consulting Psychology Journal: Practice and Research*, *62*(2), 81–93. doi:10.1037/a0019835

Zhou, M., & Lin, W. (2016). Adaptability and life satisfaction: The moderating role of social support. *Frontiers in Psychology*, *7*, 1134–1134. doi:10.3389/fpsyg.2016.01134

4 Inspiration

Amid the COVID-19 pandemic, Professor Luke O'Neill was a key person in the Irish media to reminding the population that "this too shall pass". When the TV, radio, and internet covered the news of the pandemic spreading rapidly and killing millions of people worldwide, he became a ray of sunshine in a dark sky. When people felt scared, he continued to educate them about the pandemic, the virus, and its silver lining. When people felt helpless, he began to talk about vaccines. When people forgot what it was like to hug their loved ones, walk into a shop without a mask, or enjoy a good time in a restaurant, he became the first one to talk about the end being in sight. During the pandemic, he became Ireland's positive leader, who inspired others to focus on the solution instead of dwelling on the problems. This is what the inspiration resource and this chapter is all about.

What is inspiration?

Inspiration is a resource that helps leaders inspire others to become the best versions of themselves (Figure 4.1). It differs from leaders being perceived as inspirational, which implies they are superhuman. Inspiration is not a superhuman quality, but a resource that helps leaders move themselves and their teams to resolute action. It consists of three elements: (1) self-efficacy, (2) hope and optimism, and (3) energising networks (Figure 4.2). These resources are useful when everything goes well, but particularly advantageous when individuals and teams experience setbacks. They allow leaders to refocus their team's attention on what matters and create enough fire in their belly to keep going. Without inspiration, even the best messages from

DOI: 10.4324/9781003170433-4

Figure 4.1 The Inspiration resource piece of the ALIGHT jigsaw

leaders can get lost. Thus, using the tools of inspiration can help leaders transform into positive leaders who bring about positive change.

Self-efficacy

In previous chapters, we mentioned the powerful placebo effect. Our belief that something will work for us, that our intelligence can change, or that we can further develop our strengths makes it more likely to happen. This belief is so strong that even when we do activities that aim to enhance our wellbeing, their effect is more significant when we believe in their efficacy (Mongrain & Anselmo-Matthews, 2012). The same applies to self-efficacy. Self-efficacy is our belief that we *can* accomplish something we aim to accomplish. It is not a skill, but a judgement of our abilities to reach a specific level of performance and an expectation we set up for ourselves in relation to what we can achieve in life (Bandura, 1997).

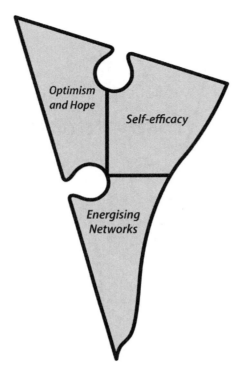

Figure 4.2 The Inspiration components

Self-efficacy is often contrasted with self-esteem. Self-esteem is our measure of self-worth, whereas self-efficacy is our judgement of abilities. Both concepts refer to a subjective evaluation of self; however, self-efficacy, according to some authors, refers to a more realistic perception of who we are (Baumeister, Campbell, Krueger, & Vohs, 2003). As such, self-efficacy is based on evidence about our capabilities, which is why past performance is the best predictor of self-efficacy (Sitzmann & Yeo, 2013). For example, past experiences showed you that other leaders were capable of honing their leadership skills over time; if they were able to do it, you believe can you too. Or you may have previously managed a small project, which boasted a successful outcome, so if you were able to do it then, you can succeed with a larger project too. Self-efficacy, then, is an ability to find evidence that fuels our belief that we or others are capable of something. Self-esteem, however, does not need to be based on any evidence. We may believe we are worthy of being listened to by others, or being acknowledged by others, and it is our belief without any specific evidence that fuels it. As such, you may be a leader who has high self-esteem (e.g. I am a very worthy person) but low efficacy (e.g. I don't think I can do it), or vice versa.

The self-efficacy research extends half a century, yet it is just as valid today as decades ago. We now have measures and research about generic efficacy, which describes the general perception of our ability (Schwarzer & Jerusalem, 1995), more specifically, efficacy about an aspect of our lives, e.g. our self-efficacy for engaging with physical exercise (Cornick, 2015). To add to it, we have professional efficacy, e.g. teachers believing that they are able to do their jobs (Roberts & Henson, 2001), and leadership self-efficacy, which refers to leaders believing in their ability to (1) start and lead change processes in groups, (2) choose effective followers and delegate responsibilities to them, (3) build and manage interpersonal relationships within the group, (4) show self-awareness and self-confidence, (5) motivate people, and (6) gain consensus of group members (Bobbio & Manganelli, 2009). This is just an example of a leader's belief to do their job to a high standard. However, these six components of leadership self-efficacy could just as well be replaced with your personal or your organisation's goals and descriptions of what is required to be a good leader. Therefore, self-efficacy beliefs can be easily extended to various aspects of our work life and, as such, affect them significantly.

A leader's self-efficacy is a significant predictor of a leader's effectiveness (Dwyer, 2019). This includes improved performance and decision-making. Leaders with higher levels of self-efficacy were able to experience less stress during work, especially when under pressure. Furthermore, when given negative feedback, they were able to embrace it more effectively than those with lower levels of self-efficacy. Finally, the feedback they received from their team was more positive, as they perceived the leader as more inspiring. The self-efficacy expectation made a significant difference in outcomes and in how much effort they put into a task (Graham & Bray, 2015). When we expect something to fail, we are less likely to work on it. Also, we do not stretch our resources to the same extent as we would if we believe that we can indeed do it.

The benefits of self-efficacy are vast to employees too. For example, self-efficacy is associated with more innovative behaviour at work as mediated by experiences of positive emotions associated with the feeling of efficacy (Mielniczuk & Laguna, 2020). It is particularly useful when the team is experiencing stressful events. When employees experience work overload, lack of support, unmanaged conflict, and other stressful situations at work, they are more likely to display counterproductive behaviours such as gossiping, self-sabotage, or in more extreme circumstances, verbal abuse, harassment, or fraud: in such circumstances, having self-efficacy moderates and mitigates the maladaptive behaviour, allowing teams to remain in control despite experiencing stress (Fida, Paciello, Tramontano, Barbaranelli, & Farnese, 2015). As such, it also protects employees against burnout (Shoji et al., 2016). In relation to the team's performance, the situation is a little more nuanced. Even though early research suggested that employees with higher self-efficacy developed behaviours to achieve higher levels of work performance (Sadri & Robertson, 1993), the recent research shows that the impact of efficacy on performance is strong in low-skilled jobs, not more complex roles (Judge, Shaw, Jackson, Scott, & Rich, 2007). Nonetheless, employees can take individual benefits from experiencing self-efficacy, be it stress reduction, creativity, or performance-related.

Most texts published about self-efficacy refer to an individual's sense of efficacy. However, the concept of collective efficacy has been growing exponentially in the last two decades. It refers to a shared belief of two or more individuals in the strength of their collective capabilities (Bandura, 1997). In other words, it is an individual's conviction that together with others they can accomplish their goals (Maddux & Kleiman, 2021). Teams may be put together; they may even be performing together for many years and truly enjoy working together. However, when a change in an organisation occurs, they may then believe that they cannot accomplish what they now need to do together.

This is what happened to one team we worked with during the recession in Ireland. Despite sharing many successes together for almost a decade, with changed economic circumstances, the team lost the belief that they could accomplish their goals together and saw their performance plummet in a matter of a few months. The managing director of the organisation blamed the market for their performance. However, the team members alluded to an additional factor affecting them: *We have never worked during a recession. We don't know how to do it.* In response to this, the leader brought in a consultant from another branch of their organisation (who had worked through a previous recession) to share with the team her beliefs as to why it would work. The team were also invited to a meeting with a branch which continued to perform. Finally, the leader convinced the team that everyone on it had unique talents to bring to the situation and together they had what it took to perform, just as they had done so before. Equipped with this powerful new belief, and seeing through other examples that it was possible, the team began to succeed, and their performance soared within three months from this intervention. This example illustrates the power of collective self-efficacy for teams in being able to make a positive change.

Even though it may seem counterintuitive, team members may experience high levels of individual self-efficacy and lower levels of collective efficacy and vice versa. For example, an individual may believe that they can accomplish their own goals; however, they may also believe that because their leader is not experienced or they do not have the expertise required on the team, or because the team does not practise good teamwork, or because they are down a staff member, that they are unable to accomplish their goals. Hence, despite individuals having high levels of self-efficacy, they may have low collective efficacy to do their job. In contrast, there may be a situation when a team has a strong collective efficacy because together they have achieved a lot; even in situations when it seemed impossible, they somehow have pulled through. They trust each other, and they trust the process of working together even though the members of the team may feel lower individual levels of self-efficacy. In these situations, they may sometimes feel like imposters or fear joining another team because they believe that it was purely the team that helped them tap into their potential – not that they did anything themselves. A positive leader is aware of these psychological undercurrents and actively makes changes when required to notice and feel self and team efficacy.

A team's social intelligence helps employees experience collective efficacy (Mohamed, 2021; Villanueva, Sánchez, & Howard, 2007). Social intelligence refers to an ability to comprehend social contexts, specifically understanding others' concerns and coping with social challenges effectively (Rahim, 2014). However, given that not all team members may have well-developed social intelligence, a positive leader needs to find alternative methods for helping teams develop collective efficacy. Another way to do it is by practising transformational leadership (Walumbwa, Lawler, Avolio, Wang, & Shi, 2005), which involves displaying charisma, inspirational motivation, intellectual stimulation, and a personal approach when communicating with a team (Bass & Avolio, 1994). Other methods include team members observing each other, which helps them improve individual performance and also develop collective efficacy (Bruton, Mellalieu, & Shearer, 2016).

There are many ways in which we can develop efficacy (Maddux & Kleiman, 2021). Firstly, the experience of performing something we did not know we could do enhances our feelings of self-efficacy. Therefore, sometimes throwing ourselves into the deep end and reflecting on how well we are doing may prove beneficial for building our confidence. Also, observing others accomplishing something may act as an ignition to start doing it ourselves. After all, if they could do it, so can we! For some, an imagined experience works well for enhancing self-efficacy, whereby they imagine themselves completing an activity or achieving a result they are hoping for. Finally, other people's verbal persuasion is yet another method for enhancing self-efficacy. When others convince us that indeed we may have transferrable skills to try something out, our belief in our abilities grows exponentially. These techniques are helpful for individuals and teams to use. Also, they can become a basis for leaders' conversations with their team; positive leaders can inspire others by reflecting on some of the accomplishments of their team and individuals, collectively imagining a positive future, and convincing everyone that they have whatever it takes to perform.

Self-efficacy usually grows with experience; however, not in all circumstances. It is very effective when we embark on a clearly defined task, complete it, and receive clear feedback regarding the completion of the task. However, it is less effective in the context of performance ambiguity (Schmidt & DeShon, 2010). Performance ambiguity is not about the lack of clarity about what our role entails. We have worked with leaders who have created employees' job descriptions and spent time explaining their role expectations clearly, and yet despite all of this their employees experienced performance ambiguity. Performance ambiguity refers to individuals' knowledge as to how well they are doing. It is not necessarily about receiving positive or negative feedback, but any feedback at all. This feedback can be self-constructed or obtained with the help of others. When feedback is received, engaging in activity boosts the sense of self-efficacy. However, when we are unsure how well we are doing, the more we complete the task, the less self-efficacy we experience; this is why clear feedback is required when positive leaders work with their team – we visit this more in Chapter 7.

As with many psychological concepts, moderation should be practised when considering both self-efficacy and collective efficacy. Too much self-efficacy may lead to complacency, whereby individuals believe in their abilities to such an extent that they do not see the need for further development (Machida & Schaubroeck, 2011). When leaders exercise high levels of belief in their abilities, it helps them produce an inspiring vision that drives their team's performance; however, it may also lead to a leader's inability to see obstacles, becoming detrimental to an organisation (Shipman & Mumford, 2011). Therefore, it is useful to use the resource of self-efficacy wisely. We can do this by reminding ourselves about self-efficacy when extra confidence is needed (e.g. to tap into our motivation to accomplish a goal), and also to practise prudence when planning to ensure potential obstacles are thought through and addressed.

Before we move to look at the next inspiration components of optimism and hope, let's take some time now to reflect on your own self-efficacy – how aware are you of your levels of self-efficacy in your work?

Reflection on practice

- *What aspects of your current role would you like to master with self-efficacy? What steps can you take over the next few weeks to do it?*

- *Who exemplifies extraordinary leadership for you? How have they developed mastery in their role?*

- *What state of mind can you adopt, or has worked for you in the past, to best help you master your goal and feel a strong sense of self-efficacy?*

Hope and optimism

Inspirational leaders need to develop both optimism *and* hope to support their team in believing that 'they can'. Optimism is an individual's expectation that everything will work out well in the future (Carver, Scheier,

Miller, & Fulford, 2009), and as such, it motivates us to keep going. On the other hand, pessimism is associated with a negative expectancy, which stops us from trying to preserve the energy. Optimism is a crucial component of inspirational leaders; however, in addition to optimism, we need hope to have the motivation to accomplish our positive future expectations and figure out a pathway to do it (Snyder, Rand, & Sigmon, 2018). Therefore, both optimism and hope work together to help leaders and team members create a positive vision of the future and find a way to get there.

Contrary to popular opinion, most of us are optimistic (Sharot, 2011), even though Freud and his colleagues did not believe this to be true for almost a century. In the 1980s a series of studies with terminally ill patients showed that even in the worst times of their lives, people's usual response to adversity was optimism, not pessimism (Taylor, 1989). It served a very important evolutionary need to continue to sustain survival. Decades later, neuroscientific research has provided evidence for this to be true (Garrett & Sharot, 2017). Therefore, optimism is a natural state of mind indicating much-needed adjustment, not delusion, as it is sometimes misunderstood.

"Scientists are often optimistic, it is part of our nature", confirms Professor Luke O'Neill

> We know that we will get somewhere if we keep trying. In science you often fail, many experiments don't work, the machine is down, your idea was wrong and if you keep at it, you will get somewhere and I knew we'd get through this (the pandemic), I knew we'd win at the end. I just wasn't sure when. A scientist is inclined to say to themselves: "that experiment didn't work, I am disappointed but I have an idea how to get out of it" and that's the nature of most scientists.

This attitude is the exact essence of optimistic thinking. It is therefore no wonder that some of the best salespeople are optimistic (Seligman & Schulman, 1986). As one of them once told us when they cold-called the 70th person who did not want their services, their optimism kept them going until the 77th person said "yes". Therefore, optimism is a driver for us not to give up, which may be why it is such an important characteristic for an inspirational leader.

Sarah Blomfield is general counsel, Europe, Middle East, and Africa (EMEA) at Evercore LLP. When Sarah was transitioning from a single professional to a professional working mum in the early 2000s, she was torn with striking a balance between being present for working and family life. Sarah talks about female role models in the workplaces offering optimism to her, including one leader, Sian Westerman, who gave her optimism to seek the career she wanted even when things seemed stacked against her gender and being a working mum. "She would say: 'Just get up and go develop the skin of a rhino' ", and this inspiration pushed Sarah onward in her career to know she could succeed regardless of whether she was a woman and a mum – she would be just as good as anybody and would prove it through balancing both career and motherhood. "Sian was right behind me, and she would back me up all of the time."

People like optimistic leaders. A team of psychologists from the University of Pennsylvania analysed nomination acceptance speeches of all Democratic and Republican presidential candidates in the United States between 1948 and 1984 and found that political leaders who displayed pessimism and rumination (obsessive negative thinking) lost nine out of ten times (Zullow & Seligman, 1990). There are several possible reasons for this. Partially, it may be because pessimism and rumination often allude to candidates' inertia, or it may also be due to the fact that pessimistic leaders make us feel helpless, and for the majority of us, it is not a desirable state of mind; alternatively, it may be because pessimistic leaders made fewer stops per day on a campaign trail, thus sabotaging their chances for election. Whatever the reason, one thing is certain: we are attracted to optimistic leaders because they make us feel like we 'can' do what they or we want to do. They motivate us to keep going, they help us believe in a better future, and they inspire us to dream. Optimism fuels positivity.

Optimism is also one of the predictors of adjustment (Brissette, Scheier, & Carver, 2002). An ability to adjust allows us to keep moving despite obstacles set in our way. The faster we can adjust, the sooner we are on our way to making a difference in our and other people's circumstances. It takes us various amounts of time to adjust; for some, it is a slow process, and for others it is so fast that they seem rarely affected by negative events (Davidson & Begley, 2012). Experienced leaders are sometimes misunderstood and seen as lacking emotions when they are very good at adjusting fast. However, their ability to do this positive adjustment inspires others and motivates them to keep going.

That orientation toward the future and an ability to see it before others is common of influential leaders (Berson, Shamir, Avolio, & Popper, 2001). When leaders and non-leaders were compared, three psychological capabilities differentiated them (Amit, Popper, Gal, Miskal-Sinai, & Lissak, 2006). Firstly, their confidence was composed of a belief that they were capable of initiating change; had low levels of anxiety, which helped them keep going without questioning themselves; and had self-efficacy, allowing them to know that they can. Secondly, they could develop stable relationships and form secure attachments. Finally, when compared with non-leaders, leaders were more likely to display proactive orientation expressed as optimism. Thus, optimism is an inherent characteristic of leadership.

This proactive optimism is not surprising. A definition of optimism states that it is an expectation that things will work out in the future (Carver et al., 2009). Without knowing that things will work out well, leaders cannot create a vision that fuels a team's inspiration to take appropriate actions. Creating a vision – an inspiring picture of the future – is about seeing the possibilities that others cannot (Murphy & Torre, 2015). This is why without optimism about the future, neither a personal nor an organisational vision can be formulated.

The good news is that, regardless of where we are right now, optimism can be learned. There are three steps we can take to do it (Seligman, 1990). The first and most challenging thing we need to do is not to blame ourselves for the bad things that happened to us. This self-blame is linked with the rumination we mentioned earlier. When we lose a business, a client, or do something silly, it is easy to drown in negative thoughts and beat ourselves up with a proverbial stick. However, it is not very useful for us because being beaten up means extra recovery time, which results in all the time lost to remedy the situation. Sometimes when coaching leaders, we see them so fixated on what they have done wrong and how bad they feel about it that they forget to think about the future and how they can fix this situation. The first step we usually ask them to take is to realise that there are extenuating circumstances in all situations. After all, we do not live in a vacuum. Our environment contributes to our behaviour in significant ways.

For example, imagine you have been rude to your team member. It is totally out of character for you, and you feel ashamed about saying the things you have said. You have a choice of ruminating about it and linking the past with an even more pessimistic future, or you can reflect on what caused your 'out of character' behaviour. Was it a sleepless night? Was it that recent constant pressure you were under? Was it your employee being particularly slow responding to you, which reminded you of someone else from the past who did not have good intentions? Although, yes, it is correct that you cannot excuse rudeness when thinking of circumstances, you are not judging the situation, nor are you making any excuses for your behaviour. Instead, you are trying to see the situation from various perspectives; you are trying to offer a more holistic and balanced view of what has happened. We need this more complex and comprehensive view of our lives to see the situation more clearly and to learn from it for the future.

The second thing you need to consider is the length of the adversity. When something terrible happens, pessimists tend to believe it will last forever, or at least a very long time, making them feel hopeless. On the other hand, optimists can see a limit to their misery, with more balanced thoughts such as: 'yes, I lost that business, but I'll soon get another deal, and maybe it will be better than the last one'; 'yes, my relationship with a colleague went off track, but I will soon figure out a way to repair it'. Optimism is associated with thinking that provides limits to the effects of the negative situation. When we see these limits, when we see that the end is in sight, we are more inspired to develop a way to act to change our circumstances.

Finally, optimistic thinking is about being able to compartmentalise the bad situation. For example, say that your job is not going well, if you are an optimist, you can see it as an aspect of your life, not your whole life. This perspective provides you more energy to act. If you are not very good at one aspect of your job and it keeps getting you into trouble, you can reflect on all the things you are very good at, which will provide the necessary balance when reviewing the situation.

Optimistic thinking is not a delusion. Instead, it is a strategy to help us have the energy and perspective to keep going. The opposite of optimism is pessimism, which results in inertia. When in a pessimistic state of mind, we are not able to see the wood for the trees and our motivation to make a change declines so that doing anything will prove to be too much effort. Optimism, therefore, is a strategy for continuing to go and grow in the face of adversity. It is a strategy for success, which makes it so inspiring to people.

In addition to optimism, we need hope. Hope can be viewed as an emotion that often arises in the most desperate of times. After 9/11, individuals reported higher levels of hope (Peterson & Seligman, 2003). Moreover, those who experienced high levels of hope before 9/11 reported a further increase in hope after this tragic event (Fredrickson, Tugade, Waugh, & Larkin, 2003). Those who experienced the opportunity for hope during quarantine periods during COVID-19 were less likely to experience distress and more likely to cope positively (Laslo-Roth, George-Levi, & Margalit, 2021). Given that hope breeds hope, a hopeful leader's impact on an organisation can be exceptionally positive.

Apart from viewing hope as an emotion, it can also be perceived as a thinking style similar to optimism. However, the difference between optimism and hope is that while optimism helps us expect the best from the future, hope gives us a pathway to get there (Carver et al., 2009; Snyder, Lopez, Shorey, Rand, & Feldman, 2003). A leader that offers hope makes their team believe that they can make change happen and, in addition, shows them pathways and options in which to do so. Sometimes, what stops people from believing in a brighter future is that they have seen in the past that something has not worked. An inspiring leader can provide them with new evidence that this time it will be different and gives them a map that they can use to take them to the place where they want to go. This direction lights up the fire in their belly, turns on new neural pathways, and taps into resources people never thought existed. This is how a leader can inspire their followers via optimism and hope.

We once worked with a chief executive officer (CEO) who transformed from being a mediocre manager into an inspirational leader in just a few months. Locked up behind closed doors, he knew his industry expertly well but could not energise his team to perform. We worked with him on his language to ensure ways he conveyed new optimism and hope. Instead of discussing what the team should do, we discussed what 'could be' and the potential pathways to get there. Soon, his team started to see a new picture of a possible optimistic future and a plan that instilled hope in them. Working together, we amplified this new attractive vision by encouraging the leader to give examples of how other organisations, similar to this one, had struggled and overcame the struggle to exceed expectations. How other people – similar to those in his organisation – have, like the phoenix, risen from the ashes. In a few weeks, there was new energy in the organisation that permeated through the team's interactions with customers who began to comment on the team's changed attitude. Not only were customers wowed by this transformation so were the employees themselves. The employees no longer just pretended they were taking notes during the team meetings, but looked at their leader with hope and enthusiasm, believing strongly that he had what it took to turn their organisation around. This is what the impact of hope looks like.

We have established that hopeful leaders create pathways for achieving positive outcomes. However, don't all leaders do it with their vision and strategy? If so, what is different between hopeful and less hopeful leaders? Hopeful leaders pursue their goals energetically with 'affective zest', which is a state of high emotional activation and enthusiasm. In contrast, less hopeful leaders tend to attend to their goals with 'affective lethargy', whereby they make progress in achieving their goals, but it lacks enthusiasm (Snyder, 2002). This affects their followers via the contagious social effect. Research has demonstrated that leaders who feel excited, enthusiastic, and energetic tend to energise their followers. As such, leaders who display hopefulness affect the hopefulness and resilience of their followers, thus inspiring them to keep going despite adversity (Norman, Luthans, & Luthans, 2005).

Apart from offering a pathway, hopeful leaders are more likely to move towards desirable goals and avoid undesirable ones (Lopez, Snyder, & Pedrotti, 2003). When they come across obstacles, they tend to experience less stress, which prevents them from panicking and changing their direction; they also tap into more effective coping strategies (Snyder & Lopez, 2005). Their coping strategies allow them to overcome their adversities faster than leaders who have not developed this skill yet. The research therefore suggests that developing and practising hopefulness can be very beneficial to leaders and their teams. Moreover, effective leadership is about a leader's ability to awaken hopeful thinking in their team (Helland & Winston, 2005) so that they can reach the height of their potential. This awakening in their teams is just one of many reasons why it is useful for positive leaders to develop hopefulness.

Reflection on practice

Think of a recent challenging project or situation you have experienced. Now, practice optimism by reflecting on:

- *What were the three to five aspects of the project or situation that could have been managed more optimistically?*

- *What action did/do you need to take for the challenge to pass more optimistically?*

- *What aspects of your life did/does the challenge not affect?*

Now, practice hope by reflecting on:

- *What is the best outcome from this challenging project or situation that you are hoping for in the future?*

- *What steps do you need to support this new best outcome?*

Energising networks

Energy is a process of emotional arousal that can be related to experiencing short-lived positive emotions, such as excitement, zest, inspiration, or joy or a longer-term mood that is an accumulation of emotions unrelated to a specific event (Cameron, 2021; Quinn & Dutton, 2005). Individuals can report high levels of energy because of internal or external processes. At an internal level, zest, vigour, and energy are attributes whereby some individuals have a more natural predisposition to experience them. It may also be triggered as an outcome of an individuals' engagement with an activity, a task, or a job. Alternatively, it may be associated with conditions that activate the external processes to energise individuals and groups of people. Let us delve deeper into all these three perspectives.

As an attribute, the energy-generating zest is one of the strongest contributors to life satisfaction, engagement, and meaning (Peterson, Ruch, Beermann, Park, & Seligman, 2007). In a workplace, individuals who experience zest at work also report satisfaction with work and view their work as a calling or a vocation (Peterson, Park, Hall, & Seligman, 2009), which is a sign of intrinsic motivation towards work. Furthermore, Peterson et al.'s study also demonstrated differences in how much zest individuals experience in the context of their profession. The highest levels of zest were noted among professionals and leaders. The lowest levels were seen among blue-collar workers and homemakers. We do not know if people's characteristics attracted them to a given profession or if the job they were doing resulted in their higher levels of zest. However, it is important to note that each member may experience varied levels of zest on a team, and a leader needs to be aware of it and help all employees tap into this resource.

Why would employers take the time to help employees enhance their level of personal energy? There are many reasons for it. Firstly, living vigorous lives predicts longevity instead of a calmer, sometimes even sluggish, life (Pressman & Cohen, 2011). This means that creating conditions at work that can help employees feel more enthusiastic in their jobs may improve their lifespan. Secondly, in a large-scale study of over 5,000 employees who were monitored over 1.5 years, those who experienced lower levels of enthusiasm for their work considered their job to be too strenuous (citing excessive work, conflicting demands, not enough time to do the work, fast work, and hard work) (Josephson & Vingård, 2007). They also reported poorer health and more sickness days (Josephson & Vingård, 2007). Thus, helping employees feel more enthusiasm for their work is good not only for them but also for their employers. That enthusiasm is what fuels the positive energy in the workplace.

In addition to this, the presence of enthusiasm and energy are contagious, and so is the lack of enthusiasm and energy (Cameron, 2021). Energy can be applied at an individual level and at a team or a network level. It is also the energy networks we live in daily which can affect us at micro, meso, and macro levels (Baker, 2019). On a micro (personal) level, some individuals have bundles of mental, emotional, spiritual, or physical energy. The productivity of these energetic employees usually excels, and they tend to have a positive influence on others, inspiring others to achieve an even higher level of performance (Cross & Parker, 2004). At the meso (relational) level, some employees in an organisation (not necessarily leaders) may have a compelling vision for the future, inspire the trust of others, and have an exquisite ability to inspire others to follow their mission. Equally, de-energising employees may be just as influential, but their negative energy will ultimately deplete others and inspire them to inertia instead of growth. Finally, at the macro (organisational) level, the energy or momentum that an organisation experiences is usually sparked by a selected few. Therefore, that energising, be it positive or negative, can occur at various levels.

Of all the types of energies (mental, emotional, spiritual, physical or relational), relational energy is the strongest, and there are many actions leaders can take to promote it in the workplace (Dutton, 2003). Firstly, it can be promoted by creating a trusting environment, abundant with psychological safety, where employees feel comfortable making mistakes. Secondly, by leaders promoting respectful engagement with their team and ensuring that everyone on the team treats others with respect. Thirdly, by enabling the team to carry out their tasks, removing the obstacles in their way of success. It is important for the team members to do the same. In one organisation we consulted for, we arranged a meaningful 'musical chairs' exchange, whereby employees in various departments moved around the room, chatting with all colleagues they regularly collaborated with and telling them what they needed from them (in terms of information, resources, and support); why they needed it; and what were or might be the consequences of not receiving this information, resources, or support on time. They finished their exchange by identifying enablers for their and others' high performance and committing to helping each other out more specifically with these energy sources. Many employees were surprised by the profound impact that their decisions or actions (or inaction) had on others. Therefore, figuring out what enables performance and then putting approaches in place so this can be transferred or received can create great relational energy on a team.

Finally, yet another way to boost relational energy is by tackling head on the connections that do not serve the team well. They include situations when there is a disrespectful engagement between team members, disabling task disruption, or false promises that fuel a lack of trust. In these situations, Dutton (2003) suggests that the problem should be called out and named. Also, an individual may try to regain a sense of control by setting up goals, creating a new working condition that supports a positive change, or new behaviour. For example, say that one employee is feeling bullied by another. The target of bullying may take control by deciding that if the bullying behaviour continues, they will take it up with the HR department (goal setting), avoid discussions other than on work-related issues (working condition), and smile at the person (changed behaviour). Other techniques include psychological disengagement from the situation that is causing energy drain, strengthening personal resources such as looking after your health, or constructing a more positive self-image. Suppose a colleague persistently does not meet deadlines they set for themselves to provide information, resources, or support to others; instead of shying away from or avoiding responsibility for this so that their colleagues expectant of the exchange feel a source of disappointment or confusion resulting in a lack of energy, in that case, a colleague can be honest and transparent that they have not or are unable to meet the deadline and create a new deadline for themselves or in tandem with their colleagues. These are just a few examples of how energy can move from negative to positive.

In addition to ensuring an energising atmosphere on the team, positive leaders need to become aware of their own energy levels and be careful that what they say does not leave their employees deflated. After all, they realise the critical impact of energy networks on employees' performance (Cameron & Plews, 2012). For example, a leader with a can-do attitude, searching for solutions and offering encouragement, may positively impact the team. If the team is meandering, disappointed about their results, or there is conflict in their midst, a positive leader thinks carefully about what they or other team members should say or do and how they can spark their team to get them going again.

"I have always been drawn to positive people", reflected Professor Luke O'Neill, "and it began with my father who was that way." Our positive leader's father was conscripted into the army during WW2 at the age of 20. He was actively fighting for the country, and all the war atrocities made him look at life in a different way. After the war, he began to appreciate small things in life, an attitude Professor O'Neill inherited from his father. Since then, he has been drawn to positive people, and many of his friends have similar attitudes. There are, of course, times when he has to work with people who are more pessimistic and do not enjoy life as much as him. He calls collaborating with them a "deadly combination" because, on the one hand, they bring his energy down; however, on the other hand, he prides himself on lifting them up. He gives them energy, which is deflating for him, but he is proud to help them a bit. These combined efforts sometimes produce good results, but they usually leave him emotionally drained. This is not unusual, as some people we interact with in our daily lives drain us, others leave us unaffected, and some inspire us. Positive leaders are the ones who keep our spirits up and whose presence lifts us and give us bundles of energy instead of getting us down.

Advice from Professor Luke O'Neill to keep the team's spirits up is by never complaining down, only by complaining up. He explained:

> Say, you are a captain, there is no point in you saying to your lieutenant; this is a bad army, there is no equipment, no weapons, no anything. That's hopeless and would demotivate him. However, if you can say to the Colonel: "Hey colonel guy, where are my weapons", something will be done about it.

Complaining to the people that report to you is a useless exercise in venting that can have dire consequences on their energy levels. The real change happens when the right resources are tapped into. This is why positive leaders think carefully as to what they say to their team members.

That awareness of leaders' words and actions also extends to knowing who the best person on the team is to help them through an energy or mindset slump. When we have energisers at work, we must recognise them and engage them in working on our mission. We once worked with a leader in the construction industry who experienced a management walkout, whereby all his leaders gave their notice at the same time and took his best people with them, leaving his business in trouble. He could not understand why this had happened; however, long coaching discussions led him to realise that while he had a great vision for the business, he was not a natural leader, and people usually did not follow him. In other words, he did not energise people, and sometimes the impact he had on his team was de-energising. Apart from committing to long-term leadership development, he also decided to restructure his organisation. He employed a deputy CEO, offered him an attractive package, and ensured that he had the natural leadership ability that prompted others to follow him. He then stepped down as his organisation's leader and saw it as an act of courage after he realised that in the energy network in the workplace, he did not contribute to it positively. Now he still makes many of the important decisions about his business but stays mainly in the background, allowing his second-in-command to run the day-to-day business. Ten years later, his organisation is thriving, and his employees are happy, as they have a different and inspirational leader who continues to keep them energised.

Reflection on practice

Consider the impact of your daily interactions on your team's energy levels. What does your team look like when they are fully energised? What have you done in the past to help them achieve this state? What changes can you make in your daily practice to energise yourself and your team?

- Who on your team has an energising effect on others? How can you use their resource more frequently and/or effectively?

Inspiration in action

Becoming an inspiring leader is not an easy task. It requires plenty of self-awareness and humility to realise that we may need help inspiring others. After all, it is rarely a lone endeavour. There are many theories of motivation. Broadly speaking, motivation is often perceived as a *force* that makes people act in desirable ways. That force may relate to intrinsic motivation finding an intrinsic drive for pursuing something (Deci & Ryan, 2012), the satisfaction of needs (Maslow, 1943), employees being treated fairly (Adams, 1963), reinforcement of positive behaviour (Skinner, 1938), or goal-setting (Locke, 2019). All these forces allow employees to act and perform to a higher level. However, the resource of inspiration differs from motivation in that it is not associated with any forces. It is about creating moments in time that spur individuals to higher levels of creativity and drive them to act. These resources, when used regularly, can spark motivation and lead to higher performance.

The inspiration resource is an amalgamation of the direct influence of leadership attitude, behaviour, and verbal communication. It is also the indirect influence of creating policies and enacting them to ensure that any conflict and de-energising behaviour does not fester in the team for too long, so that individuals on the team create networks of positive energy. For leaders to become inspiring, they need to understand and have full self-awareness of the components of the inspiration resource. They need to change, if necessary, the language they use when discussing daily situations and performance with their team. They need to become aware of their own thinking styles concerning self-efficacy and optimism. Finally, they need to act to create a hopeful pathway that will motivate their team to action and nurture an environment that allows employees to create and re-develop energising networks.

Last word

The resource of inspiration provides leaders with a tool to create self-efficacy, hope, and optimism and re-energise the workplace. Of all the resources discussed in this book, the inspiring resource is most fragile, as it is based on affect, which is short-lived. Words that people say can change the atmosphere in an instant. They can become motivating or demotivating in seconds. Individuals, teams, and organisations must remember this in the context of inspiration. In the words of playwright Arthur Miller's (2015) tragic character Eddie in *A View From the Bridge*: "You can quicker get back a million dollars that was stole than a word that you gave away". This changeable inspiration resource works against us when we do not use it correctly. At the same time, when things do not go well, it is also one resource that may have a significant and sudden positive effect on people.

References

Adams, J. S. (1963). Towards an understanding of inequity. *The Journal of Abnormal and Social Psychology*, 67(5), 422–436. doi:10.1037/h0040968

Amit, K., Popper, M., Gal, R., Miskal-Sinai, M., & Lissak, A. (2006). The potential to lead: The difference between "Leaders" and "Non-Leaders". *Megamot*, (2), 277–296. http://www.jstor.org/stable/23658399

Baker, W. E. (2019). Emotional energy, relational energy, and organizational energy: Toward a multilevel model. *Annual Review of Organizational Psychology and Organizational Behavior, 6*, 373–395. doi:10.1146/annurev-orgpsych-012218-015047

Bandura, A. (1997). *Self-efficacy: The exercise of control*. New York: W H Freeman/ Times Books/ Henry Holt & Co.

Bass, B. M., & Avolio, B. J. (1994). *Improving organizational effectiveness through transformational leadership.* Thousand Oaks, CA: Sage Publications, Inc.

Baumeister, R. F., Campbell, J. D., Krueger, J. I., & Vohs, K. D. (2003). Does high self-esteem cause better performance, interpersonal success, happiness, or healthier lifestyles? *Psychological Science in the Public Interest, 4*(1), 1–44. doi:10.1111/1529-1006.01431

Berson, Y., Shamir, B., Avolio, B. J., & Popper, M. (2001). The relationship between vision strength, leadership style, and context. *The Leadership Quarterly, 12*(1), 53–73. doi:10.1016/S1048-9843(01)00064-9

Bobbio, A., & Manganelli, A. M. (2009). Leadership self-efficacy scale: A new multidimensional instrument. *TPM-Testing, Psychometrics, Methodology in Applied Psychology, 16*(1), 3–24.

Brissette, I., Scheier, M. F., & Carver, C. S. (2002). The role of optimism in social network development, coping, and psychological adjustment during a life transition. *Journal of Personality and Social Psychology, 82*(1), 102–111. doi:10.1037/0022-3514.82.1.102

Bruton, A. M., Mellalieu, S. D., & Shearer, D. A. (2016). Observation as a method to enhance collective efficacy: An integrative review. *Psychology of Sport & Exercise, 24*, 1–8. doi:10.1016/j.psychsport.2016.01.002

Cameron, K. (2021). *Positively energising leadership: Virtuous actions and relationships that create high performance.* San Francisco: Berrett-Koehler Publishers, Inc.

Cameron, K. S., & Plews, E. (2012). Positive leadership in action: Applications of POS by Jim Mallozzi. *Organizational Dynamics, 41*, 99–105.

Carver, C. S., Scheier, M. F., Miller, C. J., & Fulford, D. (2009). Optimism. In S. J. Lopez & C. R. Snyder (Eds.), *Oxford handbook of positive psychology* (2nd ed., pp. 303–311). New York: Oxford University Press.

Cornick, J. E. (2015). Factor structure of the exercise self-efficacy scale. *Measurement in Physical Education & Exercise Science, 19*(4), 208–218. doi:10.1080/10 91367X.2015.1074579

Cross, R., & Parker, A. (2004). Charged up: Creating energy in organizations. *Journal of Organizational Excellence, 23*(4), 3–14. doi:10.1002/npr.20021

Davidson, R. J., & Begley, S. (2012). *The emotional life of your brain: How its unique patterns affect the way you think, feel, and live, and how you can change them.* New York: Hudson Street Press.

Deci, E. L., & Ryan, R. M. (2012). Self-determination theory. In P. A. M. Van Lange, A. W. Kruglanski, & E. T. Higgins (Eds.), *Handbook of theories of social psychology* (pp. 416–436). London: Sage.

Dutton, J. E. (2003). *Energize your workplace: How to create and sustain high-quality connections at work* (1st ed.). San Francisco, Great Britain: Jossey-Bass.

Dwyer, L. P. (2019). Leadership self-efficacy: Review and leader development implications. *Journal of Management Development, 38*(8), 637–650. doi:10.1108/JMD-03-2019-0073

Fida, R., Paciello, M., Tramontano, C., Barbaranelli, C., & Farnese, M. L. (2015). "Yes, I Can": The protective role of personal self-efficacy in hindering counterproductive work behavior under stressful conditions. *Anxiety, Stress & Coping, 28*(5), 479–499. doi:10.1080/10615806.2014.969718

Fredrickson, B. L., Tugade, M. M., Waugh, C. E., & Larkin, G. R. (2003). What good are positive emotions in crisis? A prospective study of resilience and emotions following the terrorist attacks on the United States on September 11th, 2001. *Journal of Personality and Social Psychology, 84*(2), 365–376. doi:10.1037/0022-3514.84.2.365

Garrett, N., & Sharot, T. (2017). Optimistic update bias holds firm: Three tests of robustness following Shah et al. *Consciousness and Cognition: An International Journal, 50*, 12–22. doi:10.1016/j.concog.2016.10.013

Graham, J. D., & Bray, S. R. (2015). Self-control strength depletion reduces self-efficacy and impairs exercise performance. *Journal of Sport & Exercise Psychology, 37*(5), 477–488. doi:10.1123/jsep.2015-0064

Helland, M. R., & Winston, B. E. (2005). Towards a deeper understanding of hope and leadership. *Journal of Leadership & Organizational Studies, 12*(2), 42–54. doi:10.1177/107179190501200204

Josephson, M., & Vingård, E. (2007). Zest for work? Assessment of enthusiasm and satisfaction with the present work situation and health – A 1.5-year follow-up study. *Work, 29*(3), 225–231.

Judge, T. A., Shaw, J. C., Jackson, C. L., Scott, B. A., & Rich, B. L. (2007). Self-efficacy and work-related performance: The integral role of individual differences. *Journal of Applied Psychology, 92*(1), 107–127. doi:10.1037/0021-9010.92.1.107

Laslo-Roth, R., George-Levi, S., & Margalit, M. (2021). Hope during the COVID-19 outbreak: Coping with the psychological impact of quarantine. *Counselling Psychology Quarterly*, 1–15. doi:10.1080/09515070.2021.1881762

Locke, E. A. (2019). What makes writing about goals work? *Academy of Management Discoveries, 5*(2), 109–110.

Lopez, S. J., Snyder, C. R., & Pedrotti, J. T. (2003). Hope: Many definitions, many measures. In S. J. Lopez & C. R. Snyder (Eds.), *Positive psychological assessment: A handbook of models and measures* (pp. 91–106). American Psychological Association. doi:10.1037/10612-006

Machida, M., & Schaubroeck, J. (2011). The role of self-efficacy beliefs in leader development. *Journal of Leadership & Organizational Studies, 18*(4), 459–468. doi:10.1177/1548051811404419

Maddux, J. E., & Kleiman, E. M. (2021). Self-efficacy: The power of believing you can. In C. R. Snyder, S. J. Lopez, L. M. Edwards, & S. C. Marques (Eds.), *The Oxford handbook of positive psychology* (3rd ed.). New York: Oxford University Press.

Maslow, A. H. (1943). A theory of human motivation. *Psychological Review, 50*(4), 370–396. doi:10.1037/h0054346

Mielniczuk, E., & Laguna, M. (2020). Positive affect mediates the relationship between self-efficacy and innovative behavior in entrepreneurs. *Journal of Creative Behavior, 54*(2), 267–278. doi:10.1002/jocb.364

Miller, A. (2015). *A view from the bridge*. London: Bloomsbury Publishing.

Mohamed, E. S. A. (2021). The impact of social intelligence and employees' collective self-efficacy on service provider's performance in the Egyptian governmental hospitals. *International Journal of Disruptive Innovation in Government, 1*(1), 58–80.

Mongrain, M., & Anselmo-Matthews, T. (2012). Do positive psychology exercises work? A replication of Seligman et al. (). *Journal of Clinical Psychology, 68*(4), 382–N.PAG. doi:10.1002/jclp.21839

Murphy, J., & Torre, D. (2015). Vision: Essential scaffolding. *Educational Management Administration & Leadership, 43*(2), 177–197. doi:10.1177/1741143214523017

Norman, S., Luthans, B., & Luthans, K. (2005). The proposed contagion effect of hopeful leaders on the resiliency of employees and organizations. *Journal of Leadership & Organizational Studies, 12*(2), 55–64. doi:10.1177/107179190501200205

Peterson, C., Park, N., Hall, N., & Seligman, M. E. P. (2009). Zest and work. *Journal of Organizational Behavior, 30*(2), 161–172.

Peterson, C., Ruch, W., Beermann, U., Park, N., & Seligman, M. E. P. (2007). Strengths of character, orientations to happiness, and life satisfaction. *The Journal of Positive Psychology, 2*(3), 149–156. doi:10.1080/17439760701228938

Peterson, C., & Seligman, M. E. P. (2003). Character strengths before and after September 11. *Psychological Science (0956–7976), 14*(4), 381–384. doi:10.1111/1467-9280.24482

Pressman, S., & Cohen, S. (2011). Positive emotion word use and longevity in famous deceased psychologists. *Health Psychology, 31*(3), 297–305.

Quinn, R. W., & Dutton, J. E. (2005). Coordination as energy-in-conversation. *Academy of Management Review, 30*(1), 36–57.

Rahim, M. A. (2014). A structural equations model of leaders' social intelligence and creative performance. *Creativity & Innovation Management, 23*(1), 44–56. doi:10.1111/caim.12045

Roberts, J. K., & Henson, R. K. (2001). A confirmatory factor analysis of a new measure of teacher efficacy. *The British Journal of Educational Psychology, 75*(Pt 4), 689–708. doi:10.1348/000709905X37253

Sadri, G., & Robertson, I. T. (1993). Self-efficacy and work-related behaviour: A review and meta-analysis. *Applied Psychology: An International Review, 42*(2), 139–152. doi:10.1111/j.1464-0597.1993.tb00728.x

Schmidt, A. M., & DeShon, R. P. (2010). The moderating effects of performance ambiguity on the relationship between self-efficacy and performance. *Journal of Applied Psychology, 95*(3), 572–581. doi:10.1037/a0018289

Schwarzer, R., & Jerusalem, M. (1995). General self-efficacy scale (GSE). In J. Weinman, S. Wright, & M. Johnston (Eds.), *Measures in health psychology: A user's portfolio. Causal and control beliefs* (pp. 35–37). Windsor, UK: NFER-NELSON.

Seligman, M. E., & Schulman, P. (1986). Explanatory style as a predictor of productivity and quitting among life insurance sales agents. *Journal of Personality and Social Psychology, 50*(4), 832–838. doi:10.1037/0022-3514.50.4.832

Seligman, M. E. P. (1990). *Learned optimism*. New York: Knopf.

Sharot, T. (2011). *The optimism bias: A tour of the irrationally positive brain*. Pantheon/Random House.

Shipman, A. S., & Mumford, M. D. (2011). When confidence is detrimental: Influence of overconfidence on leadership effectiveness. *The Leadership Quarterly, 22*(4), 649–665. doi:10.1016/j.leaqua.2011.05.006

Shoji, K., Cieslak, R., Smoktunowicz, E., Rogala, A., Benight, C. C., & Luszczynska, A. (2016). Associations between job burnout and self-efficacy: A meta-analysis. *Anxiety, Stress & Coping: An International Journal, 29*(4), 367–386. doi:10.1080/10615806.2015.1058369

Sitzmann, T., & Yeo, G. (2013). A meta-analytic investigation of the within-person self-efficacy domain: Is self-efficacy a product of past performance or a driver of future performance? *Personnel Psychology, 66*(3), 531–568. doi:10.1111/peps.12035

Skinner, B. F. (1938). *The behavior in organization.* New York: Appleton-Century-Crofts.

Snyder, C. R. (2002). Hope theory: Rainbows in the mind. *Psychological Inquiry, 13*(4), 249–275. doi:10.1207/S15327965PLI1304_01

Snyder, C. R., & Lopez, S. J. (Eds.) (2005). *The oxford handbook of positive psychology.* New York: Oxford University Press.

Snyder, C. R., Lopez, S. J., Shorey, H. S., Rand, K. L., & Feldman, D. B. (2003). Hope theory, measurements, and applications to school psychology. *School Psychology Quarterly, 18*(2), 122–139. doi:10.1521/scpq.18.2.122.21854

Snyder, C. R., Rand, K. L., & Sigmon, D. R. (2018). Hope theory: A member of the positive psychology family. In M. W. Gallagher & S. J. Lopez (Eds.), *The Oxford handbook of hope* (pp. 27–43). New York: Oxford University Press.

Taylor, S. E. (1989). *Positive illusions: Creative self-deception and the healthy mind.* New York: Basic Books/Hachette Book Group.

Villanueva, J. J., Sánchez, J. C., & Howard, V. N. (2007). Trait emotional intelligence and leadership self-efficacy: Their relationship with collective efficacy. *The Spanish Journal of Psychology, 10*(2), 349–357. doi:10.1017/S1138741600006612

Walumbwa, F. O., Lawler, J. J., Avolio, B. J., Wang, P., & Shi, K. (2005). Transformational leadership and work-related attitudes: The moderating effects of collective and self-efficacy across cultures. *Journal of Leadership & Organizational Studies, 11*(3), 2–16. doi:10.1177/107179190501100301

Zullow, H. M., & Seligman, M. E. (1990). Pessimistic rumination predicts defeat of presidential candidates, 1900 to 1984. *Psychological Inquiry, 1*(1), 52–61. doi:10.1207/s15327965pli0101_13

5 | **Grand design**

Eartha Pond is a London-based elected local government councillor, professional athlete, and educator. One of the multiple committees she is part of nominated her to be interviewed for this book as a force majeure. Eartha cherishes opportunities to support others in making a difference. She talks about having such clear meaning and purpose for her work that it does not feel like work. Eartha describes herself as someone who believes in the bigger picture, perseverant focus, and the necessity for people to make sure we achieve what we set out to do. She explains that having this grand design "provides me with the energy to be creative and to lead with integrity [. . .] to utilise the things that I'm in control of". Eartha argues that discussions leaders often have on 'time management' are futile, when the discussion we should all be having is about energy management towards what is the most purposeful goal at hand:

> To me, it's all about energy management. So, when everyone has 24 hours in the day, it's about what drives you to dedicate a specific amount of time to certain tasks that add to your purpose and how are you able to keep going. And when you've got a clear passion for something, it doesn't even seem like work. It doesn't even seem like you're doing anything – you are just doing what you love doing and what you were made to do intrinsically. [. . .] I'm doing what I'm supposed to be doing [. . .] and with that, everything's just a lot easier.

Eartha uses her grand design for the work she does to keep herself on track and focused. She is so committed to her greater purpose that she leans away from better financial gain to keep doing the work she does in education with those that are more underrepresented or for whom the educational gap is greatest. Eartha is a leader full of and directed by grand design for herself and others.

DOI: 10.4324/9781003170433-5

What is grand design?

Grand design is a leader's ability to transcend day-to-day activities into mean-ingful contributions and vice versa (Figure 5.1). There are three primary con-structs within grand design that we have identified from the research. Grand design comprises (1) meaning, which is about a positive leader's ability to develop comprehension and significance for themselves and others, where a worthwhile narrative is created; (2) purpose, which is the subcomponent of this meaning or the plot of meaning, and is the putting of meaning into action and living by our values in what we are doing in work and life; and finally, (3) catabolism, which derives from the component of purpose and is the specific action taken to deliver on the plot in order to meet the bigger narrative of meaning (see Figure 5.2). (Note we have borrowed the word catabolism from its original biological meaning of the 'breaking down' of more complex molecules into simpler ones; with catabolism here meaning for our model the 'breaking down' of purpose).

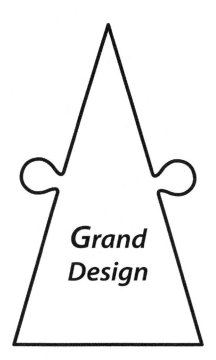

Figure 5.1 The Grand Design resource piece of the ALIGHT jigsaw

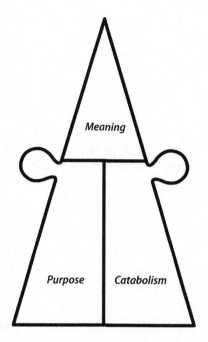

Figure 5.2 The Grand Design components

These combined resources allow leaders to achieve extraordinary performance and tap into their employees' optimum potential through a process of grand design. Again, these components are enacted at subjective, collective, and organisational levels, meaning that positive leaders can enact the components of grand design in relation to themselves, use them in their daily communication with their team, and promote them when making decisions at an organisational level. These three components lead to a grounded continuity of self – a groundedness that leads to better performance for ourselves and others than a directionless boat without a compass wandering for days adrift in the sea. We will now delve more deeply into these components, describing what they are, why they are essential, and how they show up for positive leaders, before giving you the opportunity to reflect on your own practice.

Meaning

There are many definitions of meaning. In the leadership context, meaning in life refers to the extent to which people make sense of their lives and the world around them, perceive their own lives to have intrinsic value and to be worth living, and identify highly valued and long-term aspirations towards which they endeavour (Steger, 2021). These three sub-elements of meaning are often referred to as coherence, significance, and purpose (Frank Martela & Steger, 2016). Sometimes the terms meaning and purpose are used interchangeably, which can create confusion (Steger, 2021). To separate them out more clearly, meaning can be described as the over-arching story, and purpose as a subcategory of meaning that provides the plot with more specificity. This reflects how positive leaders behave – not offering intangible pipe dream ideas but specific, clear overviews with tangibly broken-down activity and action to meet a narrative of mean-ing that is regularly reinforced. Positive leaders make the complex and abstract make sense in the way they break meaning down into purpose and purpose down into catabolic plans. The sense they make of meaning is significant and of value – it has purpose, aims, and goals and plans attached to it; they role model this and coach others to do the same. We will talk about purpose and catabolism shortly, but here we focus on the meaning-making – how leaders connect what they do to something big-ger than themselves, create the feeling that our lives are worthwhile, and know and work towards values.

Before we turn to look at values, let us first look at how positive leaders are able to connect what they do to something beyond them, something more transcendental, and feel their lives (work lives) are worthwhile. Mean-ing can be experienced through a sense of self-awareness and understand-ing: understanding of where our hedonic and eudemonic desires are fused to our understanding of ourselves and those around us and the direction within which we are heading (Steger, 2021). Positive leaders create com-prehension within meaning by offering a clear narrative and enough sense of stability and security for people to feel that there is continuity and pre-dictability to their work (Steger, 2021). Positive leaders identify a narrative and constantly reiterate it and revisit it, ensuring they and those around them are constantly aware that their work relates to something bigger than themselves and is worthwhile. Positive leaders are reflectors; they take time to reflect on their circumstances and what they are endeavouring towards. Reflection is not merely a process of describing what happened, considering how we felt, and identifying what we would do differently. Reflection is also a process of connecting what has happened to alternative causes, viewing the situation from various perspectives, and merging our and other people's behaviour with meaning (Burke & Dempsey, 2021); reflection enables the opportunity to identify that we are creating a life that is worthwhile through our work.

Positive leaders deliberately use their meaning to prioritise how they, their teams, and their organisations use time and direct energy. This prioritisation and re-prioritisation is a constant reflection for Eartha, who persistently wonders how she can make a tangible difference and put time and energy into the right something that's going to close the social gaps she sees.

> It's about identifying that I'm doing something not because I want to do it necessarily, but because there's a need for me. I've identified this task as a need for something to be improved. And it's about how can we work together collaboratively or individually in order to improve that need.

She explains that having meaning is not as easy as it might sound – and again, as with limberness, she needs to contend to it with a tough edge.

> A lot of the stuff I do is not because I *really* want to do it. Actually NO, I recognise first and foremost that here's an issue. [. . .] It's a barrier and that's a problem, and I need to find the solution. And then there's something which allows me to find a solution and that can then again help have a positive outcome on something else.

It is the meaning, then, which she has developed for herself that helps her choose and manage the challenges that might come up when pursuing her meaning.

As Eartha indicates, her meaning 'drives' her; she is someone who "believes in the bigger picture, perseverance, and a necessity to make sure what we achieve is what we set out to do." Martine, like Eartha, shares an unrelenting conviction and understanding for why she does what she does, even having spent years as a pregnant and young mum living through tough times in tiny London bedsits trying to make ends meet and manage her way in the brutal world of fashion: "For 13 years it was really hard [. . .] I got rehoused in a bedsit when I was pregnant and it was really tough [. . . but] I had a sense it was going to change. I believed in it – otherwise, I wouldn't have tortured myself like that!" Her meaning for working in the fashion industry – where difference is welcomed, embraced, and creates enticing stories – feels second nature to her and piques her creative curiosity:

> I've always been interested in people on the edges in whatever way. And that to me is what fashion is – that environment where you went, if you didn't really fit and you were a bit weird . . . you were gay, you were trans, whatever [fashion welcomed you]. And so, when I say that I enjoy that, I enjoy complex characters, I really do, and I like the diversity.

Martine's conscious and reflective awareness of her life's story and narrative enables her to keep finding meaning in her work and driving forward, knowing that what she is doing is worthwhile.

For us to feel that life has meaning, we first need to feel our actions are valuable and worthwhile and that secondly, we belong to and are working towards something greater than ourselves. Meaning is an essential element of wellbeing, in addition to being signified by connecting our work and lives to something beyond ourselves and feeling our lives are worthwhile. This meaning can thirdly be signified by our values. Moving to look at values and how positive leaders identify highly valued and long-term aspirations towards which they endeavour, experience shows us that many leaders instead struggle to recall their values. Yet without appropriate attention to awareness, development, and implementation of our values, values are unlikely to have a positive impact on workplace behaviours and practices and may even be detrimental to the individual and organisation as a whole (Thomas, 2013). For example, Thomas's research has shown that in the field of counselling, substance abuse counsellors who were not supported in identifying and aligning their values in their organisations were more likely to demonstrate unethical behaviour in their practice or leave their profession (2013).

Positive leaders have a clear understanding of what their value drivers are. Knowing our values is essential for our psychological wellbeing and performance, and is seen as our psychological keel (David, 2017). Our 'values' are the things that we deeply care about and are a helpful and genuine way to connect with our motivation systems. Our values link to our cognitive drive system – they act as cognitive motivators. A good way of thinking about values is that they are statements about what we want to be doing with our life – they offer us guidance in what we want to stand for and how we want to behave. They are leading principles that can help us to navigate our way through life. The most common sources of values include domains such as relationships, nature, hobbies, pets, religions, future aspirations, and aspects of self (Steger, 2021). Having more and a varied range of sources of meaning is considered by researchers to be optimal in life, as this is believed to broaden not just the range of meaning we experience but also the level of meaning we experience, linking to health and balance (M. F. Steger, 2021). Equally, being able to regularly recollect what matters to you over extended periods of time in a deliberate and thoughtful way has been shown in research to make people feel more likely to reap the abundant feeling of their meaningfulness in life (Steger, 2021).

If a value is truly authentic to us, then it has the potential to bring us a sense of calm and contentment as we move towards it (David, 2017). Eartha explains, "When you have got a passion for something, it doesn't even seem like work. It doesn't even seem like you're doing anything, just doing what you love and what you were intrinsically made to do". Here we see the connection between working towards our values and positive leaders' health behaviour, which we will discuss in the next chapter. If we try to work towards values that are not genuine and authentic to us, then they lose all their power. Instead of being a source of internal motivation, a 'should' value is more likely to make us feel trapped, controlled, or have us comparing ourselves to others, affecting our mental health (Harris, 2009). However, while knowing where we are going via our values might give us a sense of clarity and meaning, it does not necessarily make the journey any easier psychologically. Often the things that we care about the most can bring the greatest challenge, whether it's trying our best to lead, losing a loved one, or any number of other challenges we might experience in life. We all face times in our lives where we think, "I just can't do it" – and this goes for positive leaders too. However, rather than give up, Eartha uses her meaning to keep her moving forward to the next day:

> Instead of being negative and being sad about it [I say] I got kicked in the butt today, [and] I have the ability to get through it [. . .] tomorrow we go again; we try again to be the best version of ourselves that we can. [. . .] When you look at the bigger picture, that thing [your meaning] is actually more rewarding and more powerful than in the moment issues.

The benefits of meaning do not stop at the level of the individual; the benefits of meaning for organisations are also now widely cited (Steger, Fitch-Martin, Donnelly, & Rickard, 2015; Steger, 2012, 2016; Steger & Dik, 2010), and meaning is now often considered by organisations as just as important a considerations as wellbeing. Where organisations take efforts to encourage the development of meaning among their staff and within their organisation, the beneficial outcomes include increases in whole organisational performance through increased efforts of employees (Dik, Byrne, & Steger, 2013) and improved levels of health and the fortunes of a whole range of stakeholders, including shareholders and community members (Dik et al., 2013). Further benefits of meaning achieved at the organisational level include friendlier workplaces, increased levels of mentoring, more effective teams, and a greater focus on doing what is best for society (Steger & Dik, 2010).

Meaning is essentially the powerful narrative that we construct for our lives, and purpose – which we will discuss in the next section – is the plot detail. Before we move to look at purpose, take some time to reflect on your own meaning and the narrative you have constructed for your own life – how well does this integrate into your work and organisation?

Reflection on practice
- *What are your values?*

- *How do you integrate your values in the work that you do?*

- *How do your values play out in your broader life?*

- *How does your organisation promote the integration of your values within your work?*

Purpose

As Steger, a leading researcher into meaning, says, "If comprehension is the narrative of our stories, purpose is the plot" (2021, p. 5). Purpose is the putting of meaning into action and living by our values in what we are doing in work and life. Purpose is the superordinate, organising way of thinking with intention that offers us both a stability and an agility in pursuing what we want from life (where meaning offers us an anchor, purpose offers us a rudder to correct our course). Purpose is the reason that something exists. It is the active subcategory part of meaning, taking meaning and putting it into action. For a company, this might mean having a reason for doing business that's more than just about making money.

Take the U.S. clothing firm Patagonia, for example. Patagonia core values comprise "building the best products, causing no unnecessary harm, using business to protect nature, and not bound by convention". At Patagonia, the desire of the company is to be the change agent in the marketing and production of products that leave a difference in both society and the environment. This purpose drives all their decisions in their business, work, and how they market and position themselves. In 2021 Patagonia was described as the most reputable company in the United States, beating out 99 other prominent U.S. businesses in consumer rankings for company ethics, citizenship, and culture (Weaver, 2021). Having such a clear sense of meaning manifested by their purpose gives Patagonia a clear direction for how they move forward as an organisation, leading to this crystal-clear purpose and giving them a market edge for their offering.

Recent research has shown that it is important that people pursue a career that is in line with what they find to be 'important', rather than engaging in activities that they 'like' (Jachimowicz, To, Menges, & Akinola, 2017); thus, having a values-oriented mindset over a feelings-orientated mindset is key to finding purpose in our work. Having a purpose in life can lead to less conflict when making important decisions about life, including health, and lead to better mental health (Kang, Strecher, Kim, & Falk, 2019). Having a purpose that stems from one's meaning can reduce an aimless drifting through life or a constant change of goals in a bid to catch an undefined version of personal contentment (Donaldson, Dollwet, & Rao, 2015). Having our own purpose stops us from falling into a trap of trying to live up to socially prescribed ideals that could instead result in burnout and depression (Curran & Hill, 2019). In spite of the power of knowing one's deeper purpose, our education systems and parents often promote a focus on technical learning of knowledge and competencies without emphasis on reflecting on values, goals, and plans for what people want to get from their lives or who they want to become, fostering maladaptive perfectionism (Nurra & Oyserman, 2018; Suh, Gnilka, & Rice, 2017). So far we are generally missing a trick when it comes to fully integrating our meaning and purpose into our education and workplaces; thinking more about our values and how they are plotted in the work and decisions we take will enable much greater alignment of life for children and adults as they progress with their lives, to the advantage of the organisations they choose to resultingly work in.

What often gets in the way of developing clarity of one's purpose are social or other comparisons, consumer pressures, and cultural pressures to be or do as others (Schippers & Ziegler, 2019). Positive leaders recognise the challenge of this unsolicited pressure, and rather than mindless, auto-pilot decision-making, they support themselves and others to more mindfully reflect on what matters to each deeply, in the long term, and not just on the surface in the short term when putting their meaning into purpose. Social psychology informs us that as human beings we are socially conditioned to compare ourselves to others and to want to fit in with them (Festinger, 1954). Positive leaders lean away from this 'group think' mentality to notice the greater purpose and to align their thinking deliberately and more frequently to their values and move towards their purpose – as painful and isolating as this might sometimes be for them. Martine discussed how she had an investor pull out of buying into her brand when she shared her purpose, depicted in a manifesto for a positive culture to be not just centred around the commercial but wider health behaviour outcomes such as in sustainability, social outreach, and the wellbeing of the team. She says: "I shared the manifesto and [the investor] got really quiet . . . and they pulled out of the deal". When questioned how she felt about losing out on a lucrative deal when being so explicit about her purpose, she said: "I feel fine about it . . . I would definitely not want to find out that someone is not on board with that [our culture and values] later on". For Martine, it is much more important that those that invest and work with her are aligned to her business's purpose for the future and sustainability than take a risk for greater initial reward.

Russell highlights that we can also have too lofty an understanding of what creates purpose and that meaning can be noticed more often in our day-to-day activity if we look hard enough. He says:

You get to see lots of stats about how little meaning people find in their work on an average basis. Obviously, it's somewhat easier in some organisations than others, but I think sometimes we go too high for our meaning, we don't have to change the world all of the time. Sometimes the craft of the work can provide meaning, creating a good product that people like and buy and makes their lives a little easier – there's [purpose] in that idea. But equally, if you go too high, people being able to draw a line between their task and that meaning becomes really, really hard to do.

He talks about how something that can seem disparate from purpose – such as doing the monthly accounts – is still a key driver if you bring it down a level. He says that purpose is often found in the service that we provide to each other inside an organisation or to our customers who are hopefully part of our tribe.

And yes, we may be changing big trends in the world. We may be tackling educational disadvantage or those sorts of things. But on a day-to-day basis, I may find [purpose] in the fact that I have had a conversation with that trainee teacher who was about to quit and now they're enthused again, or we have compared the monthly accounts, the executive team was able to use them and they've cut an area of spending that was completely wasted for us as an organisation [and so on]. So I do think that you need to find meaning at a level [of purpose] where "how does what I'm doing now feels meaningful", not that I'm in some broad, fuzzy thing that's going on.

For most adults, work represents half of waking life. Feeling that what we do has a purpose – that it adds value to ourselves and our world – is therefore critical to our wellbeing (Baumeister, 1991; Treadgold, 1999; Whittington, Meskelis, Asare, Beldona, & Springer International, 2017). However, when we ignore the precarious relationship of our psychological reasoning of the place work takes in our lives, there is a danger that work can become meaningless (Bailey & Madden, 2016), losing its purpose. With a loss of purpose and instead a sense of meaninglessness, we are likely to disengage and not take pleasure or satisfaction from our work, and our wellbeing will suffer.

An ongoing tension for positive leaders is to have their own values and those of their team align with their organisation's values and vision. This tension has the potential to become magnified in VUCA (volatile, uncertain, complex, and ambiguous) times (Boniwell & Smith, 2018); purpose can get lost in times where we are under pressure. Positive leaders think about their continuity of self and support others to do so, leading to better decision-making and a more likely alignment of values, whatever the pressures. Crabb (2011) shows that alignment to values is one of the biggest drivers for individual engagement in the workplace. Eartha is single-minded about encouraging herself and others to continuously work towards purpose, so no matter what it is that might be a barrier or a blocker to it – be it class or race – nothing should stop us from pursuing our purpose. However, as we sadly know and she admits, it is much harder for some in our society than others.

Eartha works hard towards her purpose and ensures she gets a 'seat at the table' not just for her own grand design but also to role model how to access it for others. She says two things are important in this: asking for help and putting time and energy into this purpose rather than the wrong focus. She says:

> Just to prove and show that the table is for everyone, I'm going to go and sit around that table, even if it's at a detriment to me and my time and my learning just to prove to my community or whoever it is that actually if that's the case, that if you really, really want to get around, look around – like I'm not even sometimes not even super passionate about it. I'm passionate about supporting you – And to do that, I'm showing you that this thing that you're passionate about is accessible.

Eartha works hard to make sure the communities she works with realise that they all have an equal right to find their purpose and a seat at the table they want to be at, no matter what injustice and underrepresentation people may face.

Russell also argues that if people do not find this values alignment or get the autonomy, competence, and connectedness they need in their current workplace or context, it is essential to look elsewhere to fulfil our own purpose:

> Maybe part of the secret if we're lucky enough to be planning our own careers, is to go towards areas where we have greater freedom

of action so that we can behave in the ways that we want to behave [. . .] there's some thinking you need to do about where should you work? Who should you work for? And trying to find the right organisations that can [support you to] think in those sorts of terms.

Russell has been selective and particular in all of his career choices, ensuring as he progresses that the roles and organisations he works for align with his purpose.

Reflection on practice
- *One's meaning might be to work towards a life of connection, creativity, courage, curiosity, and contribution. One's purpose might be about supporting oneself to find ways to achieve connection, creativity, courage, curiosity, and contribution in the work that you do. Reflecting on the differences between meaning and purpose, what factors do you feel give your life its overall meaning versus what gives your life its ongoing purpose?*

- *How might knowing your purpose more clearly support you or others you work with in decision-making at work? Can you think of a recent example of where having a more explicit purpose may have been helpful for you or team members?*

- *Does social comparison in life or the workplace ever cloud your working towards your purpose? What supports you not to make social comparisons when it comes to your work and working towards your purpose?*

Catabolism

Whilst meaning is the story and purpose is the plot, catabolism is the commitment to paper and action of the plot; it is the writing and verbalisation of the meaning and purpose before it. We have borrowed the word catabolism from its original biological meaning of the breaking down of more complex molecules into simpler ones. Catabolism here meaning Catabolism is the act of taking the meaning and purpose (our values, passions, goals) that we have and breaking them down into tangible ways to deliver on the meaning and purpose through action and goals in our day-to-day life, such as goal attainment plans. Positive leaders regularly develop these catabolic plans, revisit and refine them, and get their teams to do so too, remaining focused (and not fixed) on what matters.

As we have mentioned, the way we live in the 21st century can distract us from our true meaning and purpose in life, where people can become regularly distracted and feel a pressure to live a picture-perfect life focused on external ideals of success instead of following what matters to them intrinsically (Schippers & Ziegler, 2019). By being catabolic, positive leaders maintain a relentless focus on their meaning and purpose. They are catabolic in breaking the macro meaning and purpose into the micro to support and sustain this focus. Positive leaders also act as reminders, supporters, and champions to others in being catabolic about our meaning and purpose.

As we have also mentioned, the three key dimensions of meaningful work that have been identified in positive psychology that can be seen to be related to the behaviour of our positive leaders are significance, the opportunity for broader purpose and for self-realisation (Martela & Pessi, 2018). We have already discussed significance when looking at meaning and broader purpose when looking at purpose, and so now let us turn to self-realisation – the catabolic part in the grand design resource. Positive leaders support the development of this self-realisation in themselves and influence their colleagues' and team members' sense of self-realisation (supporting them to know how to enact the meaning and purpose into the work in many ways). They do this through two particular methods: job crafting and delivering on purposeful work through a catabolic approach. We will now examine how these two strategies make work more meaningful and purposeful.

Job crafting relates to individuals' ability to actively reframe their work physically, cognitively, and socially to support their enjoyment, experience, and fulfilment in their work and roles (Demerouti, 2014; Vogt, Hakanen, Brauchli, Jenny, & Bauer, 2016; Wessels et al., 2019; Amy Wrzesniewski &

Dutton, 2001). This is therefore about being able to reshape or tailor your work at a physical level – for example, moving the times that you do things to different parts of the day or even more literally moving the location at which you do your job; at a cognitive level – for example, which types of cognitive tasks – deep or light in terms of cognitive load – happen when and by whom; and socially – for example, who might you do part of your role or work with or without to aid your enjoyment or fulfilment in your work. And there are many other ways this crafting can and does happen when employees are given the opportunity to craft their work in such a manner.

The beneficial implications of job crafting transcend life boundaries, which have consequences for experiencing more meaning in life (Demerouti et al., 2019). Positive leaders can and do develop job crafting for themselves and others to contribute to their teams' and organisations' catabolism and overall grand design. Organisations can do more to support their employees to craft their job by helping them identify their meaning and how it relates to what they do (Wrzesniewski, LoBuglio, Dutton, & Berg, 2013). Furthermore, positive leaders actively do this through the following seven mentioned sub-methods and more:

a. Change the way tasks are approached – if an employee can see that small actions within their role are crucial to the wider processes, mission, or goals of a team or company, it can create high personal meaning (Emmons, 1999);
b. Change the way tasks are ordered so that one structures activities in the way most conducive to personal enjoyment e.g. least enjoyable tasks first or last (Wrzesniewski, 2014);
c. Increase or decrease the number of tasks so that tasks that do not encourage meaningfulness are lessened and those that do increase (Pratt & Ashforth, 2003);
d. Increase or decrease the kinds of tasks completed (Pratt & Ashforth, 2003);
e. Change the number and nature of relationships with others encountered at work (Pratt & Ashforth, 2003);
f. Work with people more directly (Pratt & Ashforth, 2003);
g. Structure one's work towards one's future career development (Wrzesniewski, 2014).

We appreciate this is not as easy as it sounds, yet this crafting can and does happen effectively through deliberate job design.

Sarah explains that the supportive meaning-making by her former employer, along with a critical mentor Sian Westerman, were both critical in her career development as a female leader wanting to progress in her role with her own grand design. Sarah recalls being a new mother, terrified to leave the office at the end of the day – for fear that others may not think she was dedicated if she needed to head off to collect her children. She was being pulled to the side by Sian (who we discussed earlier on in Chapter 4 for her optimism) and told not to look at time in a binary way, to do what she needed to do. Sian encouraged Sarah to think about what she wanted for her own future career development and be explicit about this in what she then did in the day to day. Sian told Sarah to make a decision about whether she wanted to progress in her career, stay still, or step back; she advised that if she wanted to progress, she just needed to be proud of her purpose and meaning and state it with courage: "You've got to decide whether you want to have your cake and eat it [combining motherhood and work. . .] if you're going to give the commitment, you've got to make sure that your managers understand that". So, Sarah went and made her meaning and purpose catabolic through having direct conversations with her managers, explaining what she wanted, that she was committed to her ambitions and the firm – even if it might take her longer than those without child-caring responsibilities (which in the end it didn't) – making her grand design clear. Following this, her company promoted her through the ranks and told her that although balancing motherhood and work in the early years would be hard, they would support her until she was flying again. (And whilst as female authors and mothers we recognise this support for working parents is not always the case in our ongoing internationally unequal workplaces, stating your explicit grand design certainly worked in this instance). Sarah stayed at that company for almost 20 years and replicates these positive practices with her new team.

Catabolism is the process that breaks down the plot, ensuring that concrete plans are made to work towards the purpose. Once the best possible vision is imagined by a leader and its team, that embodies values and opportunity for purpose, the processes that positive leaders use to be catabolic include writing about the ideal future, writing down specific goal attainment plans and 'if-then' plans, and taking public commitments to the goals set (Schippers & Ziegler, 2019). Schippers and Ziegler explain that writing about the ideal future aids a broadening of mindset in being more open to opportunity; that writing down specific goal attainment plans – particularly spending longer than 15 minutes at a time doing so (Frattaroli, 2006) – as writing things down make us think about the experience of doing the thing we are writing about, which can support self-regulation and action (Balcetis & Cole, 2009); and that making public commitments to the goals set have been shown to make it more likely that people will be more self-regulating towards their goals (Balcetis & Cole, 2009). We will look further into how Schippers and Ziegler outline how these strategies work through particular methods in a moment.

Positive leaders know and say it is also important to think about when and where you do each particular task in order to manage your daily energy (Wessels et al., 2019), making strategic decisions about how to allocate your time and energy, instead of letting daily hassles make these decisions for you (Christensen, 2017). Valuable strategies for being specific and concrete include writing down things to do weekly or daily to further goals (Schippers & Ziegler, 2019). It may also be useful to make a concrete plan of action for the upcoming week and to specify for each day the hours one will spend working on the goal they have in mind (calendarising activity and work to again maintain the focus needed).

Methods highlighted that pertain to this catabolic approach include mental contrasting, broaden and build theory, and goal-setting theory (Schippers & Ziegler, 2019). Mental contrasting (Oettingen, Wittchen, & Gollwitzer, 2013) involves evaluating your implementation intentions: you can visualise and then contrast both a desirable and an undesirable future (Brodersen & Oettingen, 2017), and you can therefore visualise effectively both the goal and the obstacles to it (Sevincer, Mehl, & Oettingen, 2017). This has been described as a form of "metacognitive self-regulatory strategy of goal pursuit" (Duckworth, Kirby, Gollwitzer, & Oettingen, 2013, p. 745; Schippers, Scheepers, & Peterson, 2015), where we regulate ourselves by foreseeing different possible outcomes. One addition to the mental contrasting approach is making if-then plans (Oettingen et al., 2013; Oettingen-Spielberg, Sevincer, & Gollwitzer, 2018). The idea is that by making concrete plans and identifying obstacles as well as ways to overcome them (if-then plans), people are better able to visualise their desired future and less tempted to engage in activities distracting them from their goals (Webb, 2017).

The method of broaden and build theory is about using our experience of positive emotions to deliberately broaden our mindset and thought repertoire (Fredrickson, 2001). This can be a useful strategy because if people can imagine a better future, then you are more likely to be scanning for ways in which you can achieve this life (Schippers & Ziegler, 2019); they will have developed a more positive and optimistic mindset which is more open (Fredrickson, 2001; Meevissen, Peters, & Alberts, 2011). Over time, this broader and abundant mindset can help us acquire more skills and resources, which may lead to better health, happiness, and performance (Garland et al., 2010).

Goal-setting theory (Locke, 2019) outlines a method of how we can set, apply, and develop goal-focused behaviour. Recent research shows that goals need not be specific, as long as plans are and that a catabolic way of writing about life goals and plans in a structured way is especially effective (Locke & Schippers, 2018). Schippers and Ziegler believe that the process of writing about self-concordant goals does three things: (1) the necessity of goal-directed action is salient; (2) it starts a process of embodied cognition and dynamic self-regulation; and (3) it starts an upward spiral of goal congruence, goal attainment, and (academic) performance (2019). According to Steger's helpful unified model of meaning, you can have meaning, but without the pathways of purpose and the catabolism of that purpose, you cannot feel balanced in your meaning (2021).

Reflection on practice

- *Do you structure your day in a way that prioritises your goals?*

- *How do you make your work's meaning and purpose catabolic daily, weekly, or monthly? How clear are the links between the meaning, purpose, and catabolic day-to-day actions of your work?*

- *How often do you actively job craft to create more meaning and purpose in your work and support this in the work of others? And where could you do this more if necessary?*

- *How could you make more 'if-then' plans to better secure your goals?*

Grand design in action

A critical enabling condition for grand design is a welcome, supportive, and pro-social work environment. Positive leaders exercising their grand design resource know that being part of a community can make one feel connected to the world and that one belongs, and for them and others, science shows us that this enhances our perception of work as meaningful (Demerouti et al., 2019; Grant, Dutton, & Rosso, 2008). This pro-social atmosphere also contributes to a sense of psychological safety – which we mentioned as being critical to the limberness resource too, where human beings feel able to congruently engage their selves in their work. Otherwise, an employee can feel that they are alienated from their work and feel disengaged (Kahn, 1990; May, Gilson, & Harter, 2004; Rastogi, Pati, Krishnan, & Krishnan, 2018). Martine, like all of our positive leaders, speaks about the importance of this pro-social environment in creating grand design for her teams: "I give a lot of freedom, and I trust [my staff], I really trust their opinions, and their decision-making. I let people have bad days, and I give people space".

Workplaces and leaders can stifle the growth of their workforce's grand design if autonomy is not offered to employees, particularly if this autonomy is not offered in how they shape and craft their purpose and catabolic plans from their meaning into their work, and we see this sad missed opportunity daily in our work. The socio-cultural conditions of a person's life often stifle human development and growth (Deci, 1985; Lucey & van Nieuwerburgh, 2020; Spence & Oades, 2011). Research in a range of settings has found that organisations and environments that promote autonomous motivation instead bring about positive effects on the behaviour and outlook of their employees: persistence and maintained behaviour change; effective performance (particularly on tasks requiring creativity, cognitive flexibility, and conceptual understanding); job satisfaction; positive work-related attitudes; organisational citizenship behaviours; and psychological adjustment and wellbeing (Gagné & Deci, 2005; Wheatley, 2017). Based on this observation, a positive leader who pays attention to their own and others' autonomy, competence, and connectedness in role(s) creates more optimum conditions for grand design.

Furthermore, there is a need for grand design to be regularly reassessed and monitored and space within the organisation's delivery activity for this development work to take place. Leaders need to have the time and be

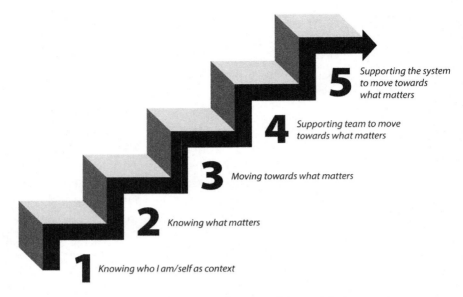

5 *Supporting the system to move towards what matters*

4 *Supporting team to move towards what matters*

3 *Moving towards what matters*

2 *Knowing what matters*

1 *Knowing who I am/self as context*

Figure 5.3 A process of meaningful grand design

encouraged to prioritise regularly assessing meaning, purpose, and catabolism in the regular and day-to-day activity of a team and organisation. At any one time, a positive leader may need to re-establish personal purpose and meaning, team meaning and purpose, or aligning this to the system and vice versa. Speaking to our positive leaders, it appears this happens regularly and at least annually – a behaviour which research says magnifies meaning (Schippers & Ziegler, 2019).

The components of meaning, purpose, and catabolism crucially fit together because it is only in having all three that a process of grand design can be fulfilled. In a process of meaningful grand design (see Figure 5.3), positive leaders demonstrate that they:

1. Know themselves well and their meaning and purpose through being able to offer a clear understanding of their own values in speech or practice for themselves or to their team in one-to-ones or team meetings;
2. Move towards values, meaning, and purpose for themselves and encourage others to do so on a daily and constantly focused basis, for example, by always making connections for others in how their values come into their work and the decisions they make and actions they take;

3. They support their teams and others to move towards what matters through encouraging job crafting, offering autonomy to others, and encouraging self-empowerment to access more meaning and purpose. For example, by getting colleagues to shape their own calendars to suit their own preferred working styles and making joint decisions on when and where different types of work can be planned, or getting team members to choose the different strands of work that most suit one another's strengths instead of allocating activity based on assumption;

4. They create meaningful connections within their team and beyond by making sure there is a 'human' side to the way they work, where there is time for connection at the start of meetings or in interactions that is not always focused on the task;

5. They are aligned and move themselves and their team towards the meaning and purpose that the system requires (and do so with passion). For example, they consider how projects and programmes of work could best or better bring a sense of coherence or significance in the way they are planned or delivered (such as drawing on specific community stakeholders for their perspectives rather than making assumptions in design); they also make explicit links to work activity and system requirements that have a wider and even transcendental purpose (e.g. explaining what a particular project's wider community outcomes will be to give broader significance to work activity).

Without all three components of grand design (meaning, purpose, and catabolism), a leader can face many insurmountable hurdles. For example, Figure 5.4 shows how the leader can consciously or unconsciously move themselves and their team away from their meaning and purpose, and indeed even cause damage to the greater system in doing do. This can happen when (1) the leader fails to know themselves well, (2) does not know what matters to them (or to others), (3) unconsciously or consciously moves away from what matters, and (4) in having a lack of coherency passes this onto the team's misdirection for themselves and moves the team away from doing what matters for the organisation and indeed the system, and (5) thus moves the system away from what matters and harms the system.

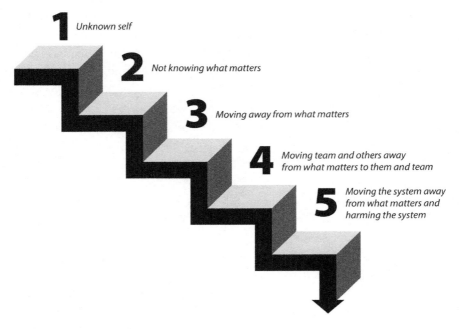

Figure 5.4 A process of meaningless design

Last word

Positive leaders with grand design can create meaningful and purposeful work for themselves, their team, and the community, which goes beyond mere words of vision and mission and touches hearts through a clear and broad purpose. They do so in a way that is clear and tangible – a catabolic way – and they do this by making the grand design explicit; articulated; co-created; and constantly reiterated, reinforced, and broken down. In the positive leadership ALIGHT framework, grand design fuses together the need for the positive leader to consider both purpose and meaning for themselves and their teams and relate this to their community and longer-term strategic priorities, as well as deliver on this through regular and tangible catabolic action.

References

Bailey, C., & Madden, A. (2016). What makes work meaningful – or meaningless. *MIT Sloan Management Review*, *57*(4), 53.

Balcetis, E., & Cole, S. (2009). Body in mind: The role of embodied cognition in self-regulation. *Social and Personality Psychology Compass*, *3*(5), 759–774. doi:10.1111/j.1751-9004.2009.00197.x

Baumeister, R. F. (1991). *Meanings of life*. New York: Guilford Press.

Boniwell, I., & Smith, W.-A. (2018). Positive psychology coaching for positive leadership. In S. Green & S. Palmer (Eds.), *Positive psychology coaching in practice* (1st ed., pp. 159–178). London: Routledge. doi:10.4324/9781315716169-10

Brodersen, G., & Oettingen, G. (2017). Mental contrasting of a negative future with a positive reality regulates state anxiety. *Frontiers in Psychology*, *8*, 1596.

Burke, J., & Dempsey, M. (2021). *Undertaking capstone projects in education: A practical guide for students*. Abingdon: Routledge.

Christensen, C. M. (2017). How will you measure your life? *Harvard Business Review Classics*.

Crabb, S. (2011). The use of coaching principles to foster employee engagement. *The Coaching Psychologist*, *7*(1), 27–34.

Curran, T., & Hill, A. P. (2019). Perfectionism is increasing over time: A meta-analysis of birth cohort differences from 1989 to 2016. *Psychological Bulletin*, *145*(4), 410–429. doi:10.1037/bul0000138

David, S. A. (2017). *Emotional agility: Get unstuck, embrace change and thrive in work and life* (Paperback ed.). London: Penguin Books Ltd.

Deci, E. L. (1985). *Intrinsic motivation and self-determination in human behavior/ Edward L. Deci and Richard M. Ryan*. New York: Plenum.

Demerouti, E. (2014). Design your own job through job crafting. *European Psychologist*, *19*(4), 237–247. doi:10.1027/1016-9040/a000188

Demerouti, E., Hewett, R., Haun, V., De Gieter, S., Rodríguez-Sánchez, A., & Skakon, J. (2019). From job crafting to home crafting: A daily diary study among six European countries. *Human Relations*, *73*(7), 1010–1035. doi:10.1177/0018726719848809

Dik, B. J., Byrne, Z. S., & Steger, M. F. (2013). *Purpose and meaning in the workplace*. Washington, DC: American Psychological Association.

Donaldson, S. I., Dollwet, M., & Rao, M. A. (2015). Happiness, excellence, and optimal human functioning revisited: Examining the peer-reviewed literature linked to positive psychology. *The Journal of Positive Psychology*, *10*(3), 185–195. doi:10.1080/17439760.2014.943801

Duckworth, A. L., Kirby, T. A., Gollwitzer, A., & Oettingen, G. (2013). From fantasy to action: Mental contrasting with implementation intentions (MCII) improves academic performance in children. *Social Psychological and Personality Science*, *4*(6), 745–753. doi:10.1177/1948550613476307

Emmons, R. A. (1999). *The psychology of ultimate concerns: Motivation and spirituality in personality*. New York: Guilford Press.

Festinger, L. (1954). A Theory of Social Comparison Processes. *Human Relations*, *7*(2), 117–140. doi:10.1177/001872675400700202

Frattaroli, J. (2006). Experimental disclosure and its moderators: A meta-analysis. *Psychological Bulletin*, *132*(6), 823–865. doi:10.1037/0033-2909.132.6.823

Fredrickson, B. L. (2001). The role of positive emotions in positive psychology: The broaden-and-build theory of positive emotions. *American Psychologist, 56*(3), 218–226. doi:10.1037/0003-066X.56.3.218

Gagné, M., & Deci, E. L. (2005). Self-determination theory and work motivation. *Journal of Organizational Behavior, 26*(4), 331–362. doi:10.1002/job.322

Garland, E. L., Fredrickson, B., Kring, A. M., Johnson, D. P., Meyer, P. S., & Penn, D. L. (2010). Upward spirals of positive emotions counter downward spirals of negativity: Insights from the broaden-and-build theory and affective neuroscience on the treatment of emotion dysfunctions and deficits in psychopathology. *Clinical Psychology Review, 30*(7), 849–864. doi:10.1016/j.cpr.2010.03.002

Grant, A. M., Dutton, J. E., & Rosso, B. D. (2008). Giving commitment: Employee support programs and the prosocial sensemaking process. *Academy of Management Journal, 51*(5), 898–918. doi:10.5465/AMJ.2008.34789652

Harris, R. (2009). *ACT made simple an easy-to-read primer on acceptance and commitment therapy.* Oakland: New Harbinger Publications.

Jachimowicz, J., To, C., Menges, J., & Akinola, M. (2017). *Igniting passion from within: How lay beliefs guide the pursuit of work passion and influence turnover.* doi:10.17605/osf.io/qj6y9

Kahn, W. A. (1990). Psychological conditions of personal engagement and disengagement at work. *Academy of Management Journal, 33*(4), 692–724. doi:10.2307/256287

Kang, Y., Strecher, V. J., Kim, E., & Falk, E. B. (2019). Purpose in life and conflict-related neural responses during health decision-making. *Health Psychology, 38*(6), 545–552. doi:10.1037/hea0000729

Locke, E. A. (2019). What makes writing about goals work? *Academy of Management Discoveries, 5*(2), 109–110.

Locke, E. A., & Schippers, M. (2018). Improving lives: Personal goal setting boosts student performance and happiness. *Academy of Management Proceedings, 2018*(1), 16790. doi:10.5465/AMBPP.2018.16790symposium

Lucey, C., & van Nieuwerburgh, C. (2020). 'More willing to carry on in the face of adversity': How beginner teachers facing challenging circumstances experience positive psychology coaching an interpretative phenomenological analysis. *Coaching: An International Journal of Theory, Research and Practice.* doi:10.1080/17521882.2020.1753791

Martela, F., & Pessi, A. B. (2018). Significant work is about self-realization and broader purpose: Defining the key dimensions of meaningful work. *Frontiers in Psychology, 9*, 363. doi:10.3389/fpsyg.2018.00363

Martela, F., & Steger, M. F. (2016). The three meanings of meaning in life: Distinguishing coherence, purpose, and significance. *The Journal of Positive Psychology, 11*(5), 531–545. doi:10.1080/17439760.2015.1137623

May, D. R., Gilson, R. L., & Harter, L. M. (2004). The psychological conditions of meaningfulness, safety and availability and the engagement of the human spirit at work. *Journal of Occupational and Organizational Psychology, 77*(1), 11–37. doi:10.1348/096317904322915892

Meevissen, Y. M. C., Peters, M. L., & Alberts, H. J. E. M. (2011). Become more optimistic by imagining a best possible self: Effects of a two week intervention. *Journal of Behavior Therapy and Experimental Psychiatry, 42*(3), 371–378. doi:10.1016/j.jbtep.2011.02.012

Nurra, C., & Oyserman, D. (2018). From future self to current action: An identity-based motivation perspective. *Self and Identity, 17*(3), 343–364. doi:10.1080/15298868.2017.1375003

Oettingen, G., Wittchen, M., & Gollwitzer, P. (2013). Regulating goal pursuit through mental contrasting with implementation intentions. In E. A. Locke & G. P. Latham (Eds.), *New developments in goal setting and task performance* (pp. 523–548). New York: Routledge/Taylor & Francis Group.

Oettingen-Spielberg, G. Z., Sevincer, A. T., & Gollwitzer, P. M. (2018). *The psychology of thinking about the future.* New York: Guilford Press.

Pratt, M., & Ashforth, B. (2003). Fostering meaningfulness in working and at work. In K. Cameron, J. Dutton, & R. Quinn (Eds.), *Positive organizational scholarship* (pp. 309–327). San Francisco, CA: Berrett-Koehler.

Rastogi, A., Pati, S. P., Krishnan, T. N., & Krishnan, S. (2018). Causes, contingencies, and consequences of disengagement at work: An integrative literature review. *Human Resource Development Review, 17*(1), 62–94. doi:10.1177/1534484317754160

Schippers, M. C., Scheepers, A. W. A., & Peterson, J. B. (2015). A scalable goal-setting intervention closes both the gender and ethnic minority achievement gap. *Palgrave Communications, 1*(1), 15014. doi:10.1057/palcomms.2015.14

Schippers, M. C., & Ziegler, N. (2019). Life crafting as a way to find purpose and meaning in life. *Frontiers in Psychology, 10*, 2778.

Sevincer, A. T., Mehl, P. J., & Oettingen, G. (2017). Well self-regulated people use mental contrasting. *Social Psychology, 48*(6), 348–364. doi:10.1027/1864-9335/a000322

Spence, G. B., & Oades, L. G. (2011). Coaching with self-determination in mind: Using theory to advance evidence-based coaching practice. *International Journal of Evidence Based Coaching & Mentoring, 9*(2), 37–55.

Steger, M., Fitch-Martin, A., Donnelly, J., & Rickard, K. (2015). Meaning in life and health: Proactive health orientation links meaning in life to health variables among American undergraduates. *Journal of Happiness Studies, 16*(3), 583–597.

Steger, M. F. (2012). Experiencing meaning in life: Optimal functioning at the nexus of well-being, psychopathology, and spirituality. In P. T. P. Wong (Ed.), *The human quest for meaning: Theories, research, and applications* (2nd ed., pp. 165–184). New York: Routledge/Taylor & Francis Group.

Steger, M. F. (2016). Creating meaning and purpose at work. In *The Wiley Blackwell handbook of the psychology of positivity and strengths-based approaches at work* (pp. 60–81). Hoboken, NJ: Wiley.

Steger, M. F. (2021). *Meaning in life: A unified model* (3rd ed.). Oxford: Oxford University Press.

Steger, M. F., & Dik, B. J. (2010). *Work as meaning: Individual and organizational benefits of engaging in meaningful work.* In P. A. Linley, S. Harrington, & N.

Garcea (Eds.), *Oxford handbook of positive psychology and work* (pp. 131–142). Oxford University Press.

Suh, H., Gnilka, P. B., & Rice, K. G. (2017). Perfectionism and well-being: A positive psychology framework. *Personality and Individual Differences, 111*, 25–30. doi:10.1016/j.paid.2017.01.041

Thomas, T. P. (2013). *The effect of personal values, organizational values, and person-organization fit on ethical behaviors and organizational commitment outcomes among substance abuse counselors: A preliminary investigation* (Ph.D. Doctor of Philosophy thesis). University of Iowa.

Treadgold, R. (1999). Transcendent vocations: Their relationship to stress, depression, and clarity of self-concept. *Press Release*.

Vogt, K., Hakanen, J. J., Brauchli, R., Jenny, G. J., & Bauer, G. F. (2016). The consequences of job crafting: A three-wave study. *European Journal of Work and Organizational Psychology, 25*(3), 353–362. doi:10.1080/1359432X.2015.1072170

Weaver, A. (2021). *Patagonia rated most reputable company in the U.S. Outside Business Journal.* Retrieved from https://www.outsidebusinessjournal.com/brands/camping-and-hiking/patagonia-rated-most-reputable-company-in-the-u-s/

Webb, C. (2017). *How to have a good day: The essential toolkit for a productive day at work and beyond.* London: Pan Books.

Wessels, C., Schippers, M. C., Stegmann, S., Bakker, A. B., van Baalen, P. J., & Proper, K. I. (2019). Fostering flexibility in the new world of work: A model of time-spatial job crafting. *Frontiers in Psychology, 10*, 505.

Wheatley, D. (2017). Autonomy in paid work and employee subjective well-being. *Work and Occupations, 44*(3), 296–328. doi:10.1177/0730888417697232

Whittington, J. L., Meskelis, S., Asare, E., Beldona, S. (2017). *Enhancing employee engagement an evidence-based approach.* New York: Springer International.

Wrzesniewski, A. (2014). Engage in job crafting. In G. M. Spreitzer & J. Dutton (Eds.), *How to be a positive leader: Small actions, big impact* (pp. 65–75). San Francisco: Berrett Koehler.

Wrzesniewski, A., & Dutton, J. E. (2001). Crafting a job: Revisioning employees as active crafters of their work. *Academy of Management Review, 26*(2), 179–201. doi:10.5465/AMR.2001.4378011

Wrzesniewski, A., LoBuglio, N., Dutton, J. E., & Berg, J. M. (2013). Job crafting and cultivating positive meaning and identity in work. In A. B. Bakker (Ed.), *Advances in positive organizational psychology* (pp. 281–302). Bingley: Emerald Group Publishing. doi:10.1108/S2046-410X(2013)0000001015

6 | Health

For Orla Deering, the first few years of running her hair and beauty business were about survival. She spent all her waking hours in the salon, working overtime, focusing on the bottom line, developing clientele and the team. However, as soon as her business was thriving and her revenue skyrocketing, she saw her passion turning obsessive affecting her health and marriage. That is when she had a choice to make: to either continue on the path of self-destruction, or change. She chose the latter. It all began with a mindfulness retreat, which helped her stop and think. Today, years later, meditation is her daily trusted companion that helps her become a better version of herself. It helps her feel calm during stormy weather; it helps her remain a good colleague to her employees; it helps her be a better mum and wife to her loved ones. Most importantly, however, meditation allows her to be authentic, to be herself, and as such, live the life she has always wanted to live.

What is health?

'Healthy leadership' is a concept that emerged over the last two decades, of which there are over a dozen definitions that can be divided broadly into two types of leadership: (1) health-promoting and (2) health-oriented (Rudolph, Murphy, & Zacher, 2020). Health-promoting behaviours relate to the leadership actions that actively promote a healthy lifestyle in an organisation (Figure 6.1). Conversely, health-oriented behaviours are actions that leaders take to ensure creation and maintenance of a healthy environment for their team. In addition to these two main conceptualisations of healthy leadership, a salutogenic leadership approach suggests that healthy leadership should go

DOI: 10.4324/9781003170433-6

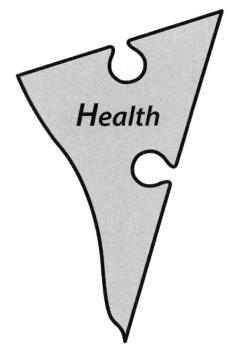

Figure 6.1 The Health resource piece of the ALIGHT jigsaw

beyond health promotion and health orientation and towards an interaction between an employee and their leader, which can be health-inducive or health-impeding (Eberz & Herbert Antoni, 2016). Therefore, the health component of the ALIGHT model consists of three elements: (1) promotion, which relates to leaders taking action to promote healthy behaviours; (2) orientation, referring to leaders taking action to ensure a healthy environment; and (3) full integration, which refers to healthy exchanges between leaders and their tribe and consideration of wider stakeholders (see Figure 6.2).

Promotion

Over the last few decades, organisations promoted health and wellbeing using various interventions. For example, there are organisations that have created virtual reality spaces to promote employees' relaxation (De Carlo, Carluccio, Rapisarda, Mora, & Ometto, 2020), others encouraged mindfulness programmes (Althammer, Reis, Beek, Beck, & Michel, 2021), online

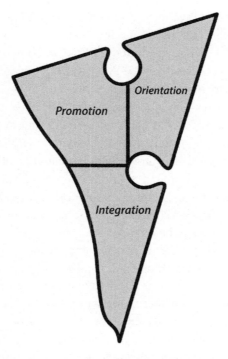

Figure 6.2 The Health components

games (Casucci, Locke, Henson, & Qeadan, 2020), or introduced a suite of cognitive-behavioural and positive psychology interventions (Lennefer, Lopper, Wiedemann, Hess, & Hoppe, 2020; Shankland & Rosset, 2017; Taylor, 2018). While these approaches are welcomed by many, they are not feasible in some organisations. A pool table or a massage room might work well, for example, in one type of company, but it may not be as effective in reducing hours and boosting wellbeing in another organisation. An alternative to it is an introduction of more integrated and evidence-based approaches to health and wellbeing, such as strengthening workplace relationships (Ejlertsson, Heijbel, Andersson, Troein, & Brorsson, 2021) or supervisors providing team support (Mohr, Hammer, Brady, Perry, & Bodner, 2021). While not all interventions work for everyone, what matters is that leaders care enough to introduce health promotion within their organisations.

Promoting health and wellness at work takes various approaches. Some organisations focus on helping employees cope with depression, anxiety, obesity, and other conditions that prevent them from living a good life. They aim to reduce the negative impact of health conditions and make employees aware of their symptoms so that they can take action to address them. For example, in a Korean organisation, office workers underwent a health promotion programme based on the World Health Organization framework, which resulted in decreased stress and cholesterol. Those who engaged with the programme fully reported changes in their body mass index, with reduced diastolic blood pressure being noted six months later (Ryu, Jung, & Moon, 2020). Other workplace occupational interventions included either one-off solutions or online health promotions (e-mental health). A review of 50 studies with occupational e-mental health interventions demonstrated lower levels of anxiety, insomnia, burnout, or alcohol misuse (Phillips, Gordeev, & Schreyögg, 2019), therefore helping employees cope more effectively with adverse mental or physical health issues by offering targeted solutions.

In contrast, instead of targeting issues, some organisations take a more proactive approach by organising a series of early interventions and introducing measures that create employees' awareness of potential illness and encouraging them to take action before the onset of disease. The outcomes of such interventions were not only effective for the health of employees but also beneficial to their employers. For example, in Australia, a programme targeting depression awareness and prevention resulted in a significant reduction of employee presenteeism a year later (Callander, Lindsay, & Scuffham, 2017). Similarly, a review of over 60 health promotion studies showed that employers can make health promotions cost-effective by targeting specific needs of their employees rather than following fads or generic health promotion strategies (Le et al., 2021). Thus, a well-thought-through health promotion strategy should be implemented to benefit both employees and their employers.

In addition to reducing and preventing health issues, positive leaders focus on helping employees grow and flourish psychologically. Reducing anxiety or preventing it from occurring keeps employees' illness at bay (moderate health), but it does not help them thrive (flourishing). Thus, their reference point is just reduction and prevention, not flourishing or thriving. Flourishing employees have well-developed psychological, social, emotional, and intellectual resources that protect them in difficult times and allow them to recover more quickly (Hone, Jarden, Schofield, & Duncan, 2014). Being at a moderate health level means they are not ill, but they are not at their subjective optimal level of wellbeing either. More importantly, however, if their health deteriorated from flourishing to moderate levels, they are more likely to develop depression within two years (Keyes, Yao, Hybels, Milstein, &

Proeschold-Bell, 2020). This means that great care should be taken to ensure that fluctuations are not too significant. Therefore, changing the reference point to tackle and prevent illness and help employees to thrive and flourish can support employees to be much better at building all the resources necessary to live a good life.

Whilst it is important for an organisation to remind their team about looking after themselves and to put structures in place that promotes employees' wellness, each individual needs to take responsibility for their action to enable their growth, health, flourishing, and thriving to take place (van der WaltFreda & Lezar, 2019). Positive leaders acknowledge the limits of their influence. Charley Stoney pointed out that "when you have an employee that works, works, works and that's all they do, you have to discuss it with them, point it out to them. But there is a limit to it". After all, it is employees' own lives, and they have a choice as to what they want to do. However, she does acknowledge that sometimes people need their leaders to give them permission to do the right thing and take some time out. But as a positive leader, you cannot force them to do it; instead, you need to role model and promote this course of action, conceding that employees need then do it for themselves. You can take a horse to the water, but you cannot make it drink; though it is much more likely the horse will drink water if you show them how.

To help colleagues find their own balance, positive leaders introduce work practices that encourage their team to relax. For example, Charley's team meets every day, but she makes sure that they don't talk about work all the time, especially on Mondays. Monday morning everyone's mind is still on the weekend, so she helps the team transition from home to work by discussing what they were up to for a significant chunk of the meeting. Orla makes sure that despite her hair salon being constantly busy, her team take regular breaks throughout the day to maintain their health. In the Royal College of Surgeons Ireland, where one of the authors of this book works (Jolanta), everyone shares positive experiences in their professional and personal lives for the previous week at weekly meetings in their department. Furthermore, during weekend and holidays nobody checks or responds to emails, thus giving everyone a break, and a simple line at the end of each email states that if you received this email outside your normal working hours, you are not expected to respond to it. Even though it might seem trivial on the surface, at a deeper level, this promotional action takes the pressure away and gives employees psychological permission not to work overtime and to hold healthy boundaries.

Promotion is vital for creating awareness of health and reminding people to look after themselves. We have seen many organisations inviting a series of ad hoc guests sharing their wisdom about wellbeing with the team. The challenge, however, is when two guests provide employees with different advice, or the type of advice that is being given is focused on one aspect of wellbeing and ignores all other facets. This is why when implementing wellbeing in organisations, it is important to follow a specific framework that will become a foundation for employees' success (Burke, 2021). These frameworks can be used for decision-making as to what health promotion initiatives should be implemented, or they may serve as measures of how well an organisation and their team are doing. Frameworks can be created by organisations after identifying employee needs, or they can be 'borrowed' from other organisations. For example, if an organisation is part of a Best Place to Work initiative, they may use their criteria for protecting employees' health as the basis for their framework. Alternatively, they may adapt it from a wellbeing campaign of organisations such as Action for Happiness, or wellbeing frameworks developed by World Health Organization (WHO), Organisation for Economic Co-operation and Development (OECD), or United Nations Sustainable Development Goals relating to ensuring healthy lives and promoting wellbeing for all. The choice is up to an organisation. What matters is that a framework exists and is followed to ensure shared language for health promotion, thus promoting a better understanding of what it is that leaders and employees are asked to do.

Sometimes the size of organisations is blamed for not implementing some of the health promotion measures. Leaders believe it is easier for a large conglomerate to engage with health promotion, whereas smaller organisations are less likely to offer their staff health promotion campaigns. Nevertheless, research indicates that size does not matter because while indeed, larger organisations offered more support, smaller organisations had a higher proportion of employees availing themselves of this support (Dale et al., 2019). This disparity of uptake is why positive leaders need to focus not on the number of interventions in an organisation, but on their own and their employees' interest in them. When their teams are interested in the health promotion programmes, they will be more likely to attend them and take on board what they have learnt from them, which may ultimately improve their health.

Recently, a series of meta-analyses were published about the effectiveness of implementing workplace health and wellbeing promotion programmes, and they yielded promising results for both employees and employers. Interventions encouraging healthy lifestyles, physical activity, and nutrition (many of which followed up with participants 12 months later or more) resulted in employees' weight loss, reduction of absenteeism generating a net benefit of €53.56 per employee, and a reduction of presenteeism of as much as 52 hours compared with a non-intervention group (Vargas-Martínez, Romero-Saldaña, & De Diego-Cordero, 2021). In addition to this, promotion programmes enhance the duration and quality of employee sleep, resulting in improved daytime performance (Robbins et al., 2019), and interventions such as yoga at work buffer teams against stress (Valencia et al., 2019). Therefore, promoting health and wellbeing in the workplace is a worthwhile exercise for positive leaders. Before we move to look at how leaders orientate health in the workplace, let us take some time to reflect on how you may promote health and wellbeing in your workplace now.

Reflection in practice

How do you look after your own health and role model this to others?

What type of health promotion programmes may you and your team be interested in, and why?

What health promotion programmes have worked for you or others in the past, and why?

Orientation

Health orientation refers to leaders' decisions to create a working environment conducive to health, be it physical or mental. Creating a healthy workplace relates to the policies employers have, habits developed by the team, and their general practice. For example, we once worked with an organisation with many impressive health-oriented policies that prevented employees from working overtime, encouraged lunch, and promoted collegiality. However, not all individual departments followed these policies. In some teams, the leader did not go out for lunch. She usually ate her sandwich at her desk while checking emails. It became a norm for the rest of the team to do the same. Moreover, some of them who did go out felt uncomfortable taking their full break entitlement, especially when they were due for promotion and saw their colleagues working through lunch. Positive leaders are there to create and support health-oriented policies and, as such, become the ambassadors for healthy work life.

In a survey with over 1,000 leaders, 7 out of 10 did not take regular micro-breaks (less than 10 minutes), and only every other leader took their lunch breaks (Burke & Dempsey, 2021a, 2021b). We have carried out similar research in three large organisations with management and non-managing team members. The results showed that most of the employees took short breaks and lunches when an organisation encouraged their work-life balance. However, when an organisation did not explicitly communicate about the importance of taking breaks, an unhealthy trend of working during lunchtime continued. This is why it is necessary for positive leaders to lead by example and give symbolic permission to their team to take regular respite and recovery during the day and after work. What they do during the break does not matter, as they need to match the employees' needs to be effective (Sonnentag & Fritz, 2015). What matters is that they take these breaks to prevent their physical, cognitive, and emotional depletion in the afternoon and maintain their wellbeing (Bosch, Sonnentag, & Pinck, 2018).

Another reason for a break is that it is a great way to ensure a better work-life balance. Employees who take their micro-breaks during the day tend to cope better with work challenges, recover faster from work, and have more energy in the evening so that they can spend quality time with their family and friends (de Bloom, Kinnunen, & Korpela, 2015; Kim, Park, & Niu, 2017). Similarly, taking regular respite over the weekend is associated with much higher work engagement and a lower likelihood of experiencing burnout the next week (Ragsdale & Beehr, 2016). Therefore, there are plenty of reasons for employees to take a break and more reasons for their leaders to encourage themselves and others to do so. Creating an environment in which employees do not feel obliged to stay at their desk during the break, or worse, work through it, can benefit the individual, their team, and their families.

Furthermore, taking micro-breaks is indirectly associated with employee performance, whereby the breaks enhance employees' positive emotions, boosting their output (Kim, Park, & Headrick, 2018). However, the effect is different for employees with various levels of engagement. Those who have difficulty engaging at work gain more out of micro-breaks than employees who are fully engaged. The performance of already fully engaged team members does not increase with an introduction of breaks. This explains why some staff head off for regular micro-breaks. Some leaders may mistakenly label them as lazy, but they follow their gut in knowing that having this quick break boosts their concentration and performance. Preventing them from taking the break may result in lower outputs. This disparity of impact of micro-breaks is yet another example of how one size does not fit all. Leaders need to understand the intricacies of employee energy, motivation, and engagement and associate with it the need to release others to help them maintain their health and increase their performance.

Sometimes, in the same organisation there may be various approaches to recovery. For example, we once collaborated with a large organisation, where according to the HR policy, all employees were permitted to take a micro-break in the morning and a one-hour lunch in the afternoon. During one of the leadership development seminars, an animated debate erupted, with some leaders saying that they stick religiously to the HR guidelines and when employees strolled in late from their breaks, they were reprimanded for their disregard of the policy. In contrast, other leaders took a more unshackled approach, whereby they were happy with employees taking many breaks or coming back late from their breaks as long as they completed what was required. Incidentally, when speaking later with the leaders who debated the issue of breaks, those who were relaxed about breaks talked about the importance of mutual trust, respect, and intrinsic motivation. Equally, employees whose leaders were strict tended to give as much as they got. They did their hours and not a minute more; when their energy was slumping, instead of renewing it by taking a visible micro-break, they found another way of switching off at their desk through procrastination: daydreaming and checking personal emails, texting, etc., which, in the long run took them more time away from work and may have negatively impacted their performance. Therefore, positive leaders need to reflect on the bigger picture of the impact of a policy instead of getting bogged down in the detail. Having healthy employees who are well-rested and focused on work can positively influence their team.

Other organisational practices also need to be considered when orienting leaders towards looking after employees' health. For example, during the COVID-19 pandemic, many employees experienced bereavement. Grief experienced by family and friends after COVID-19 is distinct from the grief experienced by employees when someone close to them dies of natural causes (Eisma, Tamminga, Smid, & Boelen, 2021). The COVID-19 pandemic exacerbated the process of bereavement due to the speed with which the virus developed, sudden intensive care admission, and additional social isolation experienced by both the sick person and their family. It resulted in many people experiencing prolonged grief disorder and persistent complex bereavement disorder, which may affect them for years to come. Amid the pandemic, employees and employers took to LinkedIn, asking how much time off should an employer give an employee whose family member died of COVID – is two to three days enough? Stories told by staff worldwide showed that some employers have led the way with compassion. Others, however, broke their employees' hearts by giving them barely one day off for a funeral and expecting them to bounce back to work, fully focused and ready to go. Positive leaders are the ones who consider the implications of their decisions in situations such as this one. They can see the impact of the working conditions they create for their team, and they are cognisant of the importance of the human factor.

Sarah explains that when she started in her role, she surveyed the level of health of her team and assessed the need for immediate resources and capacity to help the team keep up the demand being placed upon them:

> I wanted to think about quick wins for the team. So, the first thing I did was look at the resourcing, and the [team] was completely under the cosh, very busy, and constantly churning stuff out, not really breathing at all. Completing all kinds of legal agreements and sometimes up to about 15 of those a day [. . .] they couldn't really get up for breath.

Sarah immediately noticed the burden on her team as being unsustainable. She worked to manage resources, hiring an additional resource to ensure the workload became sustainable, and reinstating her team's ability to function at their best. She also specifically hired a secondee from a law firm for whom the exchange is a win-win scenario – an opportunity to gain experience and build relationships in-house with the client, considering the sustainable impact of developing working relationships over time for both parties.

The unhealthy practices can sometimes creep in so slowly that we may not be able to notice them. When Orla Deering's salon started to thrive, her team began to expand, and everything seemed to be going well at work; she came home after a busy day and found it difficult to switch off. She did not seem stressed. What she felt was an abundance of excitement. It was the excitement of tomorrow and the wonderful things she was planning to do that kept her up at night. One sleepless night turned into a week of sleeplessness, and soon, she lay awake every night and began to feel the negative effects of her work.

This is not an unusual turn of events. Neuropsychological research suggests that there is little, if any, difference in brain activation when we are excited about something and when we experience stress (Robertson, 2016). Therefore, enjoying work and thriving can bring about similar symptoms to those experienced during stress and anxiety, such as racing heart, exhaustion, trouble sleeping, headaches, high blood pressure, or stomach and digestive problems. What matters is our interpretation of the physiological reaction which defines it as stress. At this point we may consider it an undesirable state or excitement which helps us to make sense of it. Once we self-diagnose stress, our beliefs based on our prior stressful experiences flood in and change our behaviour, making us feel better or worse. If we believe that stress is good for us and it acts as a motivating factor, stress helps us cope with the situation more effectively. On the other hand, if we believe that stress is bad for us, we may bury our heads in the sand and become less effective at coping with challenges that stem from positive events. Therefore, leaders' full awareness of their thinking and avoiding reactionary autopilot is required to manage both the bad and positive events in their work lives.

The good news is that even if the positive stress makes us feel bad, there are ways to address it effectively. Firstly, the awareness of the experience of stress is important. It is easy to fall into denial and pretend we do not notice our fast-beating heart, or worse, continue to psyche ourselves up, leading to further physiological and cognitive reactions that prevent us from spreading our wings. However, once we notice it, we can do something to equalise its effect. This more active approach may be attempting mindfulness or other relaxation techniques to calm our mind down and refocus our attention from the cause of stress to the activity at hand. Past research indicates that cognitive-behavioural methods are effective in tackling this (Burke, 2018).

Cognitive-behavioural methods are associated with the awareness of entering a vicious cycle. Say we experience too much work (even though it is exciting for us), we may have a thought: "Gosh, so much to do, how will I find the time to do it?" This thought leads us to experience the emotion of excitement, followed by a physical reaction of increased heartbeat and a behaviour that propels us to keep going. This excitement continues until we get home. We lie in bed thinking the same thoughts, experiencing the same emotional and physiological reactions, and soon we find ourselves lying wide awake, too excited to sleep. After a few hours, and as we tire, our thoughts may change into more negative thoughts such as "I cannot sleep"; this will make us feel frustrated, frustration will turn our body into tiredness, and we decide to pick up the phone to check the news since we cannot sleep regardless. This is how we get stuck in a vicious cycle.

To get ourselves out of it, we need to change one aspect of the cycle (thought, feeling, physiology, or behaviour) and all other aspects will follow, turning the cycle from vicious to healthy. Say you choose to switch off your phone one hour before your sleep and consciously start winding down (changed behaviour); by the time you go to bed, your emotions will be less excitable, your thoughts will drift away from the busy work life, and your physiology will follow by reducing the levels of stress hormone in your body. Alternatively, you may choose to change your physiology and thoughts by engaging with mindfulness, which will alter your thoughts and behaviour as you begin to move and breathe more slowly. These are examples of how you can use cognitive-behavioural methods to help you manage your stress more effectively.

Reflection in practice

What daily practices help you maintain wellbeing at work?

What are your main obstacles to maintaining wellbeing?

What action can you take to overcome these obstacles?

How can you support others to prioritise and maintain their wellbeing?

Full integration

Health integration is a resource element that not all leaders can easily master. It is one thing to promote the importance of health, reminding employees to look after themselves or changing the policies and daily practices to facilitate and orientate team health and wellbeing. It is another thing to incorporate health deeply into the daily interactions between positive leaders and anyone they collaborate with. This is what full integration of health is about – considering health in all of our interactions with all of our stakeholders and in all of our systems and world.

This approach draws from decades of salutogenic research which aimed to answer an important question as to why some people experiencing daily or extreme stress remain healthy. This relates to wellness, which similar to positive psychology, focused on physical and mental health instead of pathologies. The main construct of this theory is the sense of coherence, which is an orientation towards viewing the world as comprehensible, manageable, and meaningful (Antonovsky, 1979). In other words, it is a medium for making sense of the complex world (Reimer, 2020). Furthermore, it is an individual's ability to do the following: (1) make the world predictable and explicable, (2) draw from the applicable resources, and (3) see challenges as worthy of engagement (Antonovsky, 1987). Sense of coherence, according to the author, is the reason why so many people who experience stress, sometimes a lot of stress daily, are not negatively affected by it. When individuals practise this perspective when dealing with life challenges, it helps them cope more effectively. Thus, a sense of coherence facilitates health. The full integration is a leader's approach to make the daily challenges more predictable, reassure the team of the resources at their disposal, and help them perceive their challenges as meaningful.

In recent years, we have experienced a renaissance of the sense of coherence research in the context of leadership (Eberz & Herbert Antoni, 2016; Hardy et al., 2021). Positive leaders can thus support their team by making their world coherent so that the team can deal more effectively with challenges. Through this process, they will protect their team's wellbeing by preventing them from experiencing discomfort and helping them maintain and enhance their wellness. When an organisation and their leaders can help their teams make sense of the world, especially during a crisis situation, their teams will be able to manage their emotions more effectively and experience less stress (Pelser, Bosch, & Schurink, 2016). Therefore, leaders need to enable this.

Let us now go back to the three principles of making life more coherent (Antonovsky, 1987). The first principle refers to the comprehensibility of the world. In the leadership context, a leader can support their team in coming up with a structure to their work that can be predictable to some degree. Nowadays, we often discuss the importance of flexibility and flexible work, whereby employees can choose their working hours, work from home or their office, and the options may feel endless. Yet what many employees are looking for is the opposite. They search for predictability, such as having regular hours instead of constantly changing them, having regular breaks instead of unstable structure, having some routine at work that can allow them to have more work-life balance (Kowalski & Swanson, 2018). That predictability creates a sense of security and safety (Braun-Lewensohn, Idan, Lindström, & Margalit, 2017), which helps employees deal with stressful situations more effectively. When teams do not feel they can predict the outcome of a situation and process (e.g. COVID-19 pandemic) and they experience a high level of perceived stress, their likelihood of experiencing distress is very high (Ruiz-Frutos et al., 2021). Thus, a leader can create a predictable structure, especially during highly stressful situations and can prevent a great deal of distress on their employees. This does not mean that flexible working is not appreciated by many, but rather than this flexibility too requires a consistent, predictable structure (e.g. working from home on certain days and being in an office on others with a predictable pattern).

Consider a job of a salesperson who tends to travel wherever the business takes them. One day they may be in the south of the country, the next day in the north. One day they may be home at 5, the next day at 9. This unpredictability and unstructured day may suit some, but for many, it sounds like a nightmare. However, when working in this chaotic environment, a salesperson may create routines that allow them to experience consistency and predictability. For example, they may decide to have only three meetings a day, or they may choose to limit their travel to 500 km per day. They may ensure to speak with their colleagues at specific times or have a team meeting on a specific day. This structure and routine will make a somewhat unpredictable day more predictable. When employees can expect what is coming, they will feel in control and more comfortable to organise their day. A leader can help them facilitate this daily structure. A felt locus of control is strongly linked to levels of resilience (Etilé, Frijters, Johnston, & Shields, 2021).

The second principle of the sense of coherence is manageability. It is about realising that whist individuals might not be *in* control, they can draw on the workplace resources to keep situations *under* control. For example, when we were working with an organisation during a recession, many employees felt that their lives as they knew them were no longer comprehensible and certainly not manageable. This instilled fear in them, to which some reacted by keeping their heads down and trying to work as hard as possible so that the organisation would not make them redundant; others began to voice their concerns to the management team and contacted the trade union to support them. In both cases, employees drew on the resources to keep the situation under control. Those who worked harder tapped into their inner resources to do it; those who contacted the union tapped into an external resource available to them. To feel like they are managing the situation, leaders need to show their team that resources are available to them even in the more desperate times, be it intellectual, emotional, financial, social, technological, or any other type of resources that can help them. An ability to reassure their team in these tricky circumstances will pay dividends in the future.

Finally, the third principle for making work-life coherent is finding meaning in the challenges we experience. When a team is going through changes and experiences chaos, discomfort, and confusion, a leader can help the team make sense of it by creating predictability, drawing upon resources, and making employees feel that everything they are going through is not meaningless. This results in psychological growth, learning new skills, or the experience of self-efficacy. In Chapter 5, we delved deeper into meaning-making, which is also part of the coherence process. Here, coupled with health, coherence takes on an additional meaning. Positive leaders consider health across all stakeholders and encourage their teams to do so too for their greatest level of meaning.

Martine exemplified creating a broader integrated coherence of health when her team fundraised for the charity St Giles Trust through one of their fashion creations. "I love creating stories, and recently, we collaborated with the American clothing brand and private company Stüssy to create a 40th anniversary t-shirt. We offered 40% of the profits to a charity, and one of our designers' Seanie chose St Giles." St Giles Pantry is a food hub in London providing low-cost, high-quality, and healthy food to those struggling to feed themselves and their families and those held back by poverty, addiction, and mental health. Martine said: "It was such a boost [for all of us] to be able to do that – we raised a salary for a year", and all of the team felt inspired and motivated by the broader coherence of this work. This project propelled the team onto the next project and led to the company's health-integrated decision to have a social outreach arm moving forward.

A sense of coherence is challenging to accomplish and develops slowly as we grow. Antonovsky maintained that it grows until the age of 30 and remains stable thereafter (Antonovsky, 1987). However, a more recent review of research suggests that it continues to grow for some individuals more than others (Eriksson & Mittelmark, 2016). More importantly, everyone can develop their sense of coherence. Leaders can have conversations with their team that help them make sense of the world, the same way as team members can affect each other's and their leaders' sense of coherence (Eberz & Herbert Antoni, 2016). This two-way interaction will boost everyone's and all stakeholders' wellbeing.

In 2019 Sean, the engineer specialising in water pollution that we mentioned in Chapter 1, had undertaken a beekeepers course as a way to connect with his daughter, Ciara. He subsequently got himself a beehive with 50,000 bees.

> Bees are great. They work very hard. They all work hard together and are conscious of helping other bees. When they come to the hive, they do a little wiggle dance and tell other bees where to get food. Even when they are sick, they don't die in the hive but fly away to not burden the other bees. We can all learn from their hard work and collegiality.

It was from this observation of his bees that Sean wondered if the engineers and the farmers could work just as well together. He wondered if there was a way for them to collaborate and create a healthy environment for everyone's future, and that giving them beehives to look after was a solution. Bees can only survive in a clean environment. They can fly up to a circumference of three miles from their hives, meaning that the farmers would need to keep their farms clean to help bees survive, which in turn means that the water quality would need to improve for the bees to produce honey. In further explaining more about how he was inspired to get the

'Let it Bee' project started, Sean shared how he drew on a 'full integration' health approach. Sean said:

> We identified areas we needed to target for improving watercourses. We went out and talked to the farmers in these areas. We listened to them and tried to remove all the barriers that prevented them from keeping their water clean. We wanted to help them become the solution to the environmental problem.

When the farmers said they could not use their land for any other purpose than farming, Sean and his team spoke to the government, who agreed to continue paying them a subsidy for planting hedges along the riverbank. When they had no funding for the extra plants, Sean and his team provided them with all the seeds and bulbs for thousands of plants and trees. When they said they did not know what to do with the bees, Sean provided them with the beehives, one-to-one training, and coaching from an expert on how to keep their beehives thriving. Soon, there were no obstacles for the farmers, only benefits for participating in the 'Let It Bee' programme.

Planting meadows was also not Sean's original idea. He had spoken with one of the farmers about various ways in which farmers could provide bees with a clean environment and food. On the way home, Sean received a call from the farmer, saying, "I think I have a solution to our problem. Why don't I plant a wide strip of wildflowers? It will be food for the bees and fun for my kids". With Sean's fully integrative encouragement and support, the farmer soon, rallied up his neighbouring farmers to do the same. There are now meadows in this area with thousands of more trees and hedges that prevent the farm waste from getting into the river, keeping their water clean.

Seven farmers in this area became beekeepers, and 21 farms took part in the project. The farmers' neighbours wanted to help their community and help their neighbours keep the environment clean. And Sean did not want to focus just on the farmers in the area, so he led another community education initiative called "I've planted a tree and my garden is pesticide-free". His team educated young people and their parents about the impact of pesticides on the environment and encouraged them to plant

8,000 more trees in their back gardens to help the community keep their bees alive.

In his approach to change, Sean worked off the sense of coherence principles that is part of the health resource's 'full integration' approach. He tried to make sense of the complexity of the relationship between the farming and the engineering communities. Then, in collaboration with the farmers, he created a simplified solution that they were able to contribute to. The 'Let It Bee' project structure for enhancing the water quality was predictable and easy for farmers to replicate. He then drew on the resources to remove the obstacles farmers faced and made the project meaningful to the contributing farmers and their neighbours.

Sean attributes the success of the project to the mutual trust and coherence that was built up between his team and the community. If he were working on his own or trying to coerce people into doing something they did not want to do, this project would not have taken off. It is early days, but already the 'Let It Bee' project has won the European Bee Award and has just been shortlisted for another award from a body representing 220 million farmers across Europe. This success would never have been possible if not for Sean's ability to positively lead the farmers through this change with his 'health' resource and full integration approach.

Positive leaders see the broader and more holistic conceptualisation of health orientation across all stakeholders and parts of our system and ecosystem. As Martine highlighted in our interview with her, using factories that had a transparent supply chain and developing a social outreach arm of the business to capitalise on projects such as the St Giles t-shirt project are important health integrations to her and her team. These actions support them in feeling they are orienting towards healthy behaviour not just for themselves but their broadest stakeholder, making these actions integrative. Martine argues that health in its broadest and most integrative sense is as important for her team as it is for the client: "Sustainability . . . now that is something that's really important to us, but also increasingly important to our customers". Positive leaders look at coherence and integration of health beyond the immediately obvious stakeholders and think about their community and beyond.

Reflection in practice

Consider one of the most chaotic situations you have recently experienced at work.

If the situation repeats in the future, what aspects of it will be similar to the past situation?

- *What resources will you employ to deal with it?*

- *What have you learnt from the past challenge?*

In what ways could you take more of an integrative decision-making approach to your work? Are there particular projects, programmes, or people who may benefit from this?

Health in action

Positive leaders do not promote an idealised concept of health. They do not push everyone into physical exercise or forbid unhealthy food on their premises. They realise that human beings are self-governed; therefore, they can and will decide what is good for them and when they want to bring it into their lives. Research carried out with teachers showed that what they were looking for from their leaders was not expensive mindfulness courses organised for them at work (although it was welcomed), nor having wellbeing on their weekly agenda or creating a comprehensive wellbeing policy. Instead, what impacted their personal wellbeing the most was knowing that the management cared and that support structures were in place to help employees when they needed it (Doran, Burke, & Healy, forthcoming; Lucey & van Nieuwerburgh, 2021). It is as simple as this: positive leadership is about seeing each employee clearly and showing them you care. It is about making decisions that consider health as one of the factors, rather than focusing only on the financial benefits. This care may extend to seeing the individuals, the teams, the organisation, the community, or the country. It is about adding your little bit to making the world a better place, or as one consultant called it, making positive ripples that will spread throughout.

A range of factors influence the success of workplace health promotion programmes, according to a systematic review that included over 50 research projects involving an implementation of health promotion programmes (Rojatz, Merchant, & Nitsch, 2017). These included such factors as the quality of an intervention, the resources available to team members that facilitate making health-related changes, and the individuals' commitment to interventions. Two factors in particular were of utmost importance across all stages of implementation, i.e. planning, implementation, and evaluation. They related to considering the context of interventions and leaders and organisational commitment. The context of interventions and leaders being able to both address it and act appropriately within these circumstances was the first important factor. One such context may relate to the COVID-19 crisis and leaders tweaking the interventions and their delivery accordingly to ensure that everyone has an equal opportunity to avail themselves of these interventions. Second, when an organisation is based in an economically or politically unstable environment, successful health promotion programmes addressed the ongoing issues and obstacles employees faced when attempting to mind their health. Ignoring contextual factors may deem the interventions less impactful.

At an organisational level, the factor influencing team members most was their leaders' commitment to employees' wellness. This commitment went beyond talking about wellness and towards implementing it daily: putting health-enhancing structures in place, ensuring adequate staffing so that the team can do their job within their hours of employment, not emailing the team after the official working hours ended, and taking regular breaks and other implementation actions. Any incongruence between what leaders say and do had a negative effect on their team. Therefore, it is of utmost importance for leaders to reflect on how they integrate wellbeing initiatives at work, ensuring that they are not only talked about but also implemented at many levels of an organisation.

The three elements of the health resource work in tandem with each other. However, they may also be implemented separately. For example, creating health promotion campaigns in the workplace is one of the easiest actions that leaders can take to improve their team's health. The only issue with it is that by doing it without the other two elements present, the leaders put the onus of health and wellbeing on their team. What they are inadvertently saying is that there are several tools that everyone can draw from to mind their health, and it is up to everyone to pick and choose what they need to do. In contrast, the second element, which relates to leaders' health orientation, is an acknowledgement that factors outside an individual influence their wellbeing. A positive leader who practices health orientation attempts to make changes at an environmental level to enable individuals to mind their health. Finally, the leaders practising full integration don't only promote health and create policies but enact them daily by making the busy world around them more manageable and providing resources to support their employees when required. Therefore, while each one of the health elements can be indeed applied separately, they also work in tandem with each other, supporting leaders in embedding health into the tapestry of their daily life.

Last word

For positive leaders, health is a vital resource they draw from daily to ensure they have the energy to live their lives fully and enjoy their work. They realise that only then are they able to become the best version of themselves and can they best serve their family, friends, team, organisation, or society. Health is also at the forefront of their minds in relation to other people; thus, each decision they make, each policy they set up, each action they take is informed by the impact they may have on individuals involved. Positive leaders do not leave health to their team, but acknowledge that they play a part in their team's wellness. After all, the leaders are an intricate part of the tribe network.

References

Althammer, S. E., Reis, D., Beek, S., Beck, L., & Michel, A. (2021). A mindfulness intervention promoting work – life balance: How segmentation preference affects changes in detachment, well-being, and work – life balance. *Journal of Occupational and Organizational Psychology*, 94(2), 282–308. doi:10.1111/joop.12346

Antonovsky, A. (1979). *Health, stress and coping*. San Francisco: Jossey-Bass Publishers.

Antonovsky, A. (1987). The salutogenic perspective: Toward a new view of health and illness. *Advances, 4*(1), 47–55.

Bosch, C., Sonnentag, S., & Pinck, A. S. (2018). What makes for a good break? A diary study on recovery experiences during lunch break. *Journal of Occupational & Organizational Psychology, 91*(1), 134–157. doi:10.1111/joop.12195

Braun-Lewensohn, O., Idan, O., Lindström, B., & Margalit, M. (2017). Salutogenesis: Sense of coherence in adolescence. In M. B. Mittelmark, S. Sagy, M. Eriksson, G. Bauer, J. M. Pelikan, B. Lindstrom, & G. A. Espnes (Eds.), *The handbook of Salutogenesis* (pp. 123–136). Berlin: Springer.

Burke, J. (2018). Turning stress into positive energy: An evaluation of a workplace intervention. *Positive Work and Organizations: Research and Practice.*

Burke, J. (2021). *The ultimate guide to implementing wellbeing programmes for school.* London: Routledge.

Burke, J., & Dempsey, M. (2021a). *Wellbeing in post-covid schools: Primary school leaders' reimagining of the future.* Maynooth: Maynooth University.

Burke, J., & Dempsey, M. (2021b). *One month before Covid-19 and one year after: An assessment of wellbeing of post-primary school leaders in Ireland.* Maynooth: Maynooth University.

Callander, E. J., Lindsay, D. B., & Scuffham, P. A. (2017). Employer benefits from an early intervention program for depression: A cost – benefit analysis. *Journal of Occupational and Environmental Medicine, 59*(3), 246–249. doi:10.1097/JOM.0000000000000939

Casucci, T., Locke, A. B., Henson, A., & Qeadan, F. (2020). A workplace well-being game intervention for health sciences librarians to address burnout. *Journal of the Medical Library Association, 108*(4), 605–617. doi:10.5195/jmla.2020.742

Dale, A. M., Enke, C., Buckner-Petty, S., Hipp, J. A., Marx, C., Strickland, J., & Evanoff, B. (2019). Availability and use of workplace supports for health promotion among employees of small and large businesses. *American Journal of Health Promotion, 33*(1), 30–38. doi:10.1177/0890117118772510

de Bloom, J., Kinnunen, U., & Korpela, K. (2015). Recovery processes during and after work: Associations with health, work engagement, and job performance. *Journal of Occupational and Environmental Medicine, 57*(7), 732–742. doi:10.1097/JOM.0000000000000475

De Carlo, A., Carluccio, F., Rapisarda, S., Mora, D., & Ometto, I. (2020). Three uses of virtual reality in work and organizational psychology interventions A dialogue between virtual reality and organizational well-being: Relaxation techniques, personal resources, and anxiety/depression treatments. *TPM-Testing, Psychometrics, Methodology in Applied Psychology, 27*(1), 129–143.

Doran, A., Burke, J., & Healy, C. (forthcoming). *The domino effect: The impact of school leadership on teachers' wellbeing.*

Eberz, S., & Herbert Antoni, C. (2016). Das Systemisch-Salutogene Interaktions-Modell (SSIM) – Ein ganzheitlicher Ansatz zur Erklärung und Entwicklung gesundheitsförderlicher Interaktionsdynamiken zwischen Führungskräften und Mitarbeitenden = The Systemic Salutogenic Interaction Modell (SSIM) – A holistic approach for explanation and development of health-promoting interactions between leaders and employees. *Gruppe. Interaktion. Organisation. Zeitschrift für Angewandte Organisationspsychologie (GIO), 47*(3), 265–273. doi:10.1007/s11612-016-0326-6

Eisma, M. C., Tamminga, A., Smid, G. E., & Boelen, P. A. (2021). Acute grief after deaths due to COVID-19, natural causes and unnatural causes: An empirical comparison. *Journal of Affective Disorders, 278*, 54–56. doi:10.1016/j.jad.2020.09.049

Ejlertsson, L., Heijbel, B., Andersson, I. H., Troein, M., & Brorsson, A. (2021). Strengthened workplace relationships facilitate recovery at work – qualitative experiences of an intervention among employees in primary health care. *BMC Family Practice, 22*(1), 1–10. doi:10.1186/s12875-021-01388-x

Eriksson, M., & Mittelmark, M. B. (2016). The sense of coherence and its measurement. In M. B. M. et al. (Eds.), *The handbook of salutogenesis* (pp. 97–106). New York: Springer.

Etilé, F., Frijters, P., Johnston, D. W., & Shields, M. A. (2021). Measuring resilience to major life events. *Journal of Economic Behavior & Organization, 191*, 598–619. doi:10.1016/j.jebo.2021.09.004

Hardy, L. J., Mana, A., Mundell, L., Benheim, S., Morales, K. T., & Sagy, S. (2021). Living in opposition: How women in the United States cope in spite of mistrust of federal leadership during the pandemic of Covid-19. *Journal of Community Psychology, 49*(6), 2059–2070. doi:10.1002/jcop.22544

Hone, L. C., Jarden, A., Schofield, G. M., & Duncan, S. (2014). Measuring flourishing: The impact of operational definitions on the prevalence of high levels of well-being. *International Journal of Wellbeing, 4*(1), 69–90. doi:10.5502/ijw.v4i1.4

Keyes, C. L. M., Yao, J., Hybels, C. F., Milstein, G., & Proeschold-Bell, R. J. (2020). Are changes in positive mental health associated with increased likelihood of depression over a two year period? A test of the mental health promotion and protection hypotheses. *Journal of Affective Disorders, 270*, 136–142. doi:10.1016/j.jad.2020.03.056

Kim, S., Park, Y., & Headrick, L. (2018). Daily micro-breaks and job performance: General work engagement as a cross-level moderator. *Journal of Applied Psychology, 103*(7), 772–786. doi:10.1037/apl0000308

Kowalski, K., & Swanson, J. (2018). The importance of workplace predictability for work-family balance. *Proceedings for the Northeast Region Decision Sciences Institute (NEDSI)*, 196–200.

Le, L. K.-D., Esturas, A. C., Mihalopoulos, C., Chiotelis, O., Bucholc, J., Chatterton, M. L., & Engel, L. (2021). Cost-effectiveness evidence of mental health prevention and promotion interventions: A systematic review of economic evaluations. *PLoS Medicine, 18*(5), 1–27. doi:10.1371/journal.pmed.1003606

Lennefer, T., Lopper, E., Wiedemann, A. U., Hess, U., & Hoppe, A. (2020). Improving employees' work-related well-being and physical health through a technology-based physical activity intervention: A randomized intervention-control group study. *Journal of Occupational Health Psychology, 25*(2), 143–158. doi:10.1037/ocp0000169

Lucey, C., & van Nieuwerburgh, C. (2021). 'More willing to carry on in the face of adversity': How beginner teachers facing challenging circumstances experience positive psychology coaching An interpretative phenomenological analysis. *Coaching: An International Journal of Theory, Research and Practice, 14*(1), 62–77. doi:10.1080/17521882.2020.1753791

Mohr, C. D., Hammer, L. B., Brady, J. M., Perry, M. L., & Bodner, T. (2021). Can supervisor support improve daily employee well-being? Evidence of supervisor training effectiveness in a study of veteran employee emotions. *Journal of Occupational and Organizational Psychology, 94*(2), 400–426. doi:10.1111/joop.12342

Pelser, H. J., Bosch, A., & Schurink, W. (2016). An organisational coherence model to maintain employee contributions during organisational crises. *South African Journal of Human Resource Management, 14*(1), 1–11. doi:10.4102/sajhrm.v14i1.725

Phillips, E. A., Gordeev, V. S., & Schreyögg, J. (2019). Effectiveness of occupational e-mental health interventions: A systematic review and meta-analysis of randomized controlled trials. *Scandinavian Journal of Work, Environment & Health, 45*(6), 560–576. doi:10.5271/sjweh.3839

Ragsdale, J. M., & Beehr, T. A. (2016). A rigorous test of a model of employees' resource recovery mechanisms during a weekend. *Journal of Organizational Behavior, 37*(6), 911–932. doi:10.1002/job.2086

Reimer, K. E. (2020). "Here, it's like you don't have to leave the classroom to solve a problem": How restorative justice in schools contributes to students' individual and collective sense of coherence. *Social Justice Research, 33*(4), 406–427. doi:10.1007/s11211-020-00358-5

Robbins, R., Jackson, C. L., Underwood, P., Vieira, D., Jean-Louis, G., & Buxton, O. M. (2019). Employee sleep and workplace health promotion: A systematic review. *American Journal of Health Promotion, 33*(7), 1009–1019. doi:10.1177/0890117119841407

Robertson, I. (2016). *The stress test: How pressure can make you stronger and sharper.* London: Bloomsbury Publishing.

Rojatz, D., Merchant, A., & Nitsch, M. (2017). Factors influencing workplace health promotion intervention: A qualitative systematic review. *Health Promotion International, 32*(5), 831–839. doi:10.1093/heapro/daw015

Rudolph, C. W., Murphy, L. D., & Zacher, H. (2020). A systematic review and critique of research on 'healthy leadership'. *The Leadership Quarterly, 31*(1). doi:10.1016/j.leaqua.2019.101335

Ruiz-Frutos, C., Ortega-Moreno, M., Allande-Cussó, R., Ayuso-Murillo, D., Domínguez-Salas, S., & Gómez-Salgado, J. (2021). Sense of coherence, engagement, and work environment as precursors of psychological distress among non-health workers during the COVID-19 pandemic in Spain. *Safety Science, 133.* doi:10.1016/j.ssci.2020.105033

Ryu, H., Jung, J., & Moon, J. (2020). Health promotion program for office workers with SEM based on the WHO's healthy workplace framework. *Health Promotion International, 35*(6), 1369–1382. doi:10.1093/heapro/daaa007

Shankland, R., & Rosset, E. (2017). Review of brief school-based positive psychological interventions: A taster for teachers and educators. *Educational Psychology Review, 29*(2), 363–392. doi:10.1007/s10648-016-9357-3

Sonnentag, S., & Fritz, C. (2015). Recovery from job stress: The stressor-detachment model as an integrative framework. *Journal of Organizational Behavior, 36*, S72–S103. doi:10.1002/job.1924

Taylor, M. J. (2018). Using CALMERSS to enhance teacher well-being: A pilot study. *International Journal of Disability, Development and Education, 65*(3), 243–261. doi:10.1080/1034912X.2017.1394985

Valencia, L. M. P., Weber, A., Spegel, H., Bögle, R., Selmani, A., Heinze, S., & Herr, C. (2019). Yoga in the workplace and health outcomes: A systematic review. *Occupational Medicine, 69*(3), 195–203. doi:10.1093/occmed/kqz033

van der WaltFreda, F., & Lezar, L. (2019). Flourishing and thriving for well-being. In M. Coetzee (Ed.), *Thriving in digital workspaces, emerging issues for research and practice* (pp. 85–107). New York: Springer.

Vargas-Martínez, A. M., Romero-Saldaña, M., & De Diego-Cordero, R. (2021). Economic evaluation of workplace health promotion interventions focused on Lifestyle: Systematic review and meta-analysis. *Journal of Advanced Nursing (John Wiley & Sons, Inc.), 77*(9), 3657–3691. doi:10.1111/jan.14857

7 | Tribe

Just after the start of the COVID-19 pandemic, Sarah Blomfield was head-hunted to become general counsel EMEA at Evercore. The team Sarah was going to lead had, for various reasons, undergone a turbulent year prior to her joining, and she took the role up amid the COVID-19 pandemic. Sarah instinctively – for it is a human instinct – knew that quickly building relationships and connecting with her stretched team would be crucial to her and their movement from survival as a team to thriving and optimally functioning in the ongoing challenging time that lay ahead.

Attempting to do this in the online world was Sarah's first challenge. Sarah said: "Whereas in an office environment you'd have a coffee with somebody and an informal chat and get to know them as you would anybody, the online environment made the opportunity to do this feel quite artificial at first". As she was joining them, Sarah had to think very hard about what her team's concerns would be, not just what she had to say.

> They would have been worried. They didn't know me from Adam. I hadn't had a chance to meet them informally or in a social situation, which might happen when you join a new job, you can go out for lunch or, you know, coffees, drinks after work. So, they're reading my body language online, and they're trying to work out what I'm thinking like this [online]. And that's fine if you know someone, but it's not if you don't. And it's even worse when they're your new boss.

Sarah said getting to know her team online as the pandemic continued to force working from home and online meant she transferred her usual

DOI: 10.4324/9781003170433-7

tribe ways online. Sarah is a tribal positive leader. She adapts and makes a bespoke connection and social approach to each individual she works with, so they feel heard, safe, and connected. She is sensitive to colleagues' emotional and technical needs and considers this with the best interests of all of the team and broader system in mind.

What does tribe mean?

In the current framework, tribe refers to a leader's ability to assess, initiate, foster, develop, and redevelop relationships to meet our relational needs as an individual, team, organisation, or within a system. A positive leader knows the importance of relationships to the outcomes of any given situation, project, strategy, or interaction. Tribal leaders encourage more community-based ways of supporting their teams, organisations, and communities (Figure 7.1). There are three main constructs within the tribe resource which we have identified from the research that our positive leaders demonstrate. The tribe resource of our positive leaders is about (1) connection and positive interpersonal processes, which involve ongoing and continuous everyday interactions such as being caring; (2) high-quality connections, which are deeper relational events between colleagues felt at a more physiological level; and (3) positive conflict, which is about

Figure 7.1 The Tribe resource piece of the ALIGHT jigsaw

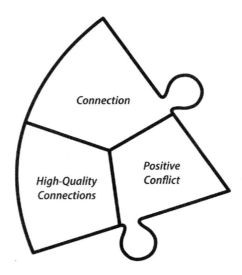

Figure 7.2 The Tribe components

leaning into and prospering from conflict, including through being gener-ous with feedback (see Figure 7.2). These three combined resources allow leaders to achieve extraordinary performance and tap into their employ-ees' optimum potential through being tribal. They are enacted at subjec-tive, collective, and organisational levels, meaning that positive leaders can enact the components of tribe in relation to themselves, use them in their daily communication with their team, and promote them when making decisions at an organisational level. These three components lead to a relational fabric – a relational fabric that leads to better performance for ourselves and others rather than a self-centred approach. We will now delve more deeply into these components, describing what they are, why they are essential, and how they show up for positive leaders before giving you the opportunity to reflect on your practice.

Connection and positive interpersonal processes

Connection in organisations is both the act and feeling of being con-nected to another in a supportive and caring relationship (Frost, Dutton, Worline, & Wilson, 2000). This focus on a shared connection can reduce any sense of fear and encourage closeness rather than strangeness (Dahl, Wilson-Mendenhall, & Davidson, 2020). The psychological evidence is increasingly showing that not only do humans like having good social connections but that connection with other people is one of the ingredients that underpins wellbeing and performance (Crocker, Canevello, & Brown, 2017) – and positive leaders know this. Good relationships can broaden opportunities, lift mood, and benefit longevity (Thoits, 2011). Even talking to those we do not know, passers-by on the street, or those whom we hardly know can boost our mood (Sandstrom & Dunn, 2014). Hari notes in his book *Lost Connections* that one of the nine key causes of depression and anxiety is disconnection from other people (Hari, 2018), which shows how much we have to lose if we ignore this. Connecting and developing relationships is a practice that is at the heart of every positive leader's tribe behaviour.

More specifically, connection can be made via positive interpersonal processes (Algoe, 2019). These take place in everyday interactions such as laughing with others, being caring, being grateful and offering gratitude, being admired, and feeling loved. These interpersonal processes create a positive emotional reaction that affects both the giver and the receiver and develops a bond (Kurtz & Algoe, 2017). Interestingly, the reaction of a partner or friend to a positive event is a heavy signifier for the person that the partner or friend is committed and will be there in the future for them (Khalifian & Barry, 2020). This is regardless of their response to a negative event, as this more important reaction to the positive event creates a greater rejuvenating sense of safety. Equally, a positive interpersonal process tends to have just as strong a value to us, if not sometimes more so, when it is other-focused and not self-focused (Algoe, 2019).

When you relax or share a moment of connection, your recovery system triggers the parasympathetic nervous system – the body's recharge button (Gilbert, 2010). One of the recovery system's key functions is for us to be social beings who can turn to one another for the mutual care we need to survive (Fredrickson, 2014). This allows us to restock our depleted energy reserves, care for one another, and have the evolutionary advantage that comes with social bonding (David, 2017) – making entry, building rapport, and establishing connection have a win-win effect. Making entry or connection is a process of establishing, building, and deepening relationships over time both formally and informally. When leaders actively build trust by sharing information, it is made easier by being friendly and open. It looks like checking in and humanising the "transaction" so instead, it becomes a human "interaction". King (2020) found that social connection – relational and trusting rather than transactional – leads to a sense of fruitful reciprocity, thus allowing all the parties involved to flourish for the better.

As Sarah explains, when she started her new role, there were no issues around the team's technical strengths, but the quality of connection and interactions of the team were a critical focus in elevating their performance to the next level. The team culture and any relational fabric joining the team together was not there and needed to be developed. "My job was to try and unravel some of this [rebuilding confidence and encouraging collaboration]. My job was to get them functioning properly as a team, collaborating properly, trusting each other, working better together, and bringing out the best in them." And this is where Sarah turned to ensuring regular connecting opportunities and behaviour.

Edmondson first coined the term psychological safety during her research study into errors made by medical teams in leading hospitals (1999). To her surprise, the data of this study unexpectedly showed higher-performing teams with better leaders had higher error rates and not lower ones. Edmondson eventually deduced through years of further research that the better teams do not make more mistakes, but are more willing and open to talk about and learn from mistakes. She described psychological safety as

> the belief that I feel the workplace context is safe for interpersonal risk taking . . . interpersonal risk taking is that I can ask a question, I can admit a mistake, I can offer a half-baked idea . . . that you can lower the threshold for speaking up . . . so that's psychological safety. It's not being nice, it's not risk free – in fact, it's the opposite, it's the willingness to take risks. Maybe the simplest way to summarise it, is that there's a sense of permission for candour.
>
> (B.E. GOOD! By BVA Nudge Unit, 2020)

Thus, the difference between mere trust and psychological safety is that trust is the vulnerability created by an individual's internal processes, whereas psychological safety relates to vulnerability created by the environment. She highlights there are the most opportunities to develop this in instances where people work together intensely and trust builds quickly and that psychological safety is difficult to create but easy to dissolve.

All positive leaders emphasise the need to offer presence, listen deeply, and be curious with colleagues, aware of the benefits that this has. Martine describes this safety she creates through her team in doing so:

> There's always a discussion ongoing in our team. I'm very honest with people and therefore I want them to be very honest with me. About whatever you think somebody might be struggling with, we talk about it. [. . .] I'm not very separate. [. . .] I'm very much a part of the team. And I'm really approachable.

For Martine, this creates transparency that keeps the environment a happy one in which to work.

The first step in being able to build connection is to be aware, appreciate, and acknowledge our evolutionary need for others; aware of both their presence, and their abundant contribution. There is a necessity to turn our awareness and attention away from the self and out to others. To appreciate the richness of thought the collective can bring us, positive leaders take time to meet, gather and collaborate, and share the diversity of ideas and perspectives. Like the coffee houses of the 1600s and beyond the Enlightenment in London, these were places in which information was exchanged for scientists, businessmen, writers, and politicians, where anyone could enter and join discussions. Coffeehouses were crucibles of creativity because of the way in which they facilitated the mixing of both people and ideas. One such debate led Isaac Newton to write his *Principia Mathematica*, which led to the development of the London stock exchange. Edward Lloyd's coffeehouse, frequented by the nautical crowd, became the insurance giant Lloyd's of London (Standage, 2013). This creativity all happened through the close interaction and development of relationships with others, and positive leaders access this connection in the way they encourage diversity of people, ideas, and experiences in the workplace.

The positive leader – as with all the ALIGHT resources – knows that diversity is more fruitful for all in evolving to our best sustainable future. An awareness and appreciation of all diversity is critical to being able to connect and be tribal. Appreciating diversity through connection bears out statistically, with more diverse companies being much more likely to outperform their industry peers on profitability over time, according to research across 1,000 companies in 15 different countries (Dixon-Fyle, Hunt, Dolan, & Prince, 2020). As Martine explains in the way her creativity springboards from connecting with a diverse team: "Another point of view is essential to having healthy conversations, healthy dialogue. Both within the team environment, and in the world, to have some points of difference and people from different and with different experiences [is an asset]". In order to encourage different opinions and diverse perspectives to come forward to enrich the work and life dialogue, Martine insists on a flat structure of connection where everybody has somebody to go to pastorally and to share ideas and ensures everybody knows they can speak up: "One of the benefits is that everyone [. . .] can throw their hat in the ring, as it were, and be like, well, this is this is my opinion. And [. . .] there's absolutely no place for politics". For Martine, the whole team is part of the whole tribe and serves the tribe and not oneself.

In joining her new team and getting to know them, Sarah is sensitive to ensure she is aware of the team's diversity, their range of skills and strengths, and ensures they can create their own grand design, giving autonomy and allowing crafting for their continual growth – not stunting it: "They had to run it all I before I joined. And so my task when I joined was to make sure that I didn't sort of suddenly take away all that they'd done in the meantime". Showing the connection skill of recognition, Sarah went out of her way to commend her team for everything they had achieved in the absence of a boss through playing to their own diversity, strengths, and skills. You know, I said, "you won't realise until you look back how much you progressed this year because you kind of had to because there was no one else to do it. So, there's no going backwards now. It's onwards and upwards". Sarah made the conscious decision not to take back stepped-up responsibilities the team had enjoyed leading on, where many were sitting on committees which gave them good exposure to their wider organisation. She explains: "I said to a senior manager, I want them to stay on because they're learning and they're making such a great contribution. So, they were worried that I would come in and say, right. Clear the decks. I'm going on all these boards, but I deliberately didn't". Sarah is aware of and supports her team to play to their diverse strengths through her connecting approach. Let us take some time now to reflect on how you make connections and build positive interpersonal processes in the workplace.

Reflection on practice

- *How often do you take time to connect with your colleagues and your team?*

- *What are the further opportunities for creating connection with your team or wider team members?*

- *What type of positive interpersonal process – gratitude, humour, play, etc. – do you have the most strength in? Which process is least authentic to you?*

High-quality connections

Expanding on positive interpersonal processes and connection, high-quality connections are micro-units of human relationships, deeper relational events. They are moments of positivity resonance, connection felt at the biological level, where both individuals involved in a connecting moment share a connection of positive affect, mutual care, and concern, with behavioural and biological synchrony (Major, Le Nguyen, Lundberg, & Fredrickson, 2018). They are social capacity builders that build our resources to endure and work with challenge for ourselves and between ourselves (Waters et al., 2021). When we experience these high-quality connections, we experience positive physiological changes that positively impact our health; prevent depression and physical illness; and enhance mental health, thriving, and cognitive performance (Major et al., 2018). High-quality connections are considered the social fabric that binds optimal work teams and organisations and fosters psychological safety, greater knowledge development and management, cohesive collaboration, attachment, and unit resilience (Waters et al., 2021). Connection and positive interpersonal processes are about the day-in and day-out of how we operate in ongoing relationships;

high-quality connections are more concerned with moments of connection where two individuals experience a sense of vitality – either through a passing exchange or a longer online call or face-to-face meeting (Jane Dutton & Heaphy, 2003).

High-quality connections are created and elevated by positive leaders who are conscious about building their connections with others. Some of these intentional and pre-prepared tribe-building strategies include removing distance by removing any distractions that might be affecting interaction between two people or in a group and instead actively focusing on the person and interaction before you; being curious and interested in the other person during the interaction with intentionality for connection; and in leading a team, purposefully designing and encouraging meetings with norms for respect and encouraging, championing, and helping one another (Waters et al., 2021), as well as active constructive responding, which we shall explain further in a moment (Gable, Reis, Impett, & Asher, 2004). These types of high-quality connections can lead to increased heart rate variability, a better response to stress, the release of the powerful bonding hormone oxytocin (Heaphy & Dutton, 2008), and improved cognitive functioning (Ybarra et al., 2008). Thinking ahead, positive leaders use their high-quality connections' mentality proactively to think about how to make the most of the interactions we have throughout the day.

To choose to connect intentionally is somewhat contrary to the norm and not always as easy as it sounds; it cannot just be taken for granted. Fredrickson, with her research on how moments of connection can create upward emotional spirals that we learn and grow from, highlights that contemporary society, with its fast-changing technology and oppressive workloads, pushes us to speed through our day at a space that's antithetical to connection (Fredrickson, 2014). A positive leader, however, reduces the speed of the day where possible and intentionally creates time and space for this connection to deepen for themselves and for those they work with. Furthermore, when they make this effort, they say this effort pays off. The benefits of high-quality connections include physical and psychological health (Ryff & Singer, 2012), greater capacity for thinking (Fredrickson, 2014), more resilience in teams (Stephens, Heaphy, Carmeli, Spreitzer, & Dutton, 2013), and greater creativity (Chiaburu & Harrison, 2008). Therefore, in intentionally creating high-quality connections, positive leaders go beyond just simple exchange of ideas between human beings – they build them up through these connections.

Some of the principles leading research has indicated that we can use when building high-quality connections include creating respectful engagement, task-enabling others, trusting in others, and being playful with others (Dutton & Spreitzer, 2014). We can create a sense of respect by being present and deeply listening to one another. We can show this active listening quality by playing back what we hear from others (i.e. summarising as we listen), asking relevant open questions, and drawing what is next from the conversation (Whetten & Cameron, 2016). By requesting and not demanding in our asks (Rosenberg, 2015), we can also create a sense of freedom and autonomy in response, which helps create high-quality connections. We can task-enable others by offering the support that they need from us either in a mentoring, coaching, or colleague capacity by giving recognition, guidance, flexibility, or whatever is needed in the moment (Dutton & Spreitzer, 2014). We can trust others by letting go of the need for controlling another to follow through in their commitments and be vulnerable that the other will do so (Dutton & Spreitzer, 2014). Finally, we can be playful with others by creating moments to be creative, explore, and have fun – a low-investment option that can build high-quality connections (Dutton & Spreitzer, 2014).

One particular strategy that research shows reaps the rewards for us in the work and wider context in building high-quality connections is Active Constructive Responding, first coined and identified and later developed by Gable's research (Gable & Reis, 2010; Gable et al., 2004). This is when we particularly tune into what is working well for a person, colleague, or friend and deliberately celebrate their success to intensify it for them and thus also deepen our connection (Passmore & Oades, 2014). It creates a process of mutual profit that Gable and colleagues term 'capitalization' (Gable & Reis, 2010). To be able to do this, we need to attentively listen for this positive news, so that when somebody shares the positive news, we don't just hear the message – we acknowledge it, provide positive feedback, and share our excitement and the emotions we feel on learning this news. The benefit of this type of listening and responding is that it creates a sense of genuineness between two parties, reaffirms the news, and offers a moment for the sharer to savour the goodness of the experience even further, as well as heightening a sense of empathy with the relationship and intensifying positive self-regard (Passmore & Oades, 2014). Furthermore, these types of connections lead to personal benefits such as increased positive emotions, better wellbeing and self-esteem, and lower levels of loneliness (Gable & Reis, 2010). The relationship benefits associated with capitalisation have been shown to result in greater bonding, "intimacy, commitment, trust, liking, closeness, and stability" (Gable & Reis, 2010, p. 197). So very often, we see in our daily lives and professional practices these golden opportunities for connection being missed, ignored, and glossed over. Positive leaders do not waste these opportunities – they actively and constructively respond at every opportunity by always listening for these deeper connecting chances and celebrating them to their fullest when shared.

Sarah talks about intentionally deepening connection and building positivity resonance to create high-quality connections with her new team eight months into her new role. She has created a weekly joint reflection and problem-solving forum for her team where no topic is off-limits for the table: "Every week we sit down, we will bring three things that we're worrying about – it could be anything. So, every Thursday at four o'clock, the four of us sit down, and I say, right, who wants to start three things?" Sarah explains that it is important for her to create a very open, full forum, far from a work in progress (WIP) meeting. Whilst not intended to be a group therapy session, Sarah says the tone of the meeting often feels therapeutic, as the team have become so intentionally supportive and empathetic. This team ambience and culture have also been built over time: "At the start, they were very cautious about it. They were really nervous about it, and they said that they weren't sure, but they went with it and now it's working really well". Sarah explains that she had to set the tone a few times: "It has to be very open, friendly, encouraging them to talk because nobody obviously likes to sort of talk about things that are bothering them, but they have to do, and I needed to understand, because then I can support". As a result of implementing this regular weekly reflection meeting, Sarah says the team work better on an emotional, professional, and collegiate level. They have moved away from the lonely, isolated, and siloed experience they were having before: "They're working together on things now, so they are thinking about how the whole team can solve a problem rather than just working on their own". The meeting also poses a strategic opportunity for Sarah to pass on soft or more confidential information in an informal way – showing how the tribe leader uses all relational channels to their optimum, celebrating those all-important achievements through active constructive responding, both one-to-one and as a team.

When a positive leader fosters family-like belonging, the quality of relationships build at a one-to-one, team, organisation, and system level through mirroring neurons of our brains (information messengers that use electrical impulses and chemical signals to transmit information between different areas of the brain and the nervous system) and create upward spirals of positive emotional contagion (Fredrickson, 2014). When this chain of effect is broken, it depletes. Reparation needs to be a regular and natural occurrence to rebolster and reinforce a deepening relationship. Sarah ensures for her team that special occasions are marked. She sets the tone by sending a gift to each team member when she started as a care package in recognition of everything they had done to keep things going before she joined. This family-like belonging continues: "To keep the connection going we have organised drinks regularly and even have a quiz, I've also sent wine at Christmas celebrations too".

Reflection on practice

- *When did you last experience a high-quality connection – where you felt you and the person you were connecting with felt physiological synchronicity of appreciation for one another? What did you do to facilitate this?*

- *Where do you feel you may be missing opportunities to build high-quality connections (either in specific situations or with particular stakeholders)?*

- *How could you plan for high-quality connections in your upcoming current work routine? What would you continue to do or to do differently?*

Positive conflict

Positive leaders know that interpersonal relationships flourish when they feature more positive communication than negative communication. A variety of studies show that a positive-to-negative ratio of at least three to one, and preferably five (or even six to one in teams), is ideal in all types of human relationships (Gottman & Silver, 1999; Losada & Heaphy, 2004). When there are approximately five positive statements for every negative one, marriages are stronger, teams are more effective, and organisational performance is higher (Fredrickson, 2009). Positive leaders know this and ensure that the focus remains appreciative in all conversations – even the tough ones – linking into abundance behaviour.

And yet the tough conversations still happen – just not as people may have imagined. These conversations are a combination of compassion and accountability. Positive leaders know that it is healthy to embrace positive conflict, being directive in working one-to-one to positively confront, and to encourage team accountability in managing underperformance (Gallo, 2021). Positive leaders also take an appreciative and strengths-based focus in conflict resolution, having a positive intent in raising and resolving the conflict. When conflict is approached constructively – with high collaboration and low avoidance – it is beneficial and results in relationship and performance gains (Kay & Skarlicki, 2020). Di Fabio (2017) highlights that healthy groups are reflected in the groups that take time to listen, tolerate different styles, and aim for win-win solutions and also highlights the research that shows such healthy groups can lead to better creative thinking. In our experience and research, psychologically flexible (limber positive leaders) manage the intricacies, uncertainties, and emotional challenges of socialising most skilfully (Doorley, Goodman, Kelso, & Kashdan, 2020). They can flex and respond to conflict and challenge when it is needed and when it is presented to them. And this is what the positive conflict component of the tribe resource does: positive leaders demonstrating positive conflict do not simply offer support; they deliberately, purposefully, and thoughtfully offer challenge, as they know that challenge (done in the right way and with the right intention) is often what leads to growth. They are pro-social in their approach to conflict and care enough about others to manage their own natural discomfort of challenging a fellow human being: the alternative – hoping the problem will go away and consequently avoiding or alienating another human being – is unthinkable to them.

As Russell mentioned in Chapter 3, positive leaders lean into positive conflict when it is called for. Martine, too, recognises that to be truly tribal in her behaviour, she needs to lean into both tough relational conversations and support. She says that kindness is giving praise when it's due and giving criticism when needed. She says: "Kindness is being transparent and honest. . . [it is not] skipping around, pretending, or ignoring, or sticking your head in the sand and ignoring the fire outside [. . .] kindness is being clear". For Martine, she says creating the positive culture she has within her award-winning team has required both the supportive edge of allowing the idiosyncrasies of people and flexibility for people to have issues – such as family issues. This positive culture is also developed by the team encouraging one another to listen deeply to each other, as well as being bounded by encouraging people to take control of their own issues when needed, and being direct when needed. She says: "It's not about always being an intermediary. It's often about being adult to adult rather than parent to child". She also highlights that when things have gone wrong or complications in relationships or work tasks have arisen, or she has made mistakes (which she is humble in conceding to), she says this is often about when there has been a lack of clarity. She says in these situations the tough-love boundaried edge of tribe is missing: the instructions were not understood or made clear.

Positive leaders show their tribe behaviour when they are consciously or unconsciously aware that challenge lands best when a relationship is in place and when efforts are being made to ensure the relationship remains in place. These leaders do not shy away from the challenge. Instead, they focus on the intention of offering the challenge – to increase the performance and impact of the task at hand. Figure 7.3 illustrates a positive relational cycle – where challenge and/or conflict is inevitable, faced up to, and worked through.

The positive relational cycle reflects the way positive leaders – as described by all the leaders we spoke to – do not shy away from conflict or confrontation, but work through this tension when it arises to create re-strengthened relationships. In this figure, we see that positive leaders always start with connecting actions, feeling connected with others. When there is a rupture – and inevitably there are always ruptures in working relationships – deliberate repair is not shied away from, but takes place intentionally, despite any uncomfortable feelings this raises. As a result, the relationship healthily moves into a state of renewal – which may or may not

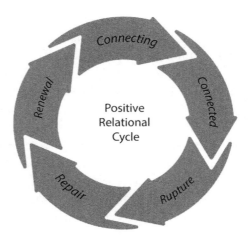

Figure 7.3 Positive relational cycle

feel uncomfortable – before ensuring connecting and connection take place again, and the relationship moves into a new and strengthened positive relational cycle.

Feedback is believed to be a significant factor in fostering intrinsic motivation (Lepper & Chabay, 1985). Looking at the effects of positive feedback on intrinsic motivation, two research syntheses showed that overall, positive feedback enhances intrinsic motivation, as it affirms a sense of competence (Deci, Koestner, & Ryan, 1999; Henderlong & Lepper, 2002). Furthermore, positive feedback has been shown to satisfy competence and autonomy needs, thereby boosting intrinsic motivation (Burgers, Eden, van Engelenburg, & Buningh, 2015). Negative feedback inversely reduces our experience of positive affect in a relationship (Fong, Patall, Vasquez, & Stautberg, 2019). Positive leaders are aware of this and again are consciously or unconsciously aware of the common triggers that put us all into defence mode: feeling excluded; feeling a lack of fairness, respect, or autonomy; feeling incompetent; feeling a lack of purpose or security; and finally a lack of rest (as we discuss in Chapter 6) (Webb, 2017). Positive leaders keep their own brain in 'discovery mode' (Webb, 2017) as much as possible and avoid sending a person into their threat system unthinkingly when offering feedback. Positive leaders being tribal in their behaviour do not miss these opportunities to help others optimally function – they offer positive feedback loops – these empower and motivate and add to self-determination.

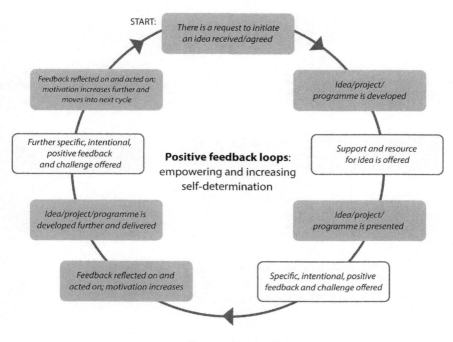

START:

There is a request to initiate an idea received/agreed

Feedback reflected on and acted on; motivation increases further and moves into next cycle

Idea/project/programme is developed

Further specific, intentional, positive feedback and challenge offered

Positive feedback loops: empowering and increasing self-determination

Support and resource for idea is offered

Idea/project/programme is developed further and delivered

Idea/project/programme is presented

Feedback reflected on and acted on; motivation increases

Specific, intentional, positive feedback and challenge offered

Figure 7.4 The positive feedback loop

In the positive feedback loop (Figure 7.4), we see that with every piece of work or idea, support and feedback are offered throughout the process to have the biggest positive effect.

In fact, recent research has shown that offering feedback – whether is it positive or negative – is more neutral than not offering feedback at all (Fong et al., 2019), so leaders – no matter how practised they are – do more good than bad in at least experimenting with this practice. Sarah, demonstrating her tribe behaviour again, explains that when she started in the role, she immediately instigated new positive feedback loops, having one to ones regularly so she and each team member could develop individual relation-ships and work through projects and challenges to empower, motivate, and strengthen work outcomes for all.

When it comes to optimally functioning, feedback that is neither pos-itive nor constructive will seriously limit the capability of the person or team at hand. Figure 7.5 shows what can happen in non-tribe behaviour and when instead there is disconnecting, downward relational behaviour. When neither support nor feedback is offered and the feedback is not

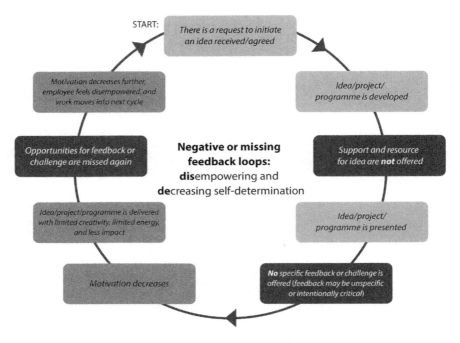

START: There is a request to initiate an idea received/agreed

Idea/project/programme is developed

Support and resource for idea are **not** offered

Negative or missing feedback loops:
disempowering and **de**creasing self-determination

Motivation decreases further, employee feels disempowered, and work moves into next cycle

Opportunities for feedback or challenge are missed again

Idea/project/programme is delivered with limited creativity, limited energy, and less impact

Motivation decreases

Idea/project/programme is presented

No specific feedback or challenge is offered (feedback may be unspecific or intentionally critical)

Figure 7.5 The negative (or missing) feedback loop

constructive, the person at the receiving end increasingly becomes demotivated, uninspired, and loses creativity. Ironically, Sarah explains that it is exactly because of negative feedback loops she experienced in her early legal career that she wanted to be different: "I came across some very flawed managers [. . .] they were not people people [. . . and it felt like] it was sink or swim". Sarah describes the way instructions would be delivered poorly through torn envelopes or written notes with no communication, or commands were shouted at her or books thrown at her – all of which she said would be equivalent to bullying now. Sarah's feedback was limited and only offered through criticism. This led to Sarah feeling "disappointed, unhappy [. . .] terrified [. . . and like she had] had the stuffing knocked out of [her]", illustrating the impact of negative or missing feedback loops. This poor feedback approach led her to change the course of her career and identify what type of culture she wanted to work in. She knew non-constructive feedback would be relationally corrosive – and as a positive leader with tribe behaviour, she knew she never wanted to be like that.

Reflection on practice

- *Reflecting on a recent conflict that you had with a colleague, where did you demonstrate a positive relational spiral or a not-so-positive relational spiral? What was missing in your intention or practice?*

- *How often do you provide feedback that is empowering and feedback that is disempowering? Reviewing the positive feedback loop, how could you increase the way you empower others when giving constructive feedback? Or indeed could you offer feedback more often, and if so, when?*

- *Preparing for an upcoming confrontation that you need to have, what do you need to do to ensure the conflict remains positive and productive, both for yourself and the other person?*

Tribe in action

Not everybody is a people person, and being relational comes more natu-rally to some than to others; the key condition is for all people to recognise the value in connecting with others even if it is not one's own strength and to learn and experiment with different ways of doing so. Several critical organisational and social conditions can support the development of tribe in leaders, including the psychological safety we have discussed in earlier chapters. Some of the wider conditions that support the development of the tribe resource in organisations include the development of a culture that promotes openness and tackles microaggression (Dixon-Fyle et al., 2020); a culture that fosters belonging where there is support for everybody no mat-ter who they are (Dixon-Fyle et al., 2020); and an organisation which sees value in time spent connecting, reflected in key performance indicators that value behaviour as well as delivery.

Promoting openness and tackling microaggressions sends out a message to employees that it's OK to be yourself and that any behaviour which stops you or others from doing so – be it bullying, harassment, racism of any form, etc. – is unacceptable. Companies that invest in their employees, managers, and leaders to support them to understand what these behaviours look like and how they can be fed back on and confronted reinforce the message that we are part of one tribe. Assessing how managers and leaders can create open, welcoming behaviour and encouraging the 360 feedback of leaders and employees in how to do this are all strategies that could promote best conditions for tribe behaviour (Dixon-Fyle et al., 2020).

Companies that build a culture in which all employees feel they can bring their true selves to work and where this is actively encouraged by its managers and leaders will support the building of diverse connections and their internal employee resource groups to foster a sense of community and belonging. This can be assessed through internal surveys or interviews. When a company gives time and role models leadership, making time for connection on a day-to-day and wider basis, this creates an environment in which leaders more freely dedicate time to being tribal. This leads to leaders creating connection through positive interpersonal processes, deepening high-quality connections, and engaging in regular and constructive positive conflict; when this is measured, it creates a positive accountability to ensure these skills, rather than being seen as 'generic' or 'soft', are given adequate credence.

Figure 7.6 provides a graphical representation of what we describe as the positive leader's 'hierarchy of relational needs' and conceptualises how positive leaders develop these three components and their tribe behaviour. It shows how the three components of tribe (connection, high-quality connections, and positive conflict) fit together. Firstly, positive leaders are consciously aware of others and their diversity and strengths; then they make efforts to make entry and to connect – to show the other their desire to connect; they then illustrate their relational understanding of the importance of high-quality connections through presence and listening; to then foster, deepen, and renew connection. It is often then as this point that – with the relational foundations strongly set – they can offer positive conflict and constructive challenge and feedback (and, where necessary, move through the positive relational cycle of connecting > connected > rupture > repair > renewal). When fluent

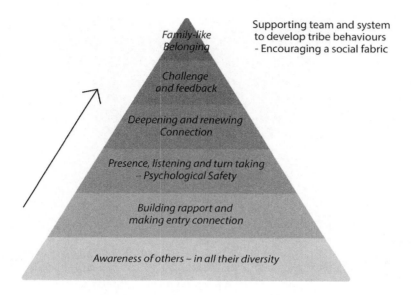

Figure 7.6 The hierarchy of relational needs

across these layers of needs – and through the three components of connection, high-quality connections, and positive conflict – the positive leaders' relationships then move to a positive state of 'belongingness' and family-like quality connections.

So what happens if any of these three components and layers of tribe are missing? The inverse of the tribe resource or behaviour can occur through intentional or unintentional, conscious or unconscious, downward relational spiral behaviours. Figure 7.7 represents the hierarchy within which this can occur: the downward relational spiral. This is where there is an overt self-focus, which can then lead to apathy towards others, followed by disconnection, and then corrosive connection, which effectively damages the relational fabric; this in turn leads to individual, team, or community alienation and ultimately isolation on all sides (Dahl et al., 2020). Sadly this can often happen unintentionally – if we at least become more mindful of our relational behaviour on others (Kay & Skarlicki, 2020), this can positively change relations from being damaged, with the downward relational spiral not being instigated. Even if we never meet the full 'hierarchy of relational needs' of tribe behaviour, our relationships will at least not fall into disrepair.

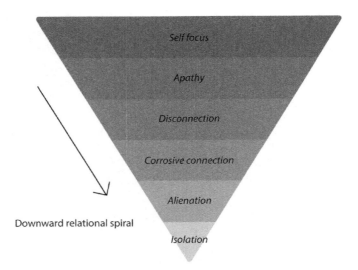

Figure 7.7 The downward relational spiral

Last word

In conclusion, positive leaders tap into the resource of tribe at every inter-action. The tribal leader taps into connecting with all they meet and every exchange they encounter because they know that these moments count. They go to lengths to deepen connection with their team members and show their self to others; they also ensure that conflict and confrontation are managed in a positive and productive way to empower, renew, and resource and to avoid disempowerment and alienation. They support their colleagues and teams to build connection with each other for the best outcomes and do not tolerate any behaviours which may damage relations or alienate any individual or group of people. They prioritise relational behaviour equally as, if not more so than, delivery or task-orientated behaviour. Positive leaders deepen their con-nections to become high-quality connections and lean into rather than shy away from conflict, creating positive conflict. Positive leaders know that their tribe is everything and that how they treat it is crucial for everybody's survival.

References

Algoe, S. B. (2019). Positive interpersonal processes. *Current Directions in Psycho-logical Science*, *28*(2), 183–188.

Baumeister, R. F., Bratslavsky, E., Finkenauer, C., & Vohs, K. D. (2001). Bad is stronger than good. *Review of General Psychology, 5*(4), 323–370. doi:10.1037/1089-2680.5.4.323

Burgers, C., Eden, A., van Engelenburg, M. D., & Buningh, S. (2015). How feedback boosts motivation and play in a brain-training game. *Computers in Human Behavior, 48*, 94–103. doi:10.1016/j.chb.2015.01.038

BVA Nudge Unit, (2020, 2 November). *B.E. GOOD!* Retrieved from https://bvanudgeunit.com/b-e-good-podcast-amy-edmondson-from-psychological-safety-to-organizational-performance/

Chiaburu, D. S., & Harrison, D. A. (2008). Do peers make the place? Conceptual synthesis and meta-analysis of coworker effects on perceptions, attitudes, OCBs, and performance. *Journal of Applied Psychology, 93*(5), 1082–1103. doi:10.1037/0021-9010.93.5.1082

Crocker, J., Canevello, A., & Brown, A. A. (2017). Social motivation: Costs and benefits of selfishness and otherishness. *Annual Review of Psychology, 68*, 299–325. doi:10.1146/annurev-psych-010416-044145

Dahl, C. J., Wilson-Mendenhall, C. D., & Davidson, R. J. (2020). The plasticity of well-being: A training-based framework for the cultivation of human flourishing. *Proceedings of the National Academy of Sciences, 117*(51), 32197. doi:10.1073/pnas.2014859117

David, S. A. (2017). *Emotional agility: Get unstuck, embrace change, and thrive in work and life* (Paperback ed.). London: Penguin Life.

Deci, E. L., Koestner, R., & Ryan, R. M. (1999). A meta-analytic review of experiments examining the effects of extrinsic rewards on intrinsic motivation. *Psychological Bulletin, 125*(6), 627–668. doi:10.1037/0033-2909.125.6.627

Di Fabio, A. (2017). Positive healthy organizations: Promoting well-being, meaningfulness, and sustainability in organizations. *Frontiers in Psychology, 8.* doi:10.3389/fpsyg.2017.01938

Dixon-Fyle, S., Hunt, V., Dolan, K., & Prince, S. (2020). *Diversity wins: How inclusion matters.* Retrieved from https://www.mckinsey.com/featured-insights/diversity-and-inclusion/diversity-wins-how-inclusion-matters

Doorley, J. D., Goodman, F. R., Kelso, K. C., & Kashdan, T. B. (2020). Psychological flexibility: What we know, what we do not know, and what we think we know. *Social and Personality Psychology Compass, 14*(12), 1–11. doi:10.1111/spc3.12566

Dutton, J., & Heaphy, E. (2003). The power of high quality connections. In K. Cameron & J. Dutton (Eds.), *Positive organizational scholarship: Foundations of a new discipline* (pp. 262–278). San Francisco: Berrett-Koehler Publishers.

Dutton, J., & Spreitzer, G. N. (2014). *How to be a positive leader: Small actions, big impact.* San Francisco: Berrett-Koehler Publishers.

Edmondson, A. (1999). Psychological safety and learning behavior in work teams. *Administrative Science Quarterly, 44*(2), 350–383. doi:10.2307/2666999

Fong, C. J., Patall, E. A., Vasquez, A. C., & Stautberg, S. (2019). A meta-analysis of negative feedback on intrinsic motivation. *Educational Psychology Review, 31*(1), 121–162. doi:10.1007/s10648-018-9446-6

Fredrickson, B. (2009). *Positivity: Groundbreaking research reveals how to release your inner optimist and thrive*. Richmond: Oneworld.

Fredrickson, B. (2014). *Love 2.0: Creating happiness and health in moments of connection*. New York: Plume.

Frost, P. J., Dutton, J. E., Worline, M. C., & Wilson, A. (2000). Narratives of compassion in organizations. *Emotion in Organizations*, *2*, 25–45.

Gable, S. L., & Reis, H. T. (2010). Good news! Capitalizing on positive events in an interpersonal context. In M. P. Zanna (Ed.), *Advances in experimental social psychology* (Vol. 42, pp. 195–257). San Diego, CA: Academic Press.

Gable, S. L., Reis, H. T., Impett, E. A., & Asher, E. R. (2004). What do you do when things go right? The intrapersonal and interpersonal benefits of sharing positive events. *Journal of Personality and Social Psychology*, *87*(2), 228–245. doi:10.1037/0022-3514.87.2.228

Gallo, A. (2021). Managers: Compassion and accountability aren't mutually exclusive. *Harvard Business Review*.

Gilbert, P. (2010). *The compassionate mind: A new approach to life's challenges*. London: Constable.

Gottman, J. M., & Silver, N. (1999). *The seven principles for making marriage work* (1st ed.). London: Weidenfeld & Nicolson.

Hari, J. (2018). *Lost connections: Why you're depressed and how to find hope*. London, England: Bloomsbury.

Heaphy, E. D., & Dutton, J. E. (2008). Positive social interactions and the human body at work: Linking organizations and physiology. *Academy of Management Review*, *33*(1), 137–162. doi:10.5465/AMR.2008.27749365

Henderlong, J., & Lepper, M. R. (2002). The effects of praise on children's intrinsic motivation: A review and synthesis. *Psychological Bulletin*, *128*(5), 774–795. doi:10.1037/0033-2909.128.5.774

Kay, A. A., & Skarlicki, D. P. (2020). Cultivating a conflict-positive workplace: How mindfulness facilitates constructive conflict management. *Organizational Behavior and Human Decision Processes*. doi:10.1016/j.obhdp.2020.02.005

Khalifian, C. E., & Barry, R. A. (2020). Expanding intimacy theory: Vulnerable disclosures and partner responding. *Journal of Social and Personal Relationships*, *37*(1), 58–76.

King, M. (2020). *Social chemistry: Decoding the patterns of human connection*. London: Hodder & Stoughton.

Kurtz, L. E., & Algoe, S. B. (2017). When sharing a laugh means sharing more: Testing the role of shared laughter on short-term interpersonal consequences. *Journal of Nonverbal Behavior*, *41*(1), 45–65. doi:10.1007/s10919-016-0245-9

Lepper, M. R., & Chabay, R. W. (1985). Intrinsic motivation and instruction: Conflicting views on the role of motivational processes in computer-based education. *Educational Psychologist*, *20*(4), 217–230. doi:10.1207/s15326985ep2004_6

Losada, M., & Heaphy, E. (2004). The role of positivity and connectivity in the performance of business teams: A nonlinear dynamics model. *The American Behavioral Scientist (Beverly Hills)*, *47*(6), 740–765. doi:10.1177/0002764203260208

Major, B. C., Le Nguyen, K. D., Lundberg, K. B., & Fredrickson, B. L. (2018). Well-being correlates of perceived positivity resonance: Evidence from trait and episode-level assessments. *Personality and Social Psychology Bulletin, 44*(12), 1631–1647. doi:10.1177/0146167218771324

Passmore, J., & Oades, L. G. (2014). Positive psychology techniques – active constructive responding. *Coaching Psychologist, 10*(2), 71–73.

Rosenberg, M. B. (2015). *Nonviolent communication: A language of life*. Encitas: Puddle Dancer Press.

Ryff, C. D., & Singer, B. (2012). *Emotion, social relationships, and health*. New York: Oxford University Press. doi:10.1093/acprof:oso/9780195145410.001.0001

Sandstrom, G. M., & Dunn, E. W. (2014). Social interactions and well-being: The surprising power of weak ties. *Personality and Social Psychology Bulletin, 40*(7), 910–922. doi:10.1177/0146167214529799

Standage, T. (2013, June 22). Social networking in the 1600s. *The New York Times*. Retrieved from www.nytimes.com/2013/06/23/opinion/sunday/social-networking-in-the-1600s.html

Stephens, J. P., Heaphy, E. D., Carmeli, A., Spreitzer, G. M., & Dutton, J. E. (2013). Relationship quality and virtuousness: Emotional carrying capacity as a source of individual and team resilience. *Journal of Applied Behavioral Science, 49*(1), 13–41. doi:10.1177/0021886312471193

Thoits, P. A. (2011). Mechanisms linking social ties and support to physical and mental health. *Journal of Health and Social Behavior, 52*(2), 145–161. doi:10.1177/0022146510395592

Waters, L., Algoe, S. B., Dutton, J., Emmons, R., Fredrickson, B. L., Heaphy, E., . . . Steger, M. (2021). Positive psychology in a pandemic: Buffering, bolstering, and building mental health. *Journal of Positive Psychology*, 1–21. doi:10.1080/1743 9760.2021.1871945

Webb, C. (2017). *How to have a good day: The essential toolkit for a productive day at work and beyond*. London: Pan Books.

Whetten, D. A., & Cameron, K. S. (2016). *Developing management skills* (9th ed.; Global ed.). Boston: Pearson Education Limited.

Ybarra, O., Burnstein, E., Winkielman, P., Keller, M. C., Manis, M., Chan, E., & Rodriguez, J. (2008). Mental exercising through simple socializing: Social interaction promotes general cognitive functioning. *Personality and Social Psychology Bulletin, 34*(2), 248–259. doi:10.1177/0146167207310454

How the ALIGHT model fits together

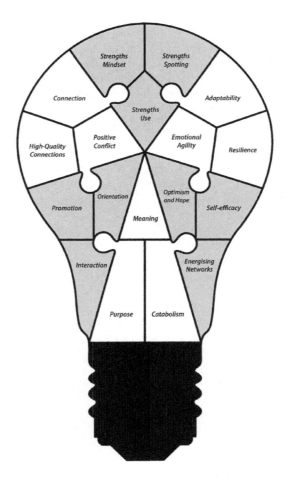

Figure 8.1 The ALIGHT Positive Leadership Model – 18 components

DOI: 10.4324/9781003170433-8

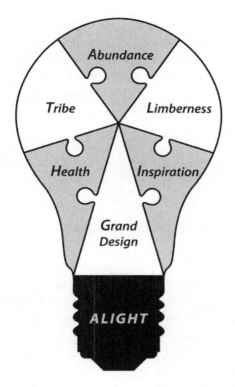

Figure 8.2 The ALIGHT Positive Leadership Model – 6 resources

Integral and integrated

When we first set out to write this book, we anticipated to see the six resources – abundance, limberness, inspiration, grand design, health, and tribe – appear in the interviews, conversations, and research we undertook. One unexpected finding was the clear interrelatedness of the six resources to one another and the lynchpin of each resource complementing the other that is required to be a sustainable positive leader (Figures 8.1 and 8.2). In many instances, the positive leaders we interviewed found it difficult to pinpoint the resources individually and often called out the overlap, interdependency, and integration of these resources. One leader, Sarah, made this very explicit:

> You can bring out all of these strands into the core of what we need to do as leaders. There's the consideration of tribe in that our teams are all people [. . .]; my job is to [be abundant], and to make sure that [the

team] want to get up and come to work and they find it meaningful. So, again, you've got the grand design element as well. And also in my job, is the importance of spreading hope and optimism. That's what I see as very, very important. But if I'm not feeling hopeful and optimistic because I just feel I'm in a downward spiral myself, I can't do that. So again, it goes into one's own levels of limberness [and health]. So it all sort of it comes together.

In reflection of the research we conducted (analysing our professional experiences, reviewing the literature, interviews, and survey development), we have identified that:

1. **All six resources go together**, outlining the essential and holistic integration of all six resources;
2. **Balance** is essential and an ongoing challenge for positive leaders working with the six resources. Balance is about how the weight of the six resources are distributed against each other in terms of daily decision making, positivity and negativity, and harmonious or obsessive passion, all to keep things steady;
3. **Volume** is relevant, as it is possible for an individual resource to be both too high and too low and require dialling up and dialling down. This volume effect offers an opportunity and requires a level of self, other, and contextual awareness and skills for positive leaders to develop each of their six resources;
4. **Clashing, collision, and unhelpful application of ALIGHT resources** is also possible, where leaders can misuse or misappropriate the resources in an unhelpful way for themselves and others.

All six resources go together

Like Niemiec has highlighted in his leading research and reflections on character strengths that they can complement each other and exist in complementary constellations (Niemiec, 2018), so too can positive leadership resources complement one another. In drawing the linkages between the different positive leadership resources and their constituent parts, it is impossible to separate all the parts out to claim that any of them on their own can create a positive leader. This is because there is consistent connection, liminality, and interaction between all the parts (as discussed in Chapters 2–7). All of our positive leaders interviewed said the resources go together and cannot be ignored one for the other. Again and again, the complementarity highlighted in the research, interviews, and surveys inspired us. Some examples that stood out to us specifically in the research review include the following:

- Grand design, abundance, and tribe – the research shows that people who report higher levels of meaning endorse and use their character strengths more, have more satisfying relationships, are more desirable friends, and assist others more (Waters et al., 2021), indicating the links between these three resources;
- Grand design and health and limberness – meaning plays an important role in all three of these resources in supporting coping with stress, trauma, and adversity (Cohen, Bavishi, & Rozanski, 2016);
- Grand design and inspiration – if you link grand design and inspiration together, you are more likely to achieve catabolic plans – if optimism is turned into concrete plans for the future with the support of hope and catabolism, there is an increased chance that this positive envisioned future will become a reality (Schippers, Scheepers, & Peterson, 2015);
- Grand design and limberness – purpose being the motivation to be committed and persevere in working toward higher-order aspirations in the face of obstacles, knowing that you may or may not reach the ultimate goal in a lifetime (Steger, 2021);
- Grand design and limberness – people who are searching for meaning are more open to new approaches to self-understanding and healing (Garland, Stainken, Ahluwalia, Vapiwala, & Mao, 2015);
- Tribe and grand design – where people most frequently nominate relationships as their first source of meaning in life (Waters et al., 2021);
- Health and tribe – intentionally strengthening pro-social qualities improves overall wellbeing (Dahl, Wilson-Mendenhall, & Davidson, 2020);
- Grand design and tribe – connect through the power of supportive work relationships and quality connections (Waters et al., 2021).

Equally if there is a total deficit in a resource area, it is impossible for a positive leader to ALIGHT with the other resources alone. Just as the acronym and mnemonic ALIGHT does not make sense when you remove a letter, removing a resource does not make sense or create any coherent impact either. Table 8.1 shares some examples of where if a resource element is missing, this has an impact on the possibility of a leader being able to reflect and enact positive leadership resources.

Table 8.1 The impact of missing resources

Resource element	Description
No Abundance	The absence of abundance would mean the leader is unable to notice their own or others' strengths, lacks the mindset to do so, and fails to take the action to develop the strengths and resources of themselves and others.
No Limberness	The absence of limberness removes the leader's capacity to adapt, emotionally regulate, or be agile with one's emotions or cognitions and prevents any growth from setbacks or positive experiences, leading to a lack of adaptive resilience.
No Inspiration	The absence of inspiration removes the leader's capacity to be optimistic about the future, reduces their confidence in succeeding, and means they fail to build hopeful pathways forward for themselves and their team. This leads to low energy and a lack of faith, commitment, and motivation to drive action – an energy-less team and leader.
No Grand Design	The absence of grand design removes a leader's sense of values, a vision for the future, clarity of goals, and an ability to help align others' values to their work or break down ambitious plans into achievable and catabolic parts.
No Health	The absence of health would mean a leader acts without regard for their own or others' health, that a leader makes decisions consciously or unconsciously that could be to the detriment of their and other's health and sustainability, reducing the capacity for them or another to realise the potential of their resources – there is a limit to the distance that the leader without health can travel.
No Tribe	The absence of tribe means the leader acts alone and without support or an understanding of the need for others to connect, leading to an inability to connect with others and resulting in their disconnection from others. The resulting alienation would prevent the leader from gathering the adequate energy or support required to make any level of ambitious plans happen, let alone in a hopeful or abundant way.

Balance: essential and a challenge

The theme of balance echoed throughout the research and application of the ALIGHT resources. Balance is both a necessity and a lever for each of the six resources. It is necessary for positive leaders to use balance in their application of these resources. They can use a balancing mindset and approach to develop the right tuning, volume, and level for which they need

Figure 8.3 The positive leadership crossroads

to apply each resource collectively for the bespoke context or situation. Every day a leader must choose the direction and balance they take in using their resources. This can feel like standing at a crossroads, waiting to make the intentional choice of the direction they want to head in (see Figure 8.3).

Some of the key themes of balance that have come through in our research were the need for:

- The balance of positive versus negative – for positive leaders to recognise the abundance in both for each of the six resources and collectively;
- The balance of passion – for positive leaders to work towards healthier and harmonious versus unhealthy, obsessive passion.

Russell explained that is it impossible to operate at 100% of our capacity and that these times are rightly limited: "I think the times that we're at 100% are quite limited actually, sometimes you just 'go through it' as well. And hopefully you want to alter the balance of that, to have more great moments and less slog". For him, it is vital that people create healthy boundaries and can switch off from work. He talks about how our perspective can be warped when we are not balanced, when we are not healthy, and how limberness can be supported – and must be supported – through health and recovery and this 'balance'. Russell highlights that people can bring self-destruction onto themselves by not prioritising their recovery and health and keeping work and their resources in balance:

> As a senior leader, judgement is probably your greatest asset and greatest contribution. So often you can see a leader who, under the constant pressure of events, has started thinking about work all the time – they have lost their sense of perspective, and their judgment has eroded within that.

Russell argues that it is essential people have a switch off, or as he describes it, a hinterland of active recovery where you can go and do something completely different to create and enable an all-important balance. For Russell himself, this has included cellar refurbishment, running, and the social side of life by seeing family, friends, and being involved in clubs and societies. "One of the ways that you could be your best at work is to put time into being your best out of work, and ensure you have proper time out of work." Let us now delve into each type of balance in turn.

The balance of positivity and negativity

Positive leadership is not about keeping positive, no matter what. In fact, this type of positivity indicates an avoidant strategy for coping with problems (David, 2017), which is not helpful at work. When a leader avoids engaging with employees' issues, the message they send them indirectly is that their issues are not important, or worse, that they are imaginary. However, there is yet another message employees receive which can negatively affect their outcomes. Working with a leader who cannot see a problem is just as frustrating as working with a leader who can only see problems. This is why positive leadership is not about pretending that everything is perfect, but acknowledging what is happening, coming up with strategies that best address the issue, and moving on.

Positive leadership is not about denying that the negative exists. Research indicates that bad is stronger than good (Baumeister, Bratslavsky,

Finkenauer, & Vohs, 2001). As leaders we are naturally inclined to pay more attention to the negative aspects of our experiences at work than the positive. We have a radar for issues that threaten our or the company's work, image, or outcomes. We may fear failure or become anxious at the thought of a challenging endeavour. All these negative notions are important aspects of our existence and powerful contributors to our leadership. They act as warning signs and protect us against danger. Without them, we would not be able to survive and would be unable to thrive at work. However, as with all in life, when disparity exists between negative and positive perception of the world, tipping heavily towards the negative for example, it blinkers views of reality. The ALIGHT framework of resources of positive leadership embraces negative experiences, as they are essential parts of leadership and self-knowledge. However, it balances it out with the positive, offering a balanced perspective of the world. A positive leader recognises their negative experience, be it anxiety or fear, and attempts to understand its source instead of reacting to it. Instead of dwelling on a negative event for a long time, a positive leader finds a constructive solution to resolving their issues promptly. They look for opportunities for all of the ALIGHT components to also shine through light a lightbulb, e.g. strengths in the situation, an optimistic take on the context, and hopeful pathways of action. What helps them achieve it is seeing a bigger picture that incorporates both negative and positive experiences. It is like walking on a balance beam: a positive leader can look ahead, see where they are heading without focusing on one leg or another, and move forward bearing each leg, and the whole body, in mind. Positive leadership focuses on emphasising the positive so that the negative is balanced, as both are needed for a leader to flourish.

The balance of passion

From interviewing our positive leaders, a clear sense of passion consistently comes through. Positive leaders do not just have a clear understanding of purpose, able to create meaning at work for themselves and others; they do it with passion. However, as with passion research in positive psychology, we can see that passion can easily get out of balance – taking a dualistic approach of being harmonious or obsessive. For example, there is a continuum of passion in grand design – from meaningless to excessive meaning. Each represents the underbelly of the extremes of grand design – meaninglessness to obsessive passion. The positive leaders we spoke with were able to evidence this spectrum too and worked hard to reach the optimum balance – as with the other positive leadership resources. For example, Russell explained the critical need to be cautious not to overexert one's own passion onto others:

> I am also aware that because I am ambitious and driven, because I love my organisation to achieve great things, that I'm always bringing in new projects and work. And I see it as my job to energise the organisation and move forward. But it does mean that because of my passion there is always more to do than can be done, and I need to be conscious of this.

Moss's writing on the subject of passion echoes this paradox of both loving one's work and being driven by one's work as "a complicated love affair" and talks of purpose-driven burnout (Moss, 2019). As illustrated, positive leaders strive and aim to get this balance right for themselves and their people. The Mayo Clinic in the United States is a non-profit organisation committed to clinical practice, education, and research. On the clinic's list of burnout risks, two out of six are related to a highly and excessively driven mindset. These risks are labelled as "You identify so strongly with work that you lack balance between your work life and your personal life" and/or "You work in a helping profession" (Mayo Clinic, 2021). This suggests how grand design in overexcess may lead to burnout if left imbalanced. A Canadian study analysed responses from 3,715 employees across 12 organisations and found that employees driven by purpose are significantly more stressed and score lower for wellbeing, resilience, and self-efficacy than those who are not (Moss, 2019). Therefore – as our positive leaders themselves highlight – grand design is only well and good when not overexerted by oneself or onto others; again, limberness comes into play.

Flexible and family-friendly work practices that recognise the need to balance work passion for quality of life particularly came to light from positive leaders during the COVID-19 pandemic. The need for flexible working patterns became essential, especially for parents often home-schooling. All positive leaders referenced this in their interviews and drove a sensitive awareness of supporting people to balance their different priorities in their teams and organisations during times of challenge whilst still working towards the bigger picture. Russell explains that the lockdowns experienced during the COVID-19 pandemic created a lack of boundaries for many at his organisation, where employees – including himself – were only ever a few yards away from their desk at any point in time.

Symbolic as well as physical boundaries can be really important for managing boundaries of work and family life. [. . .] You can role model it as well [. . .] if you're not trying to intrude on people's personal lives, not sending emails late at night, and not expecting responses. I do think that helps to establish boundaries and trust.

Russell says organisations can increase balance and support members' family lives by showing the trust that they have in people, switching towards monitoring outcomes rather than presenteeism, and always offering a level of flexibility.

Volume

No human leader is perfect, nor would anybody want them to be – we can leave this to the robots. So when we write about the capacity of the six ALIGHT resources that we have identified within positive leadership, we do not want to encourage a mandate of perfection. Instead, we prefer and would encourage readers, managers, and leaders to think about 'volumes' in which leaders may be able to apply their six powerful resources in different contexts to be more positive leaders. Thus, what is then the difference between balance and volume of the resources? Balance is about an even distribution of the weight of one thing against another to keep things steady. Volume is about the degree of loudness or the intensity of a sound. In this chapter, we are talking about the balance of the resources concerning their positive and negative values and to passion – in other words, how over or in balance the positive and negative levels, and passion (harmonious or obsessive) is of the positive leader (for example, in decision-making). In this chapter, the volume of the resources is about how much we turn up or turn down one of the resources in relation to each of the others in a given situation or context.

Our research and practice indicate that we do not expect or anticipate high volumes of positive leadership across all resources by positive leaders, but instead see positive leader resource application as nuanced and varied. Positive leaders draw on different volumes of positive leadership based on the context and are nuanced in their understanding of what volume to play at based on the context and situation. They can limberly turn up or lower the volume of the ALIGHT resource required. Positive leaders are also self admitting in highlighting that they are always on a journey to develop their positive leadership resources and components, citing greater strengths in some than others. It is this art and flexibility in utilising their resources that makes positive leadership behaviour both simple and complex.

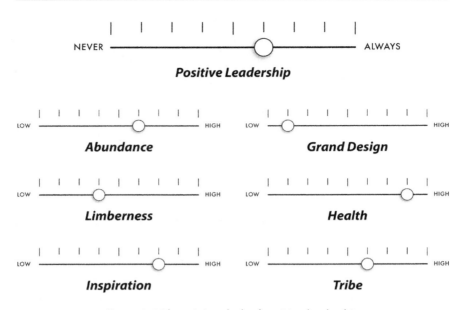

Figure 8.4 The mixing deck of positive leadership

In Figure 8.4, we illustrate that at any one time a resource is in play, it will likely be in play at different volumes across the six resources, and this will play out differently in any given context. You will also note in the figure that at no time would we anticipate from our research that an ALIGHT resource is turned all the way up or all the way down, but is instead mixed in balance for the appropriate output, given the scene in the picture (which again shows the close connection between the concepts of balance and volume when it comes to the six resources).

When it comes to the volume at which we use our resources, Russell talks about being mindful of time and what quality we can produce within it. He says that part of his role is to ensure that intense, peak moments of work are not a permanent feature of the work environment but drawn on as and when needed – turned up or down in volume – in particular circumstances.

Sometimes there's a project deadline, there's an emergency [and of course] we will be working hard for a time, and sometimes we love it as well, at that peak moment to flow [experience]. And then when you reflect and say, I have done 10 hours of solid creative work [that's great, but. . .] I'm just not sure how over an entire career, whether we can always do that?

Russell highlights that sustainability is not about always working at the same volume with all of our best resources, but working at a pace where there are ebbs and flows of our resources – where sometimes we need to step up and step back and adjust the volume in order to be sustainable across our careers.

When it comes to volume, we have noticed the following three themes of positive leaders:

- Like strengths, we can turn up too high and too low;
- Dialling up and dialling down require self, other, and contextual awareness and may link to social maturity or adult ego development;
- The volume with which we use positive leadership resources is likely related to the levels of feedback we have received over time.

In strengths research, we have seen that strengths can be both underused and overused or used optimally (Freidlin, Littman-Ovadia, & Niemiec, 2017; Niemiec, 2019). Underuse is where the volume is so low on a strength in terms of how one uses it that neither they nor others notice it; overuse is a situation where a person overdoes their strength or strengths, overusing them to such an extent that the strength(s) become their weakness (Niemiec, 2018). The field of character strengths research is examining overuse, underuse, and optimal use of character strengths (Niemiec & Pearce, 2021), and likewise we can see that positive leadership resources can also be turned up too high, too low, or used in optimal balance. (We prefer the terms high volume and low volume or in balance, as for us, as underuse and overuse have at times been confusing semantics for leaders we work with in our practice!) Again this links to the need for balance and the metaphor use in strengths research of the golden mean (Niemiec, 2019), referring to the Goldilocks principle and the need to use a strength or resource to the point that the temperature is 'just right'. This ability to consciously turn a dial up and down to manage an overuse or underuse of positive leadership resource can also be seen to be linked to a relatively new concept: 'self-connection' (Klussman, Curtin, Langer, & Nichols, 2020; Klussman, Langer, Nichols, & Curtin, 2020; Klussman, Nichols, & Langer, 2020). How self-connected you are may result in how appropriately you can turn the volume up or down in a given situation. Self-connection is a concept rooted in an active version of self-awareness and involves both accepting and aligning behaviour based on that awareness (Mead, Fisher, & Kemp, 2021). This would suggest that a positive leader, then, at best is 'self-connected' and able to align the balance and volume at which they use a resource to an optimal level for the context – aligning their behaviour to what they notice about themselves, others, and the given context.

Social maturity

Taking this self-connectedness further, it is possible that this exercising of volume links to a leader's social maturity. In a recent study (Gilbride, James, & Carr, 2020), the researchers explored how leaders – school principals – made sense of the context of their work and how it shaped their actions. As in all adults, these principals' sense-making capability is a function of ego and can change over time. Their research showed that principals reacted in different ways to critical incidents and elicited different feelings from others based on their level of adult ego development. So what is adult ego development theory? This theory proposes that the frame of reference we use as individuals to make sense of the world and how we experience it changes and develops over adulthood through specific stages and a process known as adult ego development (AED) (Loevinger & Blasi, 1976). AED suggests we move from a simple, static, and self-centred way of interpreting the world to one which is more complex, dynamic, and more social (Cook-Greuter, 2004; Gilbride et al., 2020). AED proposes a journey of adult life which sees us move from 'independence' to 'dependence' to 'inter-dependence' (Fischer & Torbert, 1995; Loevinger & Blasi, 1976). Table 8.2 highlights some examples of the more developed and socially aware layers of the adult ego. A body of research indicates that an individual's stage of AED is likely to significantly affect their leadership actions (Cook-Greuter, 2004; McCauley, Drath, Palus, O'Connor, & Baker, 2006; Rooke & Torbert, 2009). Furthermore, in Gilbride et al.'s research, the principals' leadership was perceived as much more complex, nuanced, supportive of others, and widely resourced, with the greater the development of the adult ego of the leaders involved (2020). In particular, the 'individualistic' leaders (the highest level of AED identified by the study, as no principals were identified as autonomous or integrated) were described as being comparatively "authorised, genuinely collaborative, deeply reflective, developmental, affectively aware, empathetic, engaging and perceptive" (2020, p. 16) – qualities lacking in the behaviour of the principals with earlier stages of AED. If adult ego theory is applied to how positive leaders use their six

Table 8.2 The characteristics of individuals at different later stages of adult ego development.

Name of stage	Description
Self-aware	Increased, although still limited, self-awareness and appreciation of multiple possibilities in situations; self-critical; emerging rudimentary awareness of the feelings of self and others; banal reflections on life issues, for example, God, death, relationships, and health.
Conscientious	Self-evaluated standards; reflective; responsible; empathic; long-term goals and ideals; displays and perceives true conceptual complexity; can see the broader perspective and discern patterns; principled morality; rich and differentiated inner life; mutuality in relationships; self-critical; values achievement.
Individualistic	Heightened sense of individuality; concerned about emotional dependence; tolerant of self and others; incipient awareness of inner conflicts and personal paradoxes without a sense of resolution or integration; values relationships over achievement; a vivid and unique way of expressing self.
Autonomous	Capacity to face and cope with inner conflicts; high tolerance for ambiguity; can see conflict as an expression of the multifaceted nature of people and life in general; respectful of the autonomy of the self and others; relationships seen as interdependent rather than dependent/independent; concerned with self-actualisation; recognises the systemic nature of relationships; cherishes individuality and uniqueness; expresses feelings vividly.
Integrated	Wise; broadly empathic; full sense of identity; able to reconcile inner conflicts and integrate paradoxes; self-actualised person; growth motivated; seeks to actualise potential capacities; endeavours to understand her or his intrinsic nature and to achieve integration and synergy within the self.

The pre-adult, pre-social, symbiotic and impulsive, self-protective, and conformist stages are not included (adapted and used with permission from Gilbride et al., 2020).

resources of abundance, limberness, inspiration, grand design, health, and tribe, a leader's use of these resources may be influenced by how developed one's adult ego is. This hypothesis requires continued research to explore this further.

Clashing, collision, and unhelpful use

From our research, we believe it is also possible to misuse and misappropriate the ALIGHT resources in an imbalanced and unhelpful way for the leaders and others. Much like balance and volume, our positive leaders highlighted these potential clashes, collisions, and unhelpful behaviour in our conversations with them too. This was often due to non-abundant or imbalanced abundant intention, where the self was placed before the other instead of being considered in tandem with the system. To draw this out, in Table 8.3 we propose six examples of how each of the positive leadership ALIGHT resources could be misused and misappropriated by leaders.

Table 8.3 How positive leadership ALIGHT resources could be misused

Resource	Negative outcome	Negative application	Example of clash, collision, or unhelpful use of resource
(High) Abundance (and low Tribe)	Overwhelm and overdrive	Pushing on peoples' strengths to make them overwork	A leader could highlight somebody's strengths to them and use this to encourage them to work harder, seizing their engagement but applying this too highly abundant approach for misuse, leading to overwhelm instead of flow.
Limberness (low Abundance and low Tribe)	Emotional manipulation	Adapting to manipulate, being emotionally agile to manipulate, and no growth as a result of a setback	A leader could feign adaptation in their perception of a situation and feign emotional agility – feign taking on feedback or bending to opinion to get somebody to concede to their way; there is no mutual growth in this instance, just inauthentic selfish progress.
(Misappropriated) Inspiration	Hopeless and cynical	"Empty hope and false optimism"	A leader could be optimistic, telling people 'everything will be OK' without any supporting actions or pathways of hope to truly offer hope and energy in the way forward.

Resource	Negative outcome	Negative application	Example of clash, collision, or unhelpful use of resource
(High) Grand Design (with low Tribe)	Misled and let down	Manipulation of values	A leader could manipulate a link of their own or a person's values to the work at hand to induce alignment. However, this alignment would be solely to direct energy in the short term, resulting in feelings of inauthenticity and dis-satisfaction.
(High) Health (low Limberness, low Inspiration, and low Tribe)	Confusion and ill health	"All mouth and no trousers"	A leader can talk the talk about health and say it is important to them and encourage others to see it as necessary, but not back this up through role modelling; actions; or ensuring active promotion, orientation, or integration of their colleagues' health when daily or significant decisions are made and when it matters.
Tribe (without adequate Limberness or Abundance)	Superficial and unsafe	"Everybody's friend is nobody's friend"	Using a connection that is shallow and not deep and with the intention of self-fulfilment or self-progress without real or genuine consideration to deeply connect with the other.

These clashing, collision, and unhelpful use of resources may be seen as the potential 'dark side' to developing the knowledge and practice of the positive leadership ALIGHT resources – and again emphasises the need for deeper self awareness and authenticity, and for integration and balance of all six to mitigate against the potential misuse or misappropriation of their application. Again, further research into positive leadership resources is required. This now leads us to sharing a positive leadership scale where you may now assess yourself before we move to look at where this book and the research on positive leadership needs to go next.

References

Burgers, C., Eden, A., van Engelenburg, M. D., & Buningh, S. (2015). How feedback boosts motivation and play in a brain-training game. *Computers in Human Behavior, 48*, 94–103. doi:10.1016/j.chb.2015.01.038

Cohen, R., Bavishi, C., & Rozanski, A. (2016). Purpose in life and its relationship to all-cause mortality and cardiovascular events: A meta-analysis. *Psychosomatic Medicine, 78*(2).

Cook-Greuter, S. R. (2004). Making the case for a developmental perspective. Industrial and Commercial Training. *Industrial and Commercial Training, 36*(7), 275–281. doi:10.1108/00197850410563902

Dahl, C. J., Wilson-Mendenhall, C. D., & Davidson, R. J. (2020). The plasticity of well-being: A training-based framework for the cultivation of human flourishing. *Proceedings of the National Academy of Sciences, 117*(51), 32197. doi:10.1073/pnas.2014859117

Fischer, D., & Torbert, W. M. (1995). *Personal and organisational transformations*. Maidenhead: McGraw-Hill.

Freidlin, P., Littman-Ovadia, H., & Niemiec, R. M. (2017). Positive psychopathology: Social anxiety via character strengths underuse and overuse. *Personality and Individual Differences, 108*, 50–54.

Garland, S. N., Stainken, C., Ahluwalia, K., Vapiwala, N., & Mao, J. J. (2015). Cancer-related search for meaning increases willingness to participate in mindfulness-based stress reduction. *Integr Cancer Ther, 14*(3), 231–239. doi:10.1177/1534735415580682

Gilbride, N., James, C., & Carr, S. (2020). School principals at different stages of adult ego development: Their sense-making capabilities and how others experience them. *Educational Management Administration & Leadership, 49*(2), 234–250. doi:10.1177/1741143220903724

Job burnout: How to spot it and take action. Retrieved from www.mayoclinic.org/healthy-lifestyle/adult-health/in-depth/burnout/art-20046642

Klussman, K., Curtin, N., Langer, J., & Nichols, A. L. (2020). Examining the effect of mindfulness on well-being: Self-connection as a mediator. *Journal of Pacific Rim Psychology, 14*, e5.

Klussman, K., Langer, J., Nichols, A. L., & Curtin, N. (2020). What's stopping us from connecting with ourselves? A qualitative examination of barriers to self-connection. *International Journal of Applied Positive Psychology, 5*(3), 137–152.

Klussman, K., Nichols, A. L., & Langer, J. (2020). The role of self-connection in the relationship between mindfulness and meaning: A longitudinal examination. *Applied Psychology: Health and Well-Being, 12*(3), 636–659.

Loevinger, J., & Blasi, A. (1976). *Ego development: Conceptions and theories*. San Francisco: Jossey-Bass.

McCauley, C. D., Drath, W. H., Palus, C. J., O'Connor, P. M. G., & Baker, B. A. (2006). The use of constructive-developmental theory to advance the understanding of leadership. *The Leadership Quarterly, 17*(6), 634–653.

Mead, J., Fisher, Z., & Kemp, A. H. (2021). Moving beyond disciplinary silos towards a transdisciplinary model of wellbeing: An invited review. *Frontiers in Psychology, 12*, 1652.

Moss, J. (2019, July 01). When passion leads to burnout. *Harvard Business Review*, July 01. Retrieved from https://hbr.org/2019/07/when-passion-leads-to-burnout

Niemiec, R. M. (2018). *Character strengths interventions: A field guide for practitioners*. Boston, MA: Hogrefe Publishing.

Niemiec, R. M. (2019). Finding the golden mean: The overuse, underuse, and optimal use of character strengths. *Counselling Psychology Quarterly, 32*(3–4), 453–471.

Niemiec, R. M., & Pearce, R. (2021). The practice of character strengths: Unifying definitions, principles, and exploration of what's soaring, emerging, and ripe with potential in science and in practice. *Frontiers in Psychology, 11*, 3863.

Rooke, D., & Torbert, W. R. (2009). Seven transformations of leadership. *The Essential Guide to Leadership, 41*.

Schippers, M. C., Scheepers, A. W. A., & Peterson, J. B. (2015). A scalable goal-setting intervention closes both the gender and ethnic minority achievement gap. *Palgrave Communications, 1*(1), 15014. doi:10.1057/palcomms.2015.14

Steger, M. F. (2021). Meaning in life: A unified model. In C. R. Snyder, S. J. Lopez, L. M. Edwards, & S. C. Marques (Eds.), *Oxford handbook of positive psychology* (3rd ed., pp. 959–965). Oxford: Oxford University Press.

Waters, L., Algoe, S. B., Dutton, J., Emmons, R., Fredrickson, B. L., Heaphy, E., . . . Steger, M. (2021). Positive psychology in a pandemic: Buffering, bolstering, and building mental health. *Journal of Positive Psychology*, 1–21. doi:10.1080/1743 9760.2021.1871945

ALIGHT Positive Leadership Resources Scale

Completing an assessment is not an easy endeavour. While it may be an enlightening experience for some of us, others may find it confusing, stressful, or anxiety-inducing. To ensure it will become a helpful exercise that will help you grow, you must contextualise it well. A deeper understanding of the meaning of the assessment will allow you to get the most out of it.

> **Reflection on practice**
> What do you hope to gain from assessing your own (or others') positive leadership?

Your reasons for completing this questionnaire may stem from your curiosity about yourself concerning the various positive leadership resources you use. You have read the book and may have already reflected on what resources you believe you use frequently and which ones you may wish to work on. What is important is that after reading your results, you do not focus on the ones you do not use regularly and choose to improve them. The main reason for it is that there may have been a deeply enrooted reason for you not tapping into them to date. Perhaps you have tried it before, but from your experience, you know that it did not serve you well. If this is the reason

DOI: 10.4324/9781003170433-9

for not using your resources to their full potential, consider what changes have occurred between the past and today that could result in different outcomes. Also, think about what you have learnt in the past about it. If you tried it and it did not work, what would you like to do differently to get a different outcome? These questions are essential to help you understand the best way to integrate ALIGHT into your life as a leader.

Your objective for completing this questionnaire may derive from wanting to self-improve. Whilst it is an excellent sign of your love for learning and a highly commendable motivation, bear in mind our natural inclination to search for negative situations to protect us from danger (Baumeister et al., 2001). Nevertheless, the alternative to becoming a positive leader is not dangerous; thus, this might not be a valuable motivation for this questionnaire. We do not need protection from ourselves or anyone else to become positive leaders. When you have not fully developed any of the ALIGHT resources, it does not mean that you are not entirely a leader, nor that you are in danger of failing your team or organisation in any way. All it means is that the choices you have made in the past led you in a different direction, which was more beneficial for you at the time and allowed you to develop alternative resources. Now, ask yourself how useful is it for you to develop the other ALIGHT resources further?

Just because you scored low on a specific ALIGHT resource does not mean that you should prioritise its development. If the reason for you to engage with this assessment is to enhance your wellbeing while leading others, following the logic of similar concepts in positive psychology such as character strengths, it may be more beneficial for you to continue developing the resources you are good at and want to be better at, rather than the ones that are not your strength. Also, consider how the resources you are already good at can help you work on resources you do not usually use frequently. This perspective may better enable you to reach your potential.

Your employer or an educational course may have recommended that you complete this assessment. If so, we suggest that before you embark on it, you reflect on how it can help you apart from fulfilling your duties. For example, how can it support you in becoming a positive leader or the leader you would like to be? Until you have the answer to this question, we suggest you park completing this questionnaire aside for the moment, and come back to it when you want to.

Remember that this assessment is not a measure of who you are, how worthy you are, or whether you have what it takes to be a leader. It is simply an assessment of where you are at today about using the ALIGHT resources.

It is an assessment of what choices you have made and how useful you have found them. Your score is related to all of your recent experiences, the beliefs you currently hold, and the outcomes you accomplished. Your experiences constantly change, and as you grow, you will begin to react to your circumstances differently. Everything you read, watch, talk about, and encounter in your daily life has the potential to change your beliefs.

Similarly, with a new attitude and behaviour, your outcomes will change too. This is why the questionnaire results do not measure who you are as a person, but instead where you are at this point. You are not a static object, so you can move, and grow, and make the change you want to see happen if you choose to do so.

After completing the questionnaire, you may decide to enhance aspects of your leadership behaviour, become more abundant in mindset and focused on strengths and resources, or more profoundly tribal and connect with people. This means that when you redo this assessment a few months or years later, expect that your score will be different. After all, you may tend to behave in a certain way and hold a specific attitude. However, only focused, repetitive action will help you develop new habits and the targeted elements of positive leadership and grow because all these resources are trait-like.

Sometimes people ask us where they should start with implementing changes. Should they begin with their attitude and then allow it to alter their behaviour systematically, or should they start their new behaviour before they fully believe in it and watch their attitude change as they see their outcomes changing? The answer is: whatever works for you. Some of you may need to understand each element very well before you engage with it. You may want to reflect on what you have read or explore it further by reading more books and articles or discussing it with colleagues and friends. Others, however, may wish to actively experiment with it as their source of active practice and research. You may challenge yourself and decide to experiment with introducing a new way of leading your team, and as you see the results of your changed behaviour, your attitude towards leadership will also change. The decision about where to start is all yours. What is essential is to take the first step.

Our natural reaction to an assessment is to search for weaknesses. You may try to identify the elements you did not score high on and develop practical ways to improve on them. However, in a positive leadership limber spirit and mindset, it is crucial to stop and think before jumping into this automatic reaction. Instead of asking yourself which area is the weakest, ask yourself with abundance: which area of your positive leadership is the strongest, and how can you use it to help you develop other areas? Another question to consider is: which area is the most important for you at this moment in time? Perhaps you are going through significant changes in your workplace, and the one area that you need to develop the most is, for example, limberness and its adaptability component. Even though you may have scored lower on another element, it may be the limberness you would like to focus on developing. It is vital to approach your decisions wisely after receiving your scores to consider your motivations and ambitions.

Finally, this is a self-assessment tool, meaning that you are assessing yourself on the use of positive leadership in your daily practice. While some of you may be fully aware of your attitudes and behaviour, others may have a skewed perspective on who you are. For example, instead of describing yourself as you are today, you may be describing an aspirational self. Conversely, some of your views of yourself may be underestimated, whereby you may have a limiting belief about yourself, which prevents you from seeing the real you, and perhaps comes from the past or a past experience. All these perspectives limit the effectiveness of this test, which is why we strongly encourage you to discuss the findings of your assessment with a coach, family, friends, or other leaders or colleagues you work with or know. They may offer you views that will help you grow.

Positive Leadership Assessment

If you wish to assess your skills and practices relating to the ALIGHT model, please complete the assessment below, which has undergone initial and face validation.

Read the statements carefully and decide how well they describe you on a scale from 1 (does not describe me well) to 5 (describes me very well)

1. I know my strengths well
2. I am willing to change my mind if a situation calls for it
3. I am confident in my abilities
4. I lead a meaningful life
5. Health is important to me
6. I make a conscious effort to connect with others through positive interactions, such as humour, gratitude, or kindness
7. I am aware of other people's strengths

8. I can think of different ways to respond in any given situation
9. Even when others despair, I continue to believe we can succeed
10. I can find meaning in everyday life
11. I take care of my health
12. I remove any distractions that may get in the way of connection (face to face or virtually)
13. I am able to list my own strengths
14. Even when I experience negative emotions, I can still focus on what I am doing without distraction
15. I instil confidence in others
16. I am clear about my values
17. I am satisfied with my health
18. I design meetings and all team interactions with intentionality to build in connection
19. I am able to use my strengths in many ways
20. When I experience a setback, I have difficulty moving on
21. I expect that everything will be ok in the future
22. I support others to clarify their values
23. I encourage others to take care of their health
24. My team is trustworthy
25. I believe that conflict brings negativity
26. I support others to use their strengths at work
27. I am OK with feeling sad, anxious, or angry
28. I demonstrate zest for work
29. I support others to achieve their goals
30. Health is my priority in decision-making
31. I celebrate my team's successes

Please note that questions 20 and 25 are reverse scored, i.e.

1⟹5
2⟹4
3⟹3
4⟹2
5⟹1

Abundance – sum 1, 7, 13, 19, 26 and divide by 5
Limberness – sum 2, 8, 14, 20, 27 and divide by 5

Inspiring – sum 3, 9, 15, 21, 28 and divide by 5
Grand Design – sum 4, 10, 16, 22, 29 and divide by 5
Health – sum 5, 11, 17, 23, 30 and divide by 5
Tribe – sum 6, 12, 18, 24, 25, 31 and divide by 6

The maximum average score you can reach is 5 for each resource. The higher you scored, the more you have developed this positive leadership resource to date.

Reflection on practice
What ALIGHT resources have you developed well to date?

What ALIGHT resources would be useful for you to develop over the next few months?

How will you know you have succeeded at developing them? What changes will you and others see?

What actions can you take today to develop them further?

Interventions for practice

Dependent on which element you wish to focus on, we have created a list of research-based activities you can take to develop your skills. Please note that you can alter these activities to support your team and organisation, and we would recommend working with a learning specialist or coaching psychologist with deep learning in positive psychology for the best and most ethical application. You can find out more by visiting cornelialucey.com and www.cornelialucey.com/the-book-positive-leadership-in-practice, as well as jolantaburke.com.

Abundance

1. **Strengths assessing:** Complete one of the strengths assessments to identify your strengths. Reflect on them and discuss them with your coach, colleague, significant other, or anyone you trust and who knows you to enable you to understand them. Try to figure out your top strengths and how your strengths interact with each other (Niemiec, 2018). For example, if you have well-developed courage but did not take time to develop prudence, it may explain your reckless behaviour; if you have well-developed honesty and underdeveloped compassion, it may lead to cruelty; or if you have developed tenacity but underdeveloped flexibility, it may lead to rigidity in approach. Similarly, identify the consequences of two well-developed strengths. The more you understand your strengths, the easier it will be for you to apply them.

2. **Strengths-spotting:** Spend the next week strengths-spotting. For example:
   - While watching a film or reading a book, consider the protagonists' main strengths (Niemiec & Wedding, 2014);
   - After a meeting with colleagues or clients, reflect on their main strengths;
   - Sit down with a piece of paper and map out strengths of individuals on your team;
   - Create a strengths' organisational chart, whereby strengths are assigned to all members of your team.

3. **Abundant sharing:** Begin your team meetings by going around the table and asking all colleagues to share www (what went well) for them since the last meeting, as well as on the resources that enabled their success.

4. **Reflection:** Reflect on the last week. What strengths have you used well and which ones have you forgotten to use even though they would have worked well in a given situation? When going through adversity, what strengths could you use, and how can you do it? Consider the week ahead. What strengths do you plan to use more of and how?

5. **Strength-priming:** Before a meeting, reflect on the strengths of people you are meeting (Quinlan, Vella-Brodrick, Gray, & Swain, 2019).

6. **Appreciative inquiry:** Apply a strength-based approach instead of a problem-and-solution approach when engaging in a workplace project (Lewis, Passmore, & Cantore, 2014). Instead of reflecting on problems, start a discussion with positive outcomes, resources, and strengths of

the team; then identify your ideal outcomes and potential steps you can take to engage the resources or develop them further; and then develop a plan of action for the next few weeks or months.

7. **Gratitude:** After a nasty, exhausting, tough day, reflect on what you are grateful for, despite the challenges (Waters & Stokes, 2015).

Further resources:

- Buckingham, M. (2015). *Stand out 2.0: Assess your strengths, find your edge, win at work*. Brighton, MA: Harvard Business Review Press.
- Lewis, S., Passmore, J., & Cantore, S. (2014). *Appreciative inquiry for change management: Using AI to facilitate organisational development*. Kogan Page.
- Oades, L. G., Steger, M., Fave, A. D., & Passmore, J. (2020). *The Wiley Blackwell handbook of the psychology of positivity and strengths – based approaches at work*. Hoboken, NJ: Wiley Blackwell.
- Niemiec, R. M. (2017). *Character strengths interventions: A field guide for practitioners*. Hogrefer.

Limberness

1. **Heightening awareness**: Awareness-based interventions can increase our ability to notice what is going on for us in our internal and external environment and improve outcomes related to the self-regulation of our attention. Take ten minutes every day to practise meditation, mindfulness, or the self-compassion exercise of your choice (some options include drawing from the following evidence-based programmes: acceptance and commitment therapy (mindfulness component) (Hayes, Luoma, Bond, Masuda, & Lillis, 2006), mindfulness-based cognitive therapy (mindfulness component) (Segal, Williams, & Teasdale, 2013), and mindful self-compassion (mindfulness component) (Neff & Germer, 2018)). Ideally, practise this first thing in the morning before the day's demands take over your attention.

2. **Increasing self-awareness to adapt:** Growing mindfulness in the mundane to spark curiosity and adaptivity (adapted from Langer, 1989; Stern, 2004; Niemiec, 2019). Become more aware of your perspective in mundane activities. How can you be more aware and notice your adaptation in awareness?

Routine activity	How you can be mindful in the activity	How have you adapted your perspective in the activity
Getting out of bed in the morning	Take time to notice your body and mind wakening and stretch	Noticing the mental and physical requirements of getting up in the morning, how can you adapt your perspective on this activity?
Brushing your teeth	Taking time to notice each tooth you are brushing and where and how it feels	Noticing the effects of the toothbrush and the feelings you are experiencing, how can you adapt your perspective on this activity?
Boiling the kettle/making a hot drink	For your own reflections	For your own reflections
Doing your daily exercise	For your own reflections	For your own reflections
Emailing a colleague	For your own reflections	For your own reflections
Other routine activity	For your own reflections	For your own reflections

3. **Self-reflection:** Take a piece of paper and for 20 minutes write about an emotionally charged situation that you are facing right now or have faced over the past week, month, or year. Set a timer for 20 minutes, write freely, and go wherever your mind takes you, not worrying about grammar or sense. Then throw the paper away or do not save the document. After 20 minutes, notice how different you feel after this exercise. The point is to separate your thoughts from yourself temporarily so you can step out of your experience and develop a new perspective (David, 2017, adapted from Pennebaker, 1997. See also Dahl et al., 2021).

4. **Reflecting on emotional agility in conflict:** After you have experienced conflict at work, take a piece of paper and draw circles. In each circle, enter one reason as to why you feel hurt about the situation. Next to each reason, enter what you are grateful for in relation to that hurt. Now, reflect on how this activity has allowed you to see the situations differently. Adapted from (Reivich, 2004).

5. **Positive reappraisal of the unpleasant** (McCullough, Root, & Cohen, 2006; Witvliet et al., 2010; Niemiec, 2019): Think of a minor conflict or stressful situation you are having with a colleague where you feel you have been slighted by something they said or what they are doing:

a. Write the situation in brief.

b. What strengths did you show, and how did you demonstrate them at the time of the offence?

c. What insight have you gathered from this situation in terms of learning and how you might move forward?

(Adapted from Niemiec, 2019, pp. 178–179)

6. **Increasing courage in the face of adversity:** In order to develop ways to build your resilience in the face of a challenge, try putting courage research into action (Hannah, Sweeney, & Lester, 2007; Pury, 2008):

a. Write down a problematic situation in which you would like to be courageous and take action;

b. List some positive outcomes of showing courage and taking action in this situation;

c. Think back to a time where you have shown courage and taken action in a similar situation. What was the situation, and how did it feel to act courageously?

d. What were the thoughts you had at that past courageous time of action, and what thoughts motivated you to apply your courage? How can this help now or in the future?

(Adapted from Niemiec, 2019)

7. **Mindful self-compassion:** Finding your compassionate voice (Neff & Germer, 2018). How can we work with our inner critic? We can make space for another voice, our compassionate voice or inner champion.

a. Reflect on a behaviour of yours or somebody else's that you are struggling with.

b. Put your hand on your heart and feel the warmth.

c. Decide on a phrase that helps you find your inner compassionate voice or compassionate champion, e.g. "This is difficult, and I do not want you to suffer" and say it to yourself several times.

d. When ready, write a message to yourself in the voice of your more compassionate champion; write freely and spontaneously, addressing the behaviour you would like to change (if it is your own) or how you will work with it (if it is another's). (Neff & Germer, 2018, p. 182)

Further resources:

- David, S. (2017). *Emotional agility: Get unstuck, embrace change and thrive in work and life*. London: Penguin Books Ltd.
- Hayes, S., Luoma, J., Bond, F., Masuda, A., & Lillis, J. (2006). Acceptance and Commitment Therapy: Model, processes and outcomes. *Behaviour Research and Therapy, 44*, 1–25.
- Neff, K., & Germer, C. (2018). *The mindful self-compassion workbook: A proven way to accept yourself, build inner strength, and thrive*. New York: Guilford Press.
- Niemiec, R. M. (2019). *The strengths-based workbook for stress relief*. Oakland, CA: New Harbinger.
- Segal, Z., Williams, J., & Teasdale, J. (2012) *Mindfulness-based cognitive therapy for depression*. Guilford Press.

Inspiration

1. **Self-efficacy for inspiration:** Consider yourself in the context of the inspiration resource. What actions can you take over the next few weeks to become more inspiring? Observe other people you consider inspiring and list two to three actions they take that help them do it. Write a letter to yourself providing evidence of what makes you an inspiring leader, e.g. when you inspired others or yourself. Reflect on your somatic and affective state when you become inspiring, e.g. What is your breathing like? How do you stand? How does your body feel? What emotion do you experience shortly before, during and after? All these reflections will help you develop your self-efficacy in relation to this resource (Warner & French, 2020). You can practise them in various contexts of your life by replacing the inspiration resource with other desirable outcomes.
2. **Writing about your goals:** Take a piece of paper and write about your life in the future. Imagine that you have worked hard and succeeded at accomplishing all your goals. Everything has gone as well as it possibly could. Write in detail about your life in the future. Adapted from King (2001).
3. **Best possible self:** Take a piece of paper and for 20 minutes write about you at your best. Recall a time when you were at your best, and write in detail about the situation and about the strengths you used while

being at your best. Now reflect on what you can do today to move towards the better version of yourself and commit to one action you can take. Adapted from Seligman, Steen, Park & Peterson (Seligman, Steen, Park, & Peterson, 2005).

4. **Journal writing:** Create a self-reflection journal, the objective of which is to cultivate hope (Crain & Koehn, 2012). In your journal focus on your self-care, work-life balance, and how to enhance your organisation's culture to help you and others cultivate hope.

5. **Hope profiling:** Identify resources in your workplace that can support your goal progression and, as such, help you and your team feel more hopeful about the future (O'Hara & O'Hara, 2012).

6. **The will and the way:** Identify what goal you are hoping to accomplish in the future and come up with a detailed plan on how you can make it happen (Snyder, Rand, & Sigmon, 2018).

7. **Learnt optimism:** When experiencing challenging situations, (1) consider the circumstances that affected your outcome, (2) recall a time in the past of bad things being temporary, and (3) think of your challenging situation as distinct from other situations that are not as challenging and are going well for you. Coach your team through this process of thinking, thus developing their optimism (Seligman, 1990).

8. **Energy network:** Create a map of your team's energy network, i.e. identify who energises people, what they do, and what structural and relational changes you can make to increase the energy levels on your team (Cameron, 2021).

9. **Miracle question:** If you were to wake up tomorrow as a more inspiring person than you have ever been, what changes would you see in your attitude, emotions, and behaviours? What changes can you implement in your life today to help you take a step towards becoming a more inspiring leader?

Further resources:

- Cameron, K. (2021). *Positively energising leadership: Virtuous actions and relationships that create high performance.* Barrett-Koehler Publishers.
- Lopez, S. J. (2014). *Making hope happen: Create the future you want for yourself and others.* Atria Books.
- Seligman, M. E. P. (2018). *The hope circuit: A psychologist's journey from helplessness to optimism.* Nicholas Brealey Publishing.

- Seligman, M. E. P. (2006). *Learnt optimism: How to change your mind and change your life*. Random House USA.
- Sharot, T. (2012). *The optimism bias: Why we are wired to look on the bright side*. Robinson.

Grand design

1. **Identifying values:** Take some time to ensure you know what matters to you and what your values are. You can use these questions to help you to identify them:
   a. Deep inside, what is important to you?
   b. What do you want to stand for in life?
   c. What sort of person do you want to be?
   d. What qualities would you like to cultivate?

   (Adapted from David 2017)

2. **Moving towards your values:** Write down one of your values. What have you done over the past few days that helped you move towards expressing this quality? What more could you do to move towards this quality (Flaxman & Bond, 2010)?

3. **Putting values into action:** How can you put your values into action in your work more? Remember, our values are 'big picture' directions that can guide how we live our lives. It is important to know our values, but it can be hard to think about moving towards them during day-to-day living. This is where goals come in – if we can think of some values-based goals, then we can move towards our values in a small way each day and experience the benefits for our sense of meaning and purpose. Have a go at setting yourself some small values-based goals to complete over the next week or two. As always, try to make your goals SMART – Specific, Meaningful, Achievable, Realistic, and Time-framed. Watch out for goals that are 'emotional' (e.g. I want to 'feel better') or goals that are too big and require time and resources that you do not have available (adapted from David, 2017).

4. **Planning for purpose**: Think ahead about how you would like to be remembered either at the end of your life or after you terminate your employment many years from now. What legacy would you like to leave behind? Which one of your strengths would your colleagues mention? What accomplishments would they remember? What would you like your legacy to be? Now write it all down in detail and then read it back

to help you develop realistic goals to make it happen. Adapted from Rashid and Seligman (2019).

5. **Moving purpose into catabolic action:** Having created a list of realistic goals during the previous activity which stems from your broader meaning and desired purpose, what do you now need to do to put these goals into catabolic action? Reflect on:
   a. How can you break them down, when will they happen, and what support do you need?
   b. What positive emotions can support these activities (Fredrickson, 2001)?
   c. Mental contrasting of the goals – What would happen if each goal was achieved? What would happen if each goal was not achieved (Oettingen, Wittchen, & Gollwitzer, 2013)?
   d. Finally, based on the earlier reflections, what adaptations or contingencies do you need to make to your goals? How will this affect your day-to-day work or the work of your team?

6. **Develop your sense of meaning and purpose in your work:** Reflect on and start using four or more of your strengths daily at work to help you develop a calling for work (Harzer & Ruch, 2012, 2016).

7. **Finding meaning in challenge:** Consider a challenging situation you have found yourself in. Now reflect on what the benefits were of going through this challenging situation (Helgeson, Reynolds, & Tomich, 2006).

Further resources:

- David, S. (2017). *Emotional agility: Get unstuck, embrace change and thrive in work and life.* London: Penguin Books Ltd.
- Dik, B. J., Byrne, Z. S., & Steger, M. F. (2013). *Purpose and meaning in the workplace.* Washington, DC: American Psychological Association.
- Fredrickson, B. (2009). *Positivity: Groundbreaking research reveals how to release your inner optimist and thrive.* Richmond: Oneworld.
- Harris, R. (2019). *ACT made simple: An easy-to-read primer on acceptance and commitment therapy* (2nd ed.). New Harbinger Publications.

Health

1. **Committee:** Create a health and wellbeing committee, the objective of which is to design a long- and medium-term strategy for wellbeing and

agree on a wellbeing framework relevant to your organisation (J Burke, 2021).

2. **Seminars:** Organise a series of targeted, health-promoting seminars aligned with your organisational values.

3. **Policies and procedures:** Review the policies and practices in your organisation that may impact employees' health and wellbeing.

4. **Reflection:** Reflect on your practice and the daily practice of your team that may help or hinder an individual's health.

5. **Health coaching:** Introduce and participate in health coaching programmes in your organisation to help employees reduce stress, improve sleep, and accomplish other health-related outcomes applied to individuals' specific circumstances (Röttger et al., 2017; Wright, 2007).

6. **Energy management:** List ways to manage your emotional, physical, mental, and spiritual energy at work. See an article by Schwartz and McCarthy (2007) in the further resources.

7. **Digital wellness:** Source digital programmes, the aim of which is to help people enhance their wellbeing, such as Happify (www.happify.com), RCSI health lecture series (www.rcsi.com/dublin/about/faculty-of-medicine-and-health-sciences/centre-for-positive-psychology-and-health) or Headspace (www.headspace.com/).

8. **Sense of coherence:** Tools for enhancing the sense of coherence at work include transparent communication; taking time to appreciate achievements and recognising each employee for their accomplishments; catching people when they do the right thing; and acknowledging their friendliness, justice, humour, and tolerance (Mayer & Krause, 2011).

9. **Stress mindset:** When experiencing a stressful situation, consider how stress helps you summon your focus to resolve this situation more effectively instead of focusing on how bad stress is for you. Consider resources you can tap into to help you deal with the situation. Consider your experience and what has worked well for you. Consider writing down a plan of action to resolve this issue. Now go and take the first step (Burke, 2018; Jamieson, Crum, Goyer, Marotta, & Akinola, 2018).

Further resources:

- Burke, J., Dunne, P., Meehan, T., O'Boyle, C., & van Nieuwerburgh, C. (2022). *Positive psychology and health: 50+ research-based tools for enhancing wellbeing*. Routledge.

- Frates, B., Bonnet, J. P., Joseph, R., & Peterson, J. A. (2021). *Lifestyle medicine handbook: An introduction to the power of healthy habits* (2nd ed.). Healthy Learning.
- McGonigal, K. (2015). *The upside of stress: Why stress is good for you (and how to get good at it)*. Vermilion.
- Rath, T. (2013). *Eat, move, sleep: How small choices lead to big changes*. Missionday.
- Schwarz, T., & McCarthy, C. (2007). Manage your energy, not your time. *Harvard Business Review*. Retrieved from https://hbr.org/2007/10/manage-your-energy-not-your-time

Tribe

1. **Brief loving-kindness meditation (LKM):**. Find a quiet place to sit and take some time to meditate and reflect for ten minutes on the following adapted LKM from Fredrickson (2014) aimed to support with developing kindness towards ourselves and others:
   - Place your feet flat on the floor with your spine raised towards the sky;
   - Bring your awareness to the sensations of your own heart;
   - Breathe in deeply to and from your heart, resting in the awareness of your heart bringing you new energy with each breath;
   - Visualise somebody – a child, spouse, pet – of whom the mere thought makes you smile and bring what you love about them to mind;
   - Once feelings of tenderness have taken hold, repeat the following phrases of LKM (out loud or to yourself):
     o May this one (or I, we, he, she, or they) feel safe;
     o May this one feel happy;
     o May this one feel healthy;
     o May this one live with ease.

Repeat this for a few minutes, whilst resting and breathing in love into your heart. There are many other options available online.

2. **Communicating to deepen connection:** Practice active-constructive responding to your colleagues (Gable & Reis, 2010). In other words, when they share with you good news, instead of moving on quickly from it or immediately pointing out any negatives of their news, congratulate

them with enthusiasm, take the time to celebrate their success whole-heartedly. Reflect on how this makes you feel. How do you think this makes your colleague feel?

3. **Connection through positivity:** Set out to meaningfully 'connect' with someone each day by experiencing positive emotions together (Fredrickson, 2014). Write down at the end of the day how these meaningful connections and experiences made you feel.

4. **Random acts of kindness:** Perform some random and not-so-random acts of kindness towards your colleagues at work to enhance your relations (Rowland & Curry, 2019). For example, write a note expressing thanks to a colleague, buy a colleague a coffee or snack, or buy a gift that you know somebody would like. For more information on random acts of kindness, see www.actionforhappiness.org/take-action/do-kind-things-for-others.

5. **Practising compassion for connection:** Become a compassionate leader who notices, interprets, feels, and acts compassionately and promotes compassion in organisations (Worline & Dutton, 2017). Specifically, when the team are suffering, practice the following: offer them flexible time to cope with adversity; allow employees to engage in tasks in ways that suit their circumstance; protect them from the need to divulge personal information to others by offering them a compassionate explanation; and check with an employee who is regularly suffering, reassure them and offer psychological safety, and listen.

6. **Giving more constructive and specific feedback:** As discussed, positive feedback has been shown to satisfy competence and autonomy needs, thereby boosting intrinsic motivation (Burgers, Eden, van Engelenburg, & Buningh, 2015). Reflecting on your feedback approach, how often do you give positive, constructive, and specific feedback? Reflecting on an upcoming meeting or feedback opportunity with a colleague, how could you create the opportunity for more positive, constructive feedback? See the positive feedback loop in Chapter 7 for more guidance.

7. **Practising positive conflict:** Reflect on a recent point of conflict between you and another person. To what extent you would say your positive to negative statements were at a ratio of 5:1? What could you do to increase this ratio further? How could you meet negativity in conflict with more of a kind, reaffirming, or light-hearted comment that creates a moment of reflection rather than reactivity? This will support navigating disagreements (Fredrickson, 2014; Gottman & Silver, 1999).

Further resources:

- Dutton, J., & Ragins, B. R. (2017). *Exploring positive relationships at work: Building a theoretical and research foundation*.
- Fredrickson, B. (2014). *Love 2.0: Creating happiness and health in moments of connection*. New York: Plume.
- Prilleltensky, I., & Prilleltensky, O. (2021). *How people matter: Why it affects health, happiness, love, work, and society*. Cambridge University Press.
- Worline, M. C., & Dutton, J. E. (2017). *Awakening compassion at work: The quiet power that elevates people and organizations*. Berrett-Koehler Publishers.

References

Baumeister, R. F., Bratslavsky, E., Finkenauer, C., & Vohs, K. D. (2001). Bad is stronger than good. *Review of General Psychology*, 5(4), 323–370. doi:10.1037/1089-2680.5.4.323

Burgers, C., Eden, A., van Engelenburg, M. D., & Buningh, S. (2015). How feedback boosts motivation and play in a brain-training game. *Computers in Human Behavior*, 48, 94–103. doi:10.1016/j.chb.2015.01.038

Burke, J. (2018). Turning stress into positive energy: An evaluation of a workplace intervention. *Positive Work and Organizations: Research and Practice*.

Burke, J. (2021). *The ultimate guide to implementing wellbeing programmes for school*. London: Routledge.

Cameron, K. (2021). *Positively energising leadership: Virtuous actions and relationships that create high performance*. San Francisco: Berrett-Koehler Publishers, Inc.

Crain, M., & Koehn, C. (2012). The essence of hope in domestic violence support work: A hermeneutic-phenomenological inquiry. *Journal of Mental Health Counseling*, 34(2), 170–188. doi:10.17744/mehc.34.2.am6j432352416nh8

David, S. (2017). *Emotional agility: Get unstuck, embrace change and thrive in work and life*. London: Penguin Books Ltd.

Flaxman, P. E., & Bond, F. W. (2010). A randomised worksite comparison of acceptance and commitment therapy and stress inoculation training. *Behaviour Research and Therapy*, 48(8), 816–820. doi:10.1016/j.brat.2010.05.004

Fredrickson, B. L. (2001). The role of positive emotions in positive psychology: The broaden-and-build theory of positive emotions. *American Psychologist*, 56(3), 218–226. doi:10.1037/0003-066X.56.3.218

Fredrickson, B. L. (2014). *Love 2.0: Creating happiness and health in moments of connection*. New York: Plume.

Gable, S. L., & Reis, H. T. (2010). Good news! Capitalizing on positive events in an interpersonal context. In M. P. Zanna (Ed.), *Advances in experimental social psychology* (Vol. 42, pp. 195–257). San Diego, CA: Academic Press.

Gottman, J. M., & Silver, N. (1999). *The seven principles for making marriage work* (1st ed.). London: Weidenfeld & Nicolson.

Hannah, S., Sweeney, P., & Lester, P. (2007). Toward a courageous mindset: The subjective act and experience of courage. *The Journal of Positive Psychology, 2,* 129–135. doi:10.1080/17439760701228854

Harzer, C., & Ruch, W. (2012). When the job is a calling: The role of applying one's signature strengths at work. *Journal of Positive Psychology, 7*(5), 362–371. doi:10.1080/17439760.2012.702784

Harzer, C., & Ruch, W. (2016). Your strengths are calling: Preliminary results of a web-based strengths intervention to increase calling. *Journal of Happiness Studies: An Interdisciplinary Forum on Subjective Well-Being, 17*(6), 2237–2256.

Hayes, S. C., Luoma, J. B., Bond, F. W., Masuda, A., & Lillis, J. (2006). Acceptance and commitment therapy: Model, processes and outcomes. *Behaviour Research and Therapy, 44*(1), 1–25. doi:10.1016/j.brat.2005.06.006

Helgeson, V. S., Reynolds, K. A., & Tomich, P. L. (2006). A meta-analytic review of benefit finding and growth. *Journal of Consulting and Clinical Psychology, 74*(5), 797–816. doi:10.1037/0022-006X.74.5.797

Jamieson, J. P., Crum, A. J., Goyer, J. P., Marotta, M. E., & Akinola, M. (2018). Optimizing stress responses with reappraisal and mindset interventions: An integrated model. *Grantee Submission, 31*(3), 245–261.

King, L. A. (2001). The health benefits of writing about life goals. *Personality and Social Psychology Bulletin, 27*(7), 798–807. doi:10.1177/0146167201277003

Langer, E. J. (1989). *Mindfulness*. Addison-Wesley/Addison Wesley Longman.

Lewis, S., Passmore, J., & Cantore, S. (2014). *Appreciative inquiry for change management: Using AI to facilitate organizational development* (2nd ed.). London: Kogan Page.

Mayer, C.-H., & Krause, C. (2011). Promoting mental health and salutogenesis in transcultural organizational and work contexts. *International Review of Psychiatry, 23*(6), 495–500. doi:10.3109/09540261.2011.636549

McCullough, M. E., Root, L. M., & Cohen, A. D. (2006). Writing about the benefits of an interpersonal transgression facilitates forgiveness. *Journal of Consulting and Clinical Psychology, 74*(5), 887–897. doi:10.1037/0022-006X.74.5.887

Neff, K., & Germer, C. K. (2018). *The mindful self-compassion workbook: A proven way to accept yourself, build inner strength, and thrive.* New York: The Guilford Press.

Niemiec, R. M. (2018). *Character strengths interventions: A field guide for practitioners*. Boston, MA: Hogrefe Publishing.

Niemiec, R. M., & Wedding, D. (2014). *Positive psychology at the movies 2: Using films to build character strengths and wellbeing* (2nd ed.). Boston: Hogrefe Publishing.

Oettingen, G., Wittchen, M., & Gollwitzer, P. (2013). Regulating goal pursuit through mental contrasting with implementation intentions. In E. A. Locke & G. P. Latham (Eds.), *New developments in goal setting and task performance* (pp. 523–548). New York: Routledge/Taylor & Francis Group.

O'Hara, D. J., & O'Hara, E. F. (2012). Towards a grounded theory of therapist hope. *Counselling Psychology Review, 27*(4), 42–55.

Pennebaker, J. W. (1997). Writing about emotional experiences as a therapeutic process. *Psychological Science, 8*(3), 162–166. doi:10.1111/j.1467-9280.1997.tb00403.x

Pury, C. L. S. (2008). Can courage be learned? In S. J. Lopez (Ed.), *Positive psychology: Exploring the best in people, Vol 1: Discovering human strengths* (pp. 109–130). Westport, CT: Praeger Publishers/Greenwood Publishing Group.

Quinlan, D., Vella-Brodrick, D. A., Gray, A., & Swain, N. (2019). Teachers matter: Student outcomes following a strengths intervention are mediated by teacher strengths spotting. *Journal of Happiness Studies, 20*(8), 2507–2523. doi:10.1007/s10902-018-0051-7

Rashid, T., & Seligman, M. (2019). *Positive psychotherapy workbook.* New York: Oxford University Press.

Reivich, K. (2004). *Letting go of grudges. Assignment instructions for M. E. P. Seligman's authentic happiness coaching program.* Pennsylvania: University of Pensilvania.

Rowland, L., & Curry, O. S. (2019). A range of kindness activities boost happiness. *Journal of Social Psychology, 159*(3), 340–343. doi:10.1080/00224545.2018.1469461

Röttger, S., Maier, J., Krex-Brinkmann, L., Kowalski, J., Danker-Hopfe, H., Sauter, C., & Stein, M. (2017). The benefits of sleep coaching in workplace health promotion. *Journal of Public Health (09431853), 25*(6), 685–691. doi:10.1007/s10389-017-0826-z

Schwartz, T., & McCarthy, C. (2007). Manage yoru energy, not your time. *Harvard Business Review.* Retrieved from https://hbr.org/2007/10/manage-your-energy-not-your-time

Segal, Z. V., Williams, J. M. G., & Teasdale, J. D. (2013). *Mindfulness-based cognitive therapy for depression* (2nd ed.). New York: The Guilford Press.

Seligman, M. E. P. (1990). *Learned optimism: How to change your mind and your life.* New York: Alfred A Knopf.

Seligman, M. E. P., Steen, T. A., Park, N., & Peterson, C. (2005). Positive psychology progress: Empirical validation of interventions. *American Psychologist, 60*(5), 410–421. doi:10.1037/0003-066X.60.5.410

Stern, D. N. (2004). *The present moment: In psychotherapy and everyday life.* W W Norton & Co.

Snyder, C. R., Rand, K. L., & Sigmon, D. R. (2018). Hope theory: A member of the positive psychology family. In M. W. Gallagher & S. J. Lopez (Eds.), *The Oxford handbook of hope* (pp. 27–43). New York: Oxford University Press.

Warner, L. M., & French, D. P. (2020). Self-efficacy interventions. In M. S. Hagger, L. D. Cameron, K. Hamilton, N. Hankonen, & T. Lintunen (Eds.), *The handbook of behaviour change*. Cambridge: Cambridge University Press.

Waters, L., & Stokes, H. (2015). Positive education for school leaders: Exploring the effects of emotion-gratitude and action-gratitude. *The Australian Educational and Developmental Psychologist, 32*(1), 1–22. doi:10.1017/edp.2015.1

Worline, M. C., & Dutton, J. E. (2017). *Awakening compassion at work: The quiet power that elevates people and organizations*. San Francisco: Berrett-Koehler Publishers.

Wright, J. (2007). Stress in the workplace: A coaching approach. *Work, 28*(3), 279–284.

10 The final word – for now

Never has the world been hungrier to understand better ways to work with and support one another and our wider world to be more sustainable and function optimally (Reilly, 2021). Ongoing international research by the American Gallup Organisation has consistently shown that over half of employees are either unengaged or actively disengaged in their workplace, which may be impacting their performance (Harter et al., 2021). Productivity in the UK continues to drop (Henley, 2018), and only half of UK workers feel their work is meaningful, with a third thinking it is meaningless (Dahlgreen, 2015). Furthermore, there are ongoing tensions between the generations, with younger people reporting feeling less happy and stable in their workplaces (Franklin, 2019), not to mention the VUCA (volatility, uncertainty, complexity, and ambiguity), post–COVID-19 world we live in, which significantly impacts our wellbeing. Today, more than ever, we need positive leaders to lead the way.

We have illustrated in this book that the objective of positive leadership is to get positive outcomes from ourselves, other people, our team, organisation, system, and society to address some of our current shortfalls in the system in which we operate. These positive outcomes are about reaching our subjective optimal performance. We have also highlighted that we can develop the ALIGHT model's six resources to get the best from ourselves and others – abundance, limberness, inspiration, grand design, health, and tribe – and that we all have a more significant opportunity and capability to tap into these resources than we realise. So often, we do not take the time, are not given the time, do not have the conditions to use or opportunities to develop these resources, and find ourselves sleepwalking through our leadership practice. We hope this book calls to put a different volume on your

DOI: 10.4324/9781003170433-10

actions and activities for a greater reward at work and in life for yourself and others.

The objective of this book was to provide readers with a clear evidence-based framework for positive leadership practice (the what and the why), as well as sharing the how, and to offer examples from a range of successful extraordinary ordinary leaders who depict various aspects of positive leadership (the application) which we hope we have achieved. As we have already acknowledged, whilst past research has offered us robust case studies of outcomes in terms of the extraordinary performance that positive leadership can achieve (e.g. Burke, 2020; Cameron, 2008; Murphy & Louis, 2018), we were left still with the need to understand the 'how' in which we positively lead. The ALIGHT framework offers the next step in helping us know more about the 'how', identifying six essential resources and the application and practice required for these positive leadership resources to be developed. It provides more specific, practical, and applied guidance to help organisations, HR departments, and leaders themselves know how to do the 'how'. This is not the end of the story, though; this is just the beginning of a deeper understanding of positive leadership.

We also now know that positive leaders do not just advocate positivity (referring to positive psychology v1.0, or 'positivity') or show compassion for challenging times (referring to positive psychology 2.0's embracing of the dark side of negative emotions [Lomas & Ivtzan, 2016; Sims, 2017]); positive leaders insist on a focus beyond themselves as an individual leader to look at the teams, organisations, and systems we are all part of in decision-making, aligning to the original intention and root desire of positive psychology to be systemic. Positive leaders contribute to the system around them. There is now more research to enable the field of positive psychology to offer a new understanding of positive leadership with a more effective and future-focused leadership model, of which we see the ALIGHT model and this book as one of these contributions.

The resources we have identified as being at the core of positive leadership show that this book and the concept of positive leadership is about as far as it gets for a pure domain-based argument for leadership – that we need to be knowledge experts in what we do (Goodall, 2016) in order to excel in our roles. It is not that we do not think the technical and domain-specific knowledge of leaders is critical – it is – we are just aware from our research, practice, and professional experiences that it is possible to support domain-specific knowledge within professional practices already – and organisations already tend to do so; to contend with our VUCA world more optimally, we must also think more about our deeper, human leadership capacity – how we encourage, flex and adapt, inspire, motivate, support, sustain, and relate to one another if we are going to create more profound change for everybody in the system and not just ourselves as experts (Jones, Chesley, & Egan, 2020).

The ALIGHT framework also shows us that we need better, more holistic leadership development training approaches; beyond domain-specific training and horizontal leadership training, we need to think more about vertical leadership development, which moves from a focus on the what to the 'how' leaders make sense of knowledge acquired (Gilbride, James, & Carr, 2020). Because positive leadership is not about personality traits, but rather a set of resources, we hope that more experiential, self-reflective, and jarring development programmes in enhancing positive leadership resources will be an essential part of the leadership development agenda moving forward.

We do not know many things about positive leadership yet, and more research is coming – we need further research into how the ALIGHT resources show up and how individuals and organisations develop them. We need more research into the conditions that enable and foster these resources in individuals and organisations. As just one example, we need to know does adult ego development influence how we can develop these resources? We cannot claim – and nor would we want to, given our aspiration for limberness and abundance – that our positive leadership framework is the be-all and end-all – this is just a model, not who you are, but who you could be. We do, however, say that this book ties together more evidence-based research and information than we have ever had for what positive leaders do and how to bring the best out of ourselves and others at work. This book also highlights the conscious effort, and often choice and practice required, to become a positive leader. This book is our best starter for ten on what resources the positive leader demonstrates, and over the next quarter of a century, we plan to build on this research and hope many other researchers will collaborate with us and explore positive leadership further for themselves.

The further research also starts with you – the reader – how can you practise what you have discovered about yourself or others in reading this book? We hope you will draw on the evidence in the chapters and the suggested interventions to have the courage to experiment with your own and your team's practices and influence your organisation to do so too. We also hope that you will share the stories of your experimentation with us, so we can cohere this practice-based evidence for more to learn what can work and the outcome it can have. In the words of Mother Teresa, a missionary and one of the most outstanding female leaders of our time: "I alone cannot change the world, but I can cast a stone across the water to create many ripples". So we encourage you to use this book as an opportunity to develop and cast your own positive leadership resource pebbles to create many ripples for yourself and those you work with, all so that more of us can optimally function in the workplace and our lives.

Past researchers have paved the way to defining the scope and outcomes of positive leadership. The current book aimed to broaden this perspective and contribute to the existing research by expounding the six resources leaders can tap into to develop their leadership capacity. Given that it is a theoretical framework, further research will clarify how these resources correlate with other important concepts in leadership theory and practice, such as performance, motivation, or engagement. Moreover, the framework allows us to create research-based interventions and evaluate their effectiveness using a scale we have created and validated. We hope this book will become a starting point for boosting the positive resources research and enriching leadership practice.

As we touched on in Chapter 8, for leaders to achieve their potential, they go through personal and professional development stages (Eigel & Kuhnert, 2005). Their development applies not only to the knowledge they have but ways in which they gain it and apply it in their daily practice. At an early level of leadership development, individuals view the world through a black-and-white lens, and they find it particularly difficult to perceive any shades of grey. They are thus not open to other people's opinions and tend to disregard them, or worse, consider them wrong without even taking the time to reflect on them. Leaders at level one of their development often focus on winning, regardless of whether it positively or negatively impacts others. Approximately 10% of leaders in organisations display this type of behaviour (Kegan, 1994), which can be detrimental to an organisation and their team.

At a later level or level two of leadership development, individuals become more capable of appreciating others' views and adopting their perspectives. They tend to display more empathy towards their team, reflect more on the intricacies of each situation, and do not view the world as black and white. However, their reliance on other people's opinions becomes considerable, and at this level of development, they tend to take the opinions of their trusted advisors onboard indiscriminately. This often results in inauthentic behaviour, and the more they practise this type of leadership, the more alienated they become from themselves. An example of such leaders comes from stereotypical politicians. Some political leaders tend to be so focused on creating a good image, which they hope will help them win elections, that they no longer know the person they have become. As a result, they do what is expected of them instead of what they believe is right.

At a later level or level three of leadership development, individuals take other people's views on board, but they can filter it through their own set of values, beliefs, vision for the future, and personal experience. As a result, they are more assured about what they believe is right. They do not believe everything they hear, but make their own, authentic decisions they can stand by. This type of leadership behaviour is often associated with a transformational leadership style and demonstrates a higher level of intrapersonal, interpersonal, and cognitive development.

The highest level of leadership development goes beyond this, and approximately 5% to 8% of adults aged 40 to 60 fall into this category of leaders (Kegan, 1994). These types of leaders have experienced a paradigm shift in the way they view the world. They embrace the complexity of the situations they find themselves in and can view them simultaneously from various perspectives. When making decisions, they follow their own and other people's views, and they consider the impact of their decision on the organisation and others. They can put all these perspectives into a mixing bowl, analyse them, and develop a solution that suits all the parties involved. As a result, these leaders achieve the optimal level of leadership functioning and serve the teams and communities well.

We hope that reading this book has provided you with ample opportunity to reflect on your leadership practice, levels of development, and the ALIGHT resources you use every day to amplify your own and your team's potential. We hope it helped you move or further develop your skills at a higher level of leadership development. We hope that what you have read you will now be able to filter through your value system, beliefs, and vision towards the future, to ensure that not only are you aligned with any positive leadership practice but it serves you and everyone around you well. Most importantly, however, we hope that tapping into the ALIGHT resources will help you put a dent in the VUCA world and make it a better place for future generations.

If you are interested in learning more about positive leadership and keep up to date with the latest research about it, please follow us on social media and visit our websites: www.cornelialucey.com and www.jolantaburke. com. We will leave you with a few questions to reflect on that can help you accomplish it and wish you a fulfilling journey of self-discovery.

Aligning ALIGHT resources to personal practice
- *What resources of the ALIGHT model have I already applied in my practice? What aspects of this application have worked well for me? What changes would I like to introduce in the future?*

- *What other resources of the ALIGHT model may be useful for me, my team, or my organisation to develop? How can I go about it?*

- *What are one to three things from the book that I am happy to introduce in my leadership practice today?*

References

Burke, J. (2020). *Positive psychology and school leadership: The new science of positive educational leadership.* New York: Nova.

Cameron, K. (2008). *Positive leadearship: Strategies for extraordinary performance.* San Francisco: Berrett-Koehler Publishers, Inc.

Dahlgreen, W. (2015). *37% of British workers think their jobs are meaningless.* Retrieved from https://yougov.co.uk/topics/lifestyle/articles-reports/2015/08/12/british-jobs-meaningless

Eigel, K., & Kuhnert, K. (2005). Authentic development: Leadership development level and executive effectiveness. *Monographs in Leadership and Management, 3.*

Franklin, N. (2019). *UK workers rank tenth in global happiness survey.* Retrieved from https://workplaceinsight.net/uk-workers-rank-tenth-in-global-happiness-survey/

Gilbride, N., James, C., & Carr, S. (2020). School principals at different stages of adult ego development: Their sense-making capabilities and how others experience them. *Educational Management Administration & Leadership, 49*(2), 234–250. doi:10.1177/1741143220903724

Goodall, A. H. (2016). A theory of expert leadership (TEL) in psychiatry. *Australasian Psychiatry, 24*(3), 231–234. doi:10.1177/1039856215609760

Harter, J., Schmidt, F., Agrawal, S., Blue, A., Plowman, S., Josh, P., & Asplund, J. (2021). *The relationship between engagement at work and organizational outcomes 2020 Q12 meta-analysis.* Retrieved from www.gallup.com/workplace/321725/gallup-q12-meta-analysis-report.aspx?thank-you-report-form=1

Henley, D. (2018). *Should we be happy at work?* Retrieved from www.forbes.com/sites/dedehenley/2018/04/30/should-we-be-happy-at-work/?sh=66a1f84f59ea

Jones, H. E., Chesley, J. A., & Egan, T. (2020). Helping leaders grow up: Vertical leadership development in practice. *The Journal of Values-Based Leadership, 13*(1), 8.

Kegan, R. (1994). *In over our heads: The mental demands of modern life.* Cambridge, MA: Harvard University Press.

Lomas, T., & Ivtzan, I. (2016). Second wave positive psychology: Exploring the positive-negative dialectics of wellbeing. *Journal of Happiness Studies, 17*(4), 1753–1768.

Murphy, J. F., & Louis, K. S. (2018). *Positive school leadership: Building capacity and strengthening relationships.* Canada: Teachers College Press.

Reilly, K. (2021). *Inside the battle for the hearts and minds of tomorrow's business leaders.* Retrieved from https://time.com/6105006/mba-programs-changing/

Sims, C. (2017). Second wave positive psychology coaching with difficult emotions: Introducing the mnemonic of 'TEARS HOPE'. *Coaching Psychologist, 13*(2), 66–78.

Index

Page numbers in *italics* indicate a figure and page numbers in **bold** indicate a table on the corresponding page.

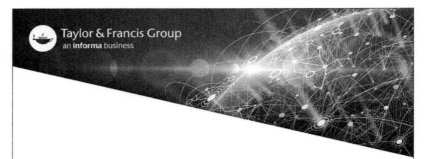